DEAD MEN'S SECRETS

Tantalising Hints of a Lost Super Race

By

JONATHAN GRAY

First published by AuthorHouse 04/07/04

ISBN: 1-4140-3749-X (e-book)
ISBN: 1-4184-2555-9 (Paperback)
ISBN: 1-4184-2556-7 (Dust Jacket)

Printed in the United States of America
Bloomington, Indiana

This book is printed on acid free paper.

DEDICATION

To that courageous band of prehistorians who have dared to say publicly what many others have known in their hearts—that their emperor has nothing on.

CONTENTS

PROLOGUE

At the time, Professor Martin Byron was in Melbourne, Australia, on a scientific lecture tour. He had just stepped under the shower, when a sharp tingle sent him scurrying to his bedside phone.

Pasadena, California. "Martin, there's been another sighting of the Black Knight. The NASA men are calling for details. Kazantsev in Moscow is pushing for an immediate expedition to the vicinity. We want you back as soon as possible."

Byron set down the receiver. So it was on again. Not sighted for twenty years. And now...He snatched up the mouthpiece and dialed another number.

I was still some fifteen minutes away from Byron's hotel apartment, which afforded time for reflection.

It was, I recalled, in October 1957, that man's most daring triumph—*Sputnik* I—had been rocketed suddenly into orbit 584 miles above the earth. With excitement, mingled almost with disbelief, millions worldwide had scanned the night sky to glimpse that shining artificial moon skimming on its path east to west against the canopy of stars. Within four months America had followed suit.

So, after aeons of tortoise-paced development, humanity had suddenly leapt off the planet; it was startling—and we were alive to see it!

Then came a bizarre discovery. It was hushed up quickly, I recalled.

I was now at Byron's hotel. The ignition key off, I sat, musing.

As tracking stations swung into action to monitor these new moons, the night sky had tossed up an awesome mystery. Another satellite was discovered already in orbit. Certainly it was neither American nor Russian—and the uncanny truth was nobody else had the technology.

French astronomer Jacques Valle of the Paris Observatory, saw it three times in 1961 and got eleven data points in forty-five seconds. It seemed to he orbiting in reverse at an altitude of over 22,000 miles above the earth.

Experts were jolted. Who put this satellite into orbit? How long had it been there?

"I'm glad you could come." smiled the professor. offering a chair. "Now *there's* something for your research. I might say the Russians have the edge on us, in this investigation. Lev Gindelis and the Pulkovo Observatory in Leningrad concur that the Black Knight is out there waiting for us to explore its cargo, and God only knows, whatever we find aboard it may change the course of history."

I shuffled intently. 'So you believe this is an intelligently placed vehicle?"

"Well, it's not a meteor, and you can rule out space junk."

Truly the last twenty-five years had plunged us into some unsettling mysteries concerning our unknown past.

I reminded Byron of that day in February 1961—the thirteenth to be precise—when Mike Mikesell, Wallace Lane and Virginia Maxey were exploring 4,300 feet up in California's Coso Mountains and stumbled upon a fossil-encrusted rock. That in itself was not unusual. But wait for this.

Expecting it to be a hollow geode stone containing crystals, they broke a diamond saw on it the next day. The surprise turned wild when, instead of crystals, they found inside the rock a mechanized device resembling a spark plug. A sophisticated relic, if you please. But the riddle was its enormous age. Authorities dated it at half a million years.

"Do you see the problem?" I asked. "Even if we dismiss such dating, this mystery object was undeniably far too old to be explained by our conventional theories."

The professor grinned. He was clearly enjoying the puzzle. "Discoveries such as these do pose awkward questions," he chuckled.

"Tell me, Martin, scientifically speaking, is it possible that things which ought not to exist, do in fact exist? Could there have been a remote era when man-made wonders were as commonplace as they are today?"

Gradually the pieces seemed to be fitting together. I was beginning to wonder, what if something very big had happened on this planet in the past—something so big it wiped traces of just about everything from the

x

face of the earth? Except for a few clues, upon which we were now stumbling?

I can imagine what you are thinking at this moment. You are probably intrigued. But skeptical. Right? Prehistoric man could never have produced such things as earth-orbiting satellites and spark plugs.

Yes, I know. The nineteenth century evolution theory was hammered into us as schoolchildren and is still taught in all places of learning. The story goes that we ascended from savages to our present civilized state by a slow, uninterrupted development.

The question now arises, Could this be a myth?

But hasn't evolution been proved? A good question. The truth is, evolution has always been only a theory. Yes, it is often presented as a fact, even though it is impossible of any really positive proof.

Would it surprise you to learn that not in one spot, but all over the world, "impossible" ancient inventions have been surfacing of late, and some of them from a technology as advanced as our own?

Did you know that nearly all writings of ancient peoples worldwide tell the same story, that of a decline from an original "Golden Age"? That a cataclysmic disaster wiped out the advanced world?

Now here is the crunch. Today diggings all over the globe show that these traditions tally with the facts. Enormous stone masses or metal fragments are there; they cannot be argued away. This is tantalizing.

Actually, the concept of an original advanced world, which gave impetus to all succeeding civilizations, is well within the framework of scientific thinking. What is more, I believe this to be such a credible reality that no longer can we evade it.

The story about to unfold concerns a technology whose citizens were rich beyond our dreams. I shall show you how a global Flood minced it to atoms. How subsequent attempts were made to revive the lost glory. And how a fiery holocaust intervening, most of the survivors became savages.

It's time the truth was out. So many theories have been foisted on so many people for so many years. We'll never know all the facts, but there's enough to ignite an explosion in conventional circles.

And when you consider we're stripping bare our secret past, our own early days on planet Earth, our very own family history, it grows exciting indeed. I suspect that as the evidence progressively interlocks, you may sense the swelling excitement of one who has suddenly touched down upon some unknown new planet.

The discoveries are explained in everyday language in order to kindle interest within the general population.

It's a tale of vast riches—forfeited, forgotten and found.

There is something ominous here. We have, early in the twenty-first century, awakened to find ourselves in the super culture arena. As we leap to new, unimagined heights, we suddenly come eyeball to eyeball with our past, awakening to the realization that we've been here before.

Last time, as now, the world scene was overshadowed with violence and corruption. The end was almost total annihilation.

One is tempted to ask, Might something like this happen again? Could a holocaust be looming of such proportions that it will parallel the first "wipeout"?

We may be better able to evaluate this question at the close of our probe. Meanwhile our excursion into the past offers a feast of hidden delights.

Let's begin.

PART ONE

HOW AN ORIGINAL
SUPER WORLD VANISHED

HOW A
WORLDWIDE
SUPER CULTURE
VANISHED IN A
COSMIC
DISASTER

Chapter 1

THE DAY THE EARTH TIPPED OVER

Sam stormed outside. Anna was such a sucker for cranks. That guy in the news interview? A world wipeout, what rot!

Why couldn't Anna be practical, like he was? Sam had built up this market garden from scratch. Sixteen thousand pineapples, the best in the south polar basin. And that clever little blackmail-well, Anna didn't know about that-but they'd soon be rich.

The hoverbus whirred into busy Adah Avenue and disgorged its load outside the Green Pyramid Hotel. Sam's favorite bar was ablaze with color. Inside, at a corner table, sat an acquaintance from the electronics plant.

Sam was still fuming at Anna's gullibility. He poured out his frustration over a beer.

"So I told her, Mal, if a worldwide flood were imminent, surely our top scientists would say so! When has nature let us down? Since time began it's been so smooth. Natural disasters? Pure fantasy, Mal. They just can't happen!"

"They do," drawled his companion. "When this mug is empty, that's a natural disaster."

Sam winced at the flippancy of that remark, and proceeded. "Anna says the end's coming, Mal. Have you heard anything so naive? That this entire planet, equable and warm from pole to pole, will suddenly change under a flood of water."

Mal peered over his flask. "How?"

"Oh, some stupid prophecy about sheets of water crashing from the sky and erupting out of the ground," Sam snorted. "Religious nonsense."

"Perhaps so," responded Mal. "But you know pal, there is enough water up there and down there." He jesticulated with his flask.

"What do you mean?" Was Sam hearing right? Was Mal a fruitcake too?

"Just this, Sam. You know why we have such an excellent climate? Why we have vegetation in such lavish exuberance, so wonderfully teeming with animal life?"

"Go on."

"It's that vapour canopy high above the planet. It filters out harmful cosmic rays and keeps our climate just right. But there's oceans of water up there- and lots more in the underground basins. If something were to disturb them…"

Sam cut in. "Rubbish. I'll believe it when the first drops fall. Look, most of earth's surface is not sea, but land, watered since time began-and quite adequately, I might say-by nothing but the gentle morning mist. It's reliable, I tell you. What can go wrong?"

"Maybe if the earth keels over," quipped Mal. "As I'm about to do." Sam bit his tongue. It was useless trying to extract sense from his companion tonight.

He glanced up at the televiewer. The news was on:

With police scanners now in 70 percent of homes, arrests for dissent had risen to six hundred per week.

A new planet had been detected beyond Pluto.

Hoodlums with a laser gun had decapitated a man on his way home. Apparently he disturbed them during a pack rape.

Today a single bomb disintegrated another entire city on the equator. Frightening, all this violence. Almost out of control.

Sam felt sick. Some cool night air, that's what he needed.

Sam pushed through the sound-activated doors and onto the street.

It was soothing…calm…fresh…He felt better. Leaflets from peace demonstrators littered the pavement. Sam watched, bemused, as one flitted above the street and up the side of the half-completed Jared Building, already towering 300 feet into the darkness.

It was partly his, thanks to photos in safe deposit; blackmailing the corporation chief had been easy; the man could ill afford a fraud scandal. Sam smiled; with his stake in the Jared Corporation, he was set for life.

And Anna, that silly woman, he wanted her so much, it hurt. Next week was the wedding. A lifetime with her.

Suddenly the pavement rocked. Sam was hurled against a guardrail.

4

He looked up. Massive buildings were swaying. Loud bursts of noise cracked the sky.

He stretched out his hand to steady himself. And felt them. SPOTS!

Sam fumbled for his neck phone, his face ashen...

Something like this was occurring on that final night of the antedeluvian era. If we are to believe later traditions, that is.

As for the worldwide greenhouse environment, geology would one day attest to it-as well as to its sudden demise.[1]

Traditions would later describe survivors of the Deluge who were like gods-that is, they were members of a superior civilization, which ceased to exist after the Great Flood. Egyptian records would contend that the reign of the "gods" before the First Dynasty was one of superior and miraculous powers.

After the Deluge, the Popol Vuh (the sacred book of the Quiche Indians of Guatemala) would record: "The first race of men before the Flood possessed all knowledge; they studied the four quarters of heaven and the round surface of the earth."[2]

Understood in this light, even Greek mythology begins to make some sense. We see it as the recollection by a degenerate race, of a vast, mighty and highly civilized empire, which in a remote past covered the world.

Pause for reflection. Can we possibly imagine that all of the peoples of all continents independently invented such a story? Did they all speak of an original Golden Age by chance, without any foundation?

Indeed, I am tempted to ask, if man evolved from beasts, then why is it that there existed a long tradition of a Golden Age instead of that of a savage past? Will anyone explain that?

Even where there was lack of writing in conditions of savagery imposed by catastrophe, the same memory of the Golden Age was passed from mouth to ear.

You may want to ask at this point, can we really place much credence in ancient legends?

Surprisingly, a great deal. Too often, I'm afraid, we have been prone to dismiss folklore and mythology out of hand. But is this not unscientific, especially since traditions have often led us to discover physical remains?

LEGENDS ARE USUALLY BASED
ON A CORE OF FACT

Pertinently, William Prescott, the great Americanologist, reminds us: "A nation may pass away and leave only the memory of its existence, but the stories of science it has gathered up will endure forever."[3]

You see, folklore is a fossil of history; it preserves history in the guise of colorful tales. Far from being a collection of fables, it is a recital of actual past events, even though from generation to generation some facts have become distorted or forgotten.

Professor I.A. Efremov, of the Soviet Union, cautions that "historians must pay more respect to ancient traditions and folklore." He accuses Western scientists of snobbishness in rejecting the tales of the "common people."[4]

We must face it: legends are usually based on a core of fact.

Take the legend of Troy. No scholar took The Iliad or The Odyssey of homer as history. But Schliemann, putting faith in it, discovered the "mythical" city of Troy. The *Iliad* spoke of a cup decorated with doves which Odysseus used. In a shaft Schliemann found that 3,600-year-old cup.

Herodotus told a fabulous story of a distant country where griffins guarded a golden treasure. This land (Altai, or Kin Shan) has now been found, together with ancient gold mines, and decorations from a high culture prominently display the griffin. The vague myth is seen to be a fact.

Mexican Indian legends spoke of a sacred well of sacrifice, into which maidens and jewelry were hurled. Historians dismissed this as a mere tale, until the well, at Chichen Itza, was discovered in the nineteenth century.

More than any document, the Bible was assailed as a collection of fanciful myths. Yet, to the embarrassment of the critics, archaeological discoveries proved time and again that the fabled cities, mythical persons and impossible events were true and reliable reporting in every detail. Indeed, the Bible can now be regarded as the most accurate and trustworthy source of history we possess.

OUR ANCESTRAL MEMORY
OF THE GOLDEN ERA

If we are to credit the collective testimony of all ancient races, man's early history was truly an incredible one. It was a Golden Age of advanced civilization, of original giants who had superior intelligence and technology.

This appears to have been a universal truth, known to everyone in ancient times.

Sacred records affirm that at the very beginning (soon after the fall from Paradise) men possessed extraordinary mental abilities. Beginning with the raw earth, they mastered a high level of civilization in just the first six generations of their existence. In that short time they were able to build cities, play complex musical instruments and smelt metals. Indeed, with their scientific complexes, these earliest men, it seems, were no fools.

We might well wonder to what degree they further developed and refined this technology in the final few centuries before the Flood struck. Were the miracles of science as common as they are now? A perfectly valid question, I think.

Imagine it, if you can. Paved rainbow cities whose "houses of crystal" reflected every spectral hue; and we're talking about air travel, computers and plastics.

Did you know that when Alexander Graham Bell gave us the telephone, he hinted that it had been done before? "The old devices have been reinvented," he observed.[5]

Yes, you read it right. That is exactly what Bell said.

In fact the question was pressed further by the eminent British scientist Frederick Soddy, winner of a Nobel Prize in physics. He wondered whether the ancients might "not only have attained our present knowledge, but a power hitherto unmastered by us?"[6]

PHYSICAL REMAINS ALSO

Where did Bell and Soddy get their information? Quite possibly from some musty old records.

Nevertheless, our quest is not based on ancient texts and reports, but on accepted scientific discoveries. There are recently discovered artifacts that cannot be dismissed, namely, objects of metal sitting in museums, unquestionably made in the ancient world, that would have required very advanced technology to produce. A technology not to be repeated until our day.

The weight of evidence grows daily-evidence that all the major secrets of modern technology were known, and forgotten, long ago. Evidence that early man did create a society that surpassed ours in all aspects of development.

The entire world is really a 'dead man's tomb', a treasure hunter's paradise. As we prize open the coffin, suspense builds. Slowly we're lifting the lid on a lost technology which almost smacks of science fiction. We come face to face with such absurdities as brain transplants, colonies on Mars and invisible men. And we wonder, What next?

Admittedly, such concepts almost strain credibility. We are tempted to ask, Could the ancients have really advanced so far?

It may help to consider our own age.

As recently as a hundred years ago, were not most of today's inventions totally unknown, even unbelievable? Since then the spawning has been sudden-and rapid. What is more, the present age of basic discoveries is hardly at its end. It is forecast that just fifteen years hence our present accumulated knowledge will have doubled. Do you grasp what that means?

How, then, can one possibly conceive of the state of knowledge attained by the antedeluvians before the Deluge struck?

THE DELUGE

A world war was raging at the time.

In the thirty-fourth century B.C., a catastrophe of incredible magnitude intervened, causing the world to wobble and ripping the crust of the earth to shreds. A great Flood swept the whole planet.

November 17, 3398 B.C. [7] That day was probably like most others: temperate, balmy.

In one longitude, millions were dining…entertaining…relaxing. Precisely at 8 P.M. the earth gave an enormous shudder.

Prodded by an outside force, the planet tilted on its axis, and amidst lightning and the worst thunder ever heard by man, the pristine vapour canopy began to disintegrate. A floodgate of rain was released upon the earth.

There could be no gentle rising of water. Cosmic forces of horrific violence came unleashed.

With a dreadful shock, large land masses with their populations slipped into the sea. The surface of the entire globe became as a giant maelstrom, in which continents and seas were churned up together.

Attended by a screaming hurricane, tidal waves of 6,000 feet swept toward the poles. A blanket of lava and asphyxiating gases extinguished all life.

This cataclysm wiped the Mother Civilization from the face of the earth and consigned its products to a watery grave forever.

Not only were the antedeluvian people buried, but their technological achievements were destroyed, including all form of machinery and construction.

It is quite possible that areas which were most densely populated were submerged by the sea or buried under thousands of feet of debris. It has been scientifically estimated that over 75 percent of the earth's surface is sedimentary in nature, extending, as in India, to 60,000 feet deep.

Indeed, the earth, torn and twisted and shaking, was not to quiet down for centuries. With no less than three thousand volcanoes in eruption, a dense cloud of dust enshrouded the earth, blocking out the sun and distorting the climate for hundreds of years. Thus began the Ice Age. [8]

Of the human race a mere handful remained; Indeed, their survival was in every sense a miracle.

Forewarned, they had salvaged what records they might: a compilation of knowledge which, in due course, would be imparted to their descendants.

Now for the sake of the reader who is unfamiliar with this event, it should be stressed that the global Flood catastrophe is one of the key facts of all history. Not only is there a mass of geological evidence-it has left an indelible impression on the memory of the entire human race. [9]

An analysis of some 600 individual Flood traditions reveals a widespread concurrence on essential points:

- the prior corruption of mankind,
- a Flood warning unheeded by the masses,
- a survival vessel,
- the preservation of up to eight people with representative animal life,
- the sending forth of a bird to determine the suitability of re-emerging land,
- significance in the rainbow,
- descent from a mountain,
- and the repopulation of the whole earth from a single group of survivors.

Especially remarkable is the persistence of that biblical name Noah. And this is particularly so when you consider the ultimate language differences between peoples, and the extreme local distortions which developed in Flood legends.

Yet the name survived virtually unchanged in such isolated places as Hawaii (where he was called Nu-u), the Sudan (Nuh), China (Nu-Wah), the

Amazon region (Noa), Phrygia (Noe) and among the Hottentots (Noh and Hiagnoh).

Think about this. Did each of these nations independently concoct the same name for its flood-surviving ancestor? Or did these widely separated peoples refer back to the same family of survivors?

The table of nations in Genesis 10 records the gradual dispersion of Noah's descendants and lists names, thus offering clues to their history and dwelling place. It contends that all nations of the earth have sprung from the family of Noah. [10]

Professor W.F. Albright, internationally recognized archaeological authority, describes this as an astonishingly accurate document...[which] shows such remarkable 'modern' understanding of the ethnic and linguistic situation in the modern world, in spite of all its complexity, that scholars never fail to be impressed with the author's knowledge of the subject. [11]

So, in a nutshell, there is good reason to believe that, after the Deluge, mankind sprang from a single group of people. Chapters 2 to 6 will confirm that these were not idiots, imbeciles or illiterates; they were in a civilized state, with an enormous cultural heritage, before they separated. Chapter 5 traces their ultimate slide into oblivion; while Chapters 7 to 9 raise three challenging questions that need to be answered.

Thus prepared, we shall more intelligently evaluate clues salvaged from the ancient world; an exercise to which the major portion of this work is devoted.

WHY
THE FIRST
CITIES SUDDENLY
HATCHED OUT
OF NOWHERE,
FULLY
MATURE

Chapter 2

SEARCH

Quick, jump!" shrieked Ed. "Get in, will you!" His jeep door was flung open. I glanced back hurriedly. A fierce-eyed mob was closing the gap.

It had happened so fast. Camera strung, I was exploring a fertility temple near Calcutta. To stumble upon a sacrificial blood rite was, to put it mildly, unexpected.

Some hawk-eyed watcher raised the alarm and in seconds, I was the focus of an inflamed pursuit. The foremost devotee was now so close you could hear him panting. A quick sideward glance…the glint of a raised knife…Persuasion enough! I leapt into the moving vehicle; it screeched to top gear and flew.

Hours later my heart still pounded madly; but now the excitement had shifted. Four bizarre coincidences were startling enough…but a fifth? Was a world-shaking event soon to break, affecting all of us?

I had been pondering some old prophecies which declared the end of modern civilization to be already known. The prophecies claimed credibility on the basis of a certain past event.

Naturally, before one can begin to consider such prophecies seriously, it must at least be established that the ancient event to which they are linked did in fact occur.

I knew Ed Savage to be a bulldog of an archaeologist. Even so, his announcement startled me to no end.

That evening I quizzed him over vegetable curry and iced mango juice.

"Putting it simply," he began, "the commonly held view is that we came up from savage, Stone Age beginnings. It was a slow but steady development to civilization."

11

He wiped dahl from his fingers. "Well naturally I expected on-site investigation of the very first cultures to verify this 'fact.' But what really emerged was something quite different. The coincidence in each case is simply this: all cultures began suddenly—and fully developed! A long preliminary period is *not* supported by archaeology."

"But..." I faltered, groping for words.

"Before cities on earth," he continued, "there was nothing; nothing, I tell you, but a clean slate."

"Are you telling me the evidence points to *no transition whatsoever* between the ancient civilizations and any primitive forebears?"

"Precisely! They did not rise to their peak. They were at their peak *from the beginning.*"

"Hogwash!" I snapped. "There has to be trial and error, refinement, evolution."

"SUDDEN" APPEARANCE

Edgar went on. "At first I could not believe it either; there was but one pattern—the 'sudden' appearance of civilizations worldwide. Five coincidences, or one pattern; call it what you like."

"Meaning?" I looked at him.

"Well, there was Egypt. *About 3000 B.C., Egypt sprang into existence suddenly, fully developed—that is, without transition from a primitive state, with a fantastic ready-made high society.*

"Great cities, enormous temples," he continued. "Pyramids of overwhelming size. Colossal statues with tremendous expressive power. Luxurious tunnels and tombs. Splendid streets flanked by magnificent sculptures. Perfect drainage systems. A decimal system at the very start. A ready-made writing, already perfected. A well-established naming system (in which each Pharaoh had as many as five names). Society already divided into specialist classes. An army, civil service and hierarchy minutely organized. A court exhibiting all the indications of well-defined precedence and form."

Edgar stirred his dish. "In the remotest period of which there are records, I tell you Egypt shows a level of civilization which is inexplicable. It sounds crazy I know, but it's a fact!"

I emptied my glass without tasting it, and poured another. "What if..."

"Go on," said Edgar.

"Oh, forget it. I need a stroll in the night air."

12

Outside was coal black. An almost eerie stillness. Above, the Milky Way floatcd brilliantly close. A gentle, warm breeze brushed my face. My mind wafted back...back...back.

Inexplicable, he said. Inexplicable unless...Suddenly it flashed. 'That's it!" I heard myself shouting, glad that nobody could hear me. "Yes, it *is* inexplicable, unless Egypt received her heritage basically from somewhere else." Egypt came from a clearly established civilization.

Triumphantly I strode back inside. Ed politely heard me out. "So she got it from someone else, eh?" The archaeologist ran a finger under his collar and swallowed. "Just, uh..." He cleared his throat and tried again. "...just who was Egypt's invisible mother?"

I have to admit, it stopped me for a moment.

"It wasn't only Egypt," he went on. "Take a look at Sumeria. *The appearance around 3000 B.C. of Sumerian civilization was likewise sudden, unexpected and out of nowhere.*

"H. Frankfort (Tell Uqair) called it 'astonishing.' Pierre Amiet (Elam) termed it 'extraordinary.' A. Parrot (Sumer) described it as 'a flame which blazed up so suddenly.' Leo Oppenheim (Ancient Mesopotamia) stressed 'the astonishingly short perio the civilization had arisen. Joseph Campbell *(The Masks of God)* summed it up this way: 'With stunning abruptness...there appears in this little Sumerian mud garden...the whole cultural syndrome that has since constituted the germinal unit of all the high civilizations of the world." 'd' within which [12]

Ed crumpled the napkin on his plate. "There's your second coincidence.

"But I've also been examining the evidence unearthed in *Harappa and Mohenjo-Daro,"* Ed stated. "They were *the key centers of the Indus Valley civilization. These also appear to have suddenly sprung up with no clear-cut traces of having evolved from primitive beginnings.* Your third coincidence."

The archaeologist opened his mouth and closed it again. "Perhaps I've got an overwrought imagination," he said carefully, "but there's one possibility I must explore. Do you think some explosive, unknown event might lie behind all this?

"You see, *the Maya of Central America* are in it, too. The Mayan calendar goes back to approximately the same time (c. 3000 B.C.). And sure enough, at the outset of Mayan culture, their script was *already perfect."*

Another bombshell. I arose and leaned against the plaster wall, studying the evidence, sighing. "Four very odd coincidences. You said there were five."

"Indeed there are. The megalith builders of *northwest Europe* appeared at precisely the same time. The achievements they demonstrated were identical, that is, the 'simultaneous discovery of Pythagorean triangles, a precise calendar, a true compass-bearing for north, knowledge of the movement of celestial bodies (possibly including knowledge that the world was round) and a minutely accurate system of measurement.' [13]

"Well, Jon, there's no disputing the facts. Just wish I had an answer.

The very next day Edgar was Nepal-bound; one thing seemed sure, our next meeting would be memorable.

That night I couldn't sleep. My head was throbbing, the mystery deepening.

How was all this possible? So many instant civilizations. I took a map, encircled these suddenly appearing, ready-made cultures and stared at them.

A COMMON ORIGIN?

Was there any connection between them?

I began to sift every available isolated piece of information. Over the next few months the search would lead through scores of countries. Meanwhile, back of my mind the thought kept surfacing: what of the prophecies?

Something told me there was a connection, though I knew not where. As for a possible link between the "instant" civilizations, eight clues emerged.

1. *Symbols and hieroglyphics,* identical worldwide, bore the marks of a common heritage. Everywhere the swastika, snake and sun combinations, as well as numerous specialized and intricate glyphs were repeated with no chance of coincidence.[14]
2. Likewise, similar *systems of writing* were in use—again all over the globe, even on isolated islands. This was striking.
3. And *languages* had similarities. The older these were, the more they resembled each other. Practically all languages have connections through both vocabulary and construction. In almost every language are many words containing similar root words or combinations beyond what mere chance would allow. (Take, for instance, the names of the constellations. I found these were substantially the same whether in Mexico, Africa or Polynesia.)
4. The *calendars* of Egypt and faraway Peru both had eighteen months of twenty days, with a five-day holiday at year's end.
5. I also took into account the great similarities in *buildings,* not only in construction but in astronomical alignment. Sphinxes in Egypt and

Yucatan; pyramids on every continent and on remote islands; monoliths and stone circles also worldwide and often quarried elsewhere in the world. I was struck by similarity even as to original purpose. The Tower of Babel was built (according to Josephus, first-century Jewish historian) to provide shelter should another Deluge destroy the earth. And regarding the Toltec pyramids, the Mexican chronicler, Ixtlilxochitl, states: "After men had multiplied, they erected a very high 'zacuali,' which is today a tower of great height, in order to take refuge in it should the second world be destroyed." Now I ask you, without a common source, why should the purpose be identical in Babylon and Mexico? [15]

6. *Customs* again were similar, as in burial, mummification, circumcision, or in binding babies' heads to produce an elongated skull. (The Maya, Incas, Celts, Egyptians and Basques did this.)

7. *Forms of religious observance* bore more striking similarities.

8. Finally I added to the list *worldwide traditions of early history.* Traditions of a Garden of Delight, a Golden Age, a global Flood, one original language, a tower where sudden language confusion resulted in a dispersal—clearly these bore the marks of a common source.

Of one thing I was certain. The origins of cultures that were so different and so widely dispersed could not wholly be explained by borrowing and imitation.

The Russian poet Valeri Brussov seemed to express it well: "At the bases of the oldest cultures of mankind we must look for a single influence…We must look back beyond antiquity for an X, for a still unknown cultural world that set the engine we know in motion.

"The Egyptians, the Babylonians, the Greeks and Romans were all our teachers, but who were our teachers' teachers?"[16]

My attention was riveted. Here were several fully developed cultures, apparently related, suddenly appearing out of nowhere.

Well, how does one deal with such a discovery? I must confess, my curiosity was exploding. One more search was imperative. This time I had to track down the common source of any footprints leading to these cultures.

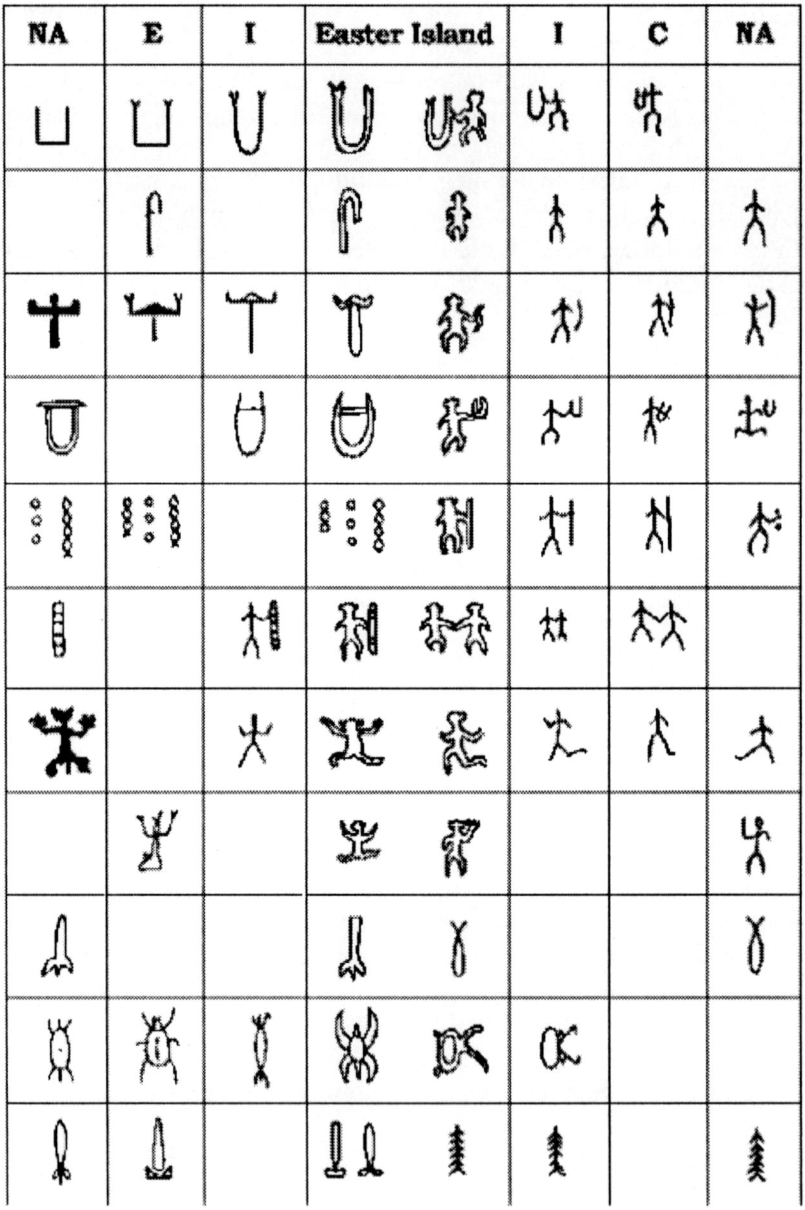

Fig. 2—1. Comparison by Larry E. Arnold of scripts from ancient North American rock art (NA). Egypt (E), China (C). Indus Valley (I) and Easter Island indicates a common origin.

SOURCE OF THE FOOTPRINTS

Fortunately, after 5,000 years, there were prints still visible enough to read.

The evidence fairly tumbled out.

Language was the first clue. It was soon apparent that root words in almost every language had their origins in the Middle East.

Written signs added to the evidence. A single system of signs used over an extensive area of the earth by the Stone-writers originated likewise in the Middle East.

Anthropology provided another helpful clue. I discovered that the best reconstructions by anthropologists located man's point of origin close to the center of the Europe-Asia-Africa land mass.

Archaeological finds clinched it. *Agriculture* had spread all over the world from, where else, but the Middle East highlands. In every instance plants, shrubs and fruit-bearing trees basic to survival and advancement came out of the Middle East first. *Botanical genetic studies* "confirm the archaeological finds and leave no doubt." [17]

There it was. Our beginnings were in the Middle East highlands.

I suggested this to Ed Savage when next we met. The first thing he did was throw at me a tricky question:

"So tell me, then, why did agriculture begin in the difficult arc of mountains and highlands? Doesn't it make you wonder? Why was it not begun on the fertile, easily cultivated plains and valleys?"

It was a natural enough question. During my search I had found other scholars expressing surprise at this most odd discovery.

"Have you considered a worldwide Deluge?" he suggested.

"You don't mean Noah's Flood?" I snorted.

"Just that," clipped Ed. "It does shed some light on things."

"Jon, don't you see? Survivors of such a Deluge (an event most scholars have overlooked) would still be in the mountains. The lowlands were not yet dry enough following the global Flood."

"And did you know, biblical sources not only point to Ararat (Armenia) as the landing place of the Flood survivors, but state that they landed 'in the mountains.'" [18]

Ed unfolded a world map; I elbowed over it on the table. He pointed out the pertinent areas. "Artifacts uncovered suggest that settled communities extended from the Americas in the west to Thailand in the east by 3000 B.C. And overlaying that is a proven pattern of high cultures from Spain to Pakistan."

I stared, somewhat intrigued, at the map. *Armenia, the dispersion point, lay almost precisely in the middle.*

(I would later discover that other researchers had reached a similar conclusion. As says Howells: "If we look, first of all, for that part of the world which was the hothouse of the races, we can make only one choice. All the visible footsteps lead away from Asia. ") [19]

"Ed," I asked, "could this perhaps be the key to your five coincidences?"

"Oh, I hardly think so. How?"

I recited to Edgar the succession of discoveries made since our last meeting.

1. Each of the first civilizations appeared suddenly, already fully developed. (Ed's find.)
2. A connection existed between them.
3. Their footprints led back to the Middle East mountains.

The archaeologist thought a minute, eyes narrowed, working through all the angles. Gradually a smile formed on those weathered lips. "By gum, man, you've hit it! Only one thing could explain their high level of civilization. Those nations got their heritage basically from the world that was wiped out in the Deluge. They continued where the generation of the biblical Noah left off!"

"Those Flood survivors must have carried sufficient knowledge of the antedeluvian era to give a rapid start to the new cultures that sprang up 'out of nowhere' soon after." He clicked his fingers. "And the timing. Four hundred years—all it needed. The oldest civilizations appear just long enough after the Deluge for a population density to support a culture."

Of course we could hardly claim to be first. Sir Leonard Woolley notched up a similar observation years before: "It was confidently expected that the widely held view of a gradual development would be proved, but the whole evidence has been to the contrary; indeed, it has grown to such proportions where we contact the most ancient civilizations that we find the peak was reached soon after the flood." [20]

The *sudden* appearance of civilization is itself a memorial to history's one great catastrophe. More importantly, the Flood is a historical event of tremendous testimonial importance to modern man.

As in the days of Noah, the world has reached an unprecedented stage of material and technical progress. Then, as now, skepticism, corruption and violence abound.

Ancient prophecies treat Noah and the Flood as a prototype of the coming sudden and fearful end of the present world.

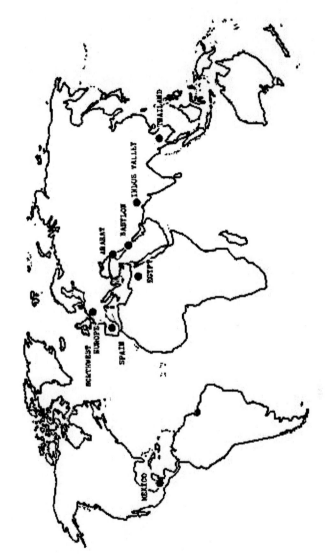

Fig. 2— 2. From central dispersion point (Ararat), descendants of the flood survivors took with them advanced knowledge that enabled new civilization centers to sprout suddenly.

20

For example: "As the days of Noah were, so shall also the coming of the Son of man be. For as in the days that were before the flood they were eating and drinking, marrying and giving in marriage, until the day that Noah entered into the ark, and knew not until the Flood came, and took eating and drinking, marrying and giving in marriage, until the day that Noah entered into the ark, and knew not until the Flood came, and took them all away; so shall also the coming of the Son of man be." (Matt. 24:37-39.)

Other prophecies project that as the first world perished by water, so the present world shall be destroyed by fire (2 Pet. 3:3-7). And as this second world emerged from the Deluge stripped of its original glory, so shall emerge from the final fire, a new world cleansed of evil, misery and death, and restored to a perfection which shall transcend even its original glory.

WORLD ORDER FROM THE RUINS

It goes without saying that the small group of bewildered survivors from the Deluge could hardly reproduce all of the aspects of the pre-Flood technology. Nevertheless they would have bequeathed to their migrating descendants the information of which they had personal or recorded knowledge.

We know that the very earliest grains show genetic evidence of sophisticated manipulation; that is, they were already uniform and highly specialized immediately after the Flood.

In an attempt to reconstruct the antedeluvian technology, the semblance of an integrated global civilization emerged in various parts of the world. Its achievements were astonishing; in some spheres, penetrating knowledge which our science has scarcely begun to nudge.

I filed the results of my search under "C" for "Confirmed" and sat by the fire, watching the coals on the hearth. It was time to call the Jigsaw Team together.

HOW
SOMEBODY
MAPPED OUR
WHOLE PLANET
BEFORE
"HISTORY"
BEGAN!

Chapter 3

MYSTERIOUS MESSAGES IN THE CANYON

The year is 1799. The explorer Humboldt is paddling down the wild waters of the upper Orinoco. Formidable cliffs press upon him from both sides. Suddenly he glimpses, etched in the rock high above, an array of strange messages.

Humboldt asks the natives what it means. Their reply is so startling, he almost tips out of his canoe.

Exactly 130 years later, Halil Edhem, Director of the National Museums of Turkey, is cleaning out debris in the Topkapi Palace in Istanbul. He comes upon the dusty fragments of an old map. Examination shows that it was compiled by an Admiral Piri Reis in 1513, from portions of much older maps.

Not until 1956, however, is the map subjected to a serious analysis. The Hydrographic Office of the U.S. Navy issues a statement. What it reveals is almost unbelievable.

Just twelve years later, Richard Nixon arrives in China. A cultural exchange is initiated with America. Interest is awakened in an ancient Chinese document, the *Shan Hai King*. Something which this old manuscript reveals is enough to rock you off your seat.

All these seemingly unrelated events would come together with compelling force on October 17, 1984. On that day, I strolled into the foyer of a l Hong Kong hotel for a rendezvous with the Jigsaw Team. Five men and one woman were converging with results of separate investigations into some very strange recent discoveries.

Phillip Corderoy was a cartographer; Denise Tagg a linguist of no mean accomplishment; Paul Heron a mathematician; Jacob Wajsmann a keen student of prehistory; and Charlie Perch a Scotland Yard-trained detective who had turned to genealogy more from passion than from pecuniary ambitions. His innate skepticism would render Perch all the more valuable for critical analysis.

As it turned out, we would spend four days in a tight little suite, advancing the pieces each of us held of the jigsaw puzzle, then slowly keying them together until a clear picture developed—a picture which would prove more startling than any of us ever expected.

...Corderoy snapped open his briefcase, withdrew a sheaf of papers and squinted at us over his spectacles.

"I want you each to take a gander at these maps. There are fourteen of them, all from the Medieval and Renaissance period." Corderoy laid them on the table.

"This one is *the Zeno map, drawn in 1380.* See how accurately it outlines the coasts of Norway, Sweden, Denmark, Germany, Scotland, as well as the exact latitude and longitude of a certain number of islands."

"Just a minute, Phil," Heron cut in. "The chronometer, necessary to determine longitude, was not invented until 1765."

"He's right," said Perch. "That is why the readings of Columbus were all inaccurate."[1]

"Nevertheless, the Zeno map is most accurate," insisted Corderoy. "And notice, the topography of Greenland is shown free of glaciers as it was prior to the Ice Age. Unknown rivers and mountains shown on this Zeno map have since been located in probes of the French Polar Expedition of 1947-1949. What do you think of that?"

Silence.

"See this photograph? It shows *a Chinese map on stone from 1137,* formed on a spherical grid.

"And this is *the Camerio map of 1502,* which uses the same spherical grid."

Miss Tagg looked agitated. "Listen, Phil, in the Middle Ages they thought the earth was flat. Are you certain these are not modern fakes?"

"No chance of a mistake, I assure you. But just wait till you see this." Corderoy passed around another sheet.

"Now, here's *the Zauche map of 1737.* It shows Antarctica free of—"

Wajsmann interjected. "Impossible, Phil. Antarctica's existence was not verified until 1819!"

Corderoy grinned. "I expected that. Nevertheless, this map does show that continent—and *completely free of ice* to boot. Surprisingly, it is shown not as one continent but two islands separated by a strait from the Ross to the Weddell Seas (a fact which was not established until the Geophysical Year, 1968). Also shown are islands of the Mid-Atlantic Ridge, now known to lie on the bottom of the ocean.

"Now here's a map drawn *in 1531 by Orontius Fineus,* in which the dimensions of the Antarctic land mass correspond very closely to those on the best modern maps. The map indicates that the center of Antarctica was beginning to fill with ice when its source maps were drawn. It shows rivers and fjords in Antarctica where today mile-thick glaciers flow.

"Next, notice this *Mercator chart of 1569;* it depicts only the Antarctic coast left uncovered by glaciers.

"I really don't follow you," said Heron. 'The events you're describing are Ice Age, cave man era and all that. Yet you admitted these are Renaissance maps."

Corderoy burst into laughter. "That's right. But I think you'll agree these particular maps are infinitely superior to the regular maps made at that time. Now I'll share a secret. You see, my friends, many of the Medieval and Renaissance mapmakers admitted they were copying from sources whose origins were unknown.

"These maps are a scientific achievement far surpassing the abilities of the navigators and mapmakers of the Renaissance, Middle Ages, the Arab world, or any ancient geographers. They are the product of an unknown people antedating recognized history.

"Now, here's a very exciting map, copied *in 1559. The Hadji Ahmed map* shows Antarctica and the Pacific coast of the United States of America with extreme accuracy. It also depicts the land bridge that once existed between Siberia and Alaska.

"This Andrea Benincasa map (1508) indicates that Northern Europe was being covered by the Ice Age glaciation's furthest advance.

"Here is *the Iehudi Ibn ben Zara map of 1487.* Notice these remnants of glaciers in Britain? And the detailed profiles of islands in the Mediterranean and Aegean Seas? Those islands are still there—but now under water.

"The Hamy King chart (1502) indicates northern Siberian rivers emptying into the Arctic Ocean (but which are now all under ice). It also shows glacial actions in the Baltic countries. What are today huge islands in Southeast Asia are shown on this map joined to land (which they once were). And you know what? The map even shows an ancient Suez Canal!

'Ptolemy's map of the North depicts a glacial sheet advancing across south-central Greenland; and at the same time it shows glaciers retreating from northern Germany and southern Sweden.

"Do you see? This all could only have come from the findings of surveying parties that tracked the areas before, during and after the Ice Age.

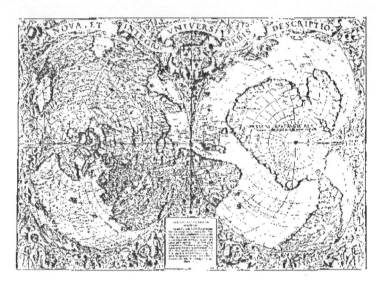

Fig. 3-1a. The Orontius Fineus map. Its greatest error is that Antarctica is drawn too large, possibly a copyist's mistake, although mountains and other details, not rediscovered until 1958, are accurately presented.

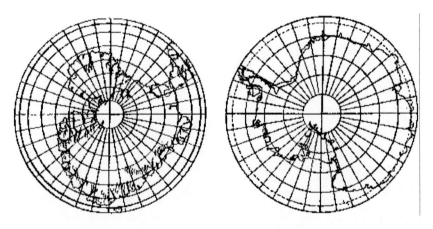

Fig. 3-1b. Antarctica on the Orontius Fineus map of 1531 (left) reduced to the same scale and grid as modern map of Antarctica.

26

During the Ice Age, according to the evolutionary theory, humans were grunting savages.

"The Gloreanus map (1510) shows not only the exact line of the Atlantic coast of America from Canada to Tierra del Fuego, but also the whole length of the Pacific coast.

"The King Jaime World Chart (1502) shows the Sahara Desert as a fertile land with large lakes, rivers and cities (which, at a remote period, it was).

"Then there's this *Dulcert map of 1339,* tracing from Ireland to the Don River of Eastern Europe; I tell you, this map shows precision beyond understanding.

"But there's one more. Its a beauty."

With a teasing twinkle, Corderoy eyed us each in turn, arose from his chair and ambled over to the window. He stood there gazing over the harbor toward Victoria Peak with its skirt of skyscrapers. He just stood there and said nothing. It was as though we were no longer with him.

"Come on, Phil. We're waiting. What's this trump of yours?"

Corderoy turned, still smirking, and rejoined us. He felt for something in his briefcase and plopped it on the table.

"This is the *Piri Reis chart of 1513,"* he began. "After its discovery, Captain Arlington H. Mallery, an American authority on cartography, asked the U.S. Hydrographic Office to examine it. The U.S. Navy, through Commander Larsen, subsequently issued this statement." Corderoy took his notes and read to us.

"'The Hydrographic Office of the Navy has verified an ancient chart—it's called the Piri Reis map, that goes back more than 5,000 years. It's so accurate, only one thing could explain it—a worldwide survey. The Hydrographic Office couldn't believe it, either, at first. But they not only proved the map genuine, it's been used to correct errors in some present-day maps.'"

Corderoy grew excited. "I say if ever there were a treasure map, this is it. Just crammed with priceless gems. It tells the story of ancient coastlines, as well as the surprising exploits of our ancestors five thousand years ago.

"Piri Reis stated that his copy was a composite from twenty ancient maps. So let's explore it."

I took a pad and noted the following features:

1. South America and Africa in correct relative longitude and latitude. Not only were the Caribbean, Spanish, African and South American

coasts in correct positions relative to each other, but even isolated land areas, like Cape Verde Island, the Azores, the Canary Islands, as well as topographies of the interiors—mountain ranges, peaks, rivers, plateaus. All were accurately positioned by longitude and latitude.

2. The coastline of Queen Maud Land in Antarctica. The islands and bays of the depicted coastline are the same as they appear below the Antarctic ice sheet (as recently revealed by seismic echo soundings). Pictured in great detail are regions scarcely explored today, including a mountain range that remained undiscovered until 1952. Interestingly, the map shows two bays where the modern seismic map showed lands. However, when the experts were asked to check their measurements, they found that the ancient map was correct, after all. One thing was crystal clear. Either somebody had mapped Antarctica before the ice cap covered the continent, or else the ice-covered continent was mapped with very sophisticated instruments. [2]

3. The Isle of Pines, Andros Island, San Salvador, Jamaica, the mouth of the Amazon and the island of Morajo are all correctly shaped and perfectly located in latitude and longitude.

4. A major error appeared to be Greenland, shown as three islands. But during the International Geophysical Year it was proved that this correctly represented the state of affairs about 3000 B.C.

5. Every mountain range in northern Canada and Alaska was recorded on this ancient map—including some ranges which the U.S. Army Map Services did not have on their maps. But the U.S. Army has since found them!

6. The ancient source-maps were drawn using a circular grid based on spherical trigonometry, with the focal point situated in Egypt. The copiest Piri Reis (unfamiliar with circular projection) shifted and spliced the original grid to compensate for the curvature. Any modern spheroid projection on a flat surface would cause the same distortion. (Notice this in the accompanying comparison between Piri Reis and a modern map.)

Corderoy pressed the point. Was this not compelling proof of the map's validity? Clearly it came from an advanced ancient technology and *its grid system is similar to air navigation maps.*

Even so, we cannot know how many times it was imperfectly copied.

"Now listen to this," said Corderoy. "The Piri Reis map projection was based on *an overestimate of 4 1/2 degrees* in the circumference of the earth.

Only one geographer in the ancient world had made that overestimation: the Greek Eratosthenes.

"When the Piri Reis map is redrawn to correct the Eratosthenes error, all existing longitude errors on the map are thereby reduced to almost zero.

"This can mean only one thing. Do you see? The Greeks who mapped according to Eratosthenes' circumference had before them source maps which had been drawn without that error. Thus, the geographical knowledge on which the Piri Reis map is based ultimately originated not with the Greeks but with an earlier people who possessed a more advanced science of mapmaking than even the Greeks!"

"That's brilliant!" exclaimed Perch. "Couldn't do better myself. What you're saying is that while Greece and Rome were developing new civilizations, the vestiges of an older one, seemingly worldwide in scope, was vanishing. It left these maps, which were partly incomprehensible. So later cartographers altered them. Yes, I can see that."

"There's just one more thing," said Corderoy. "The evidence indicates that what we have here is only part of an original world map."

He paused.

"Whew!" whistled Wajsmann.

So here it was—evidence of science in an early epoch, which is considered to have had none. Here were physical fragments of the amazing knowledge of a super culture long vanished.

We spread out six pieces of the jigsaw—facts which were now apparent concerning those early explorers:

1. They possessed a knowledge of cartography comparable to our own.
2. They knew the correct shape and size of the earth.
3. They possessed a knowledge of cartography comparable to our own.
4. They knew the correct shape and size of the earth.
5. They used spherical trigonometry in their mathematical measurements.
6. They utilized ultramodern methods of projection (exact coordinates).
7. They must have had at their disposal advanced geodetic instruments (and trained specialists to use them) to measure longitude and latitude (totally lost and not developed in the modern world until the end of the eighteenth century).[3]

Fig. 3-2a. The Piri Reis map, dated 1513 but compiled from world maps of ancient times.

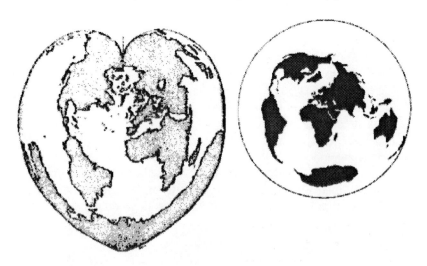

Fig. 3-2b. For comparison a global projection based on Cairo, complied from NASA sources.
Copy of the Hadji Ahmed globe.

8. They must have been organized and directed on a global scale.

The picture falling into place was this. Almost *5,000* years ago somebody undertook a survey of the whole planet. The technology at their disposal was very sophisticated.

Breakfast next morning was in a small restaurant off Nathan Road. Rice congee and fried pastries. Different!

Wajsmann had uncovered some little-known data which quite rocked us. Back in our room, he elaborated.

"Did you know that thousands of years ago people in India knew faraway England as 'the Island of the White Cliffs'? Their *Vishnu Purana* reveals a close acquaintance with Europe. The geographical contours of the Americas and the North Polar zone are also described in detail."

"That interests me, Jacob." All eyes turned to Denise Tagg. "My family was Irish, so I've had a penchant for the most ancient Irish legends. And you know what? They agree. They say that Ireland was visited by men from India—the Dravidians—who came not as invaders but as surveyors."

Wajsmann nodded. "The Maya of Guatemala divided a spherical earth into five major continents: Africa, Europe-Asia, North and South America and Australia.

"And in second-century Greece, Flavius Philostratus wrote, 'If the land be considered in relation to the entire mass of water, we can show that the earth is the lesser of the two.' Now, I ask you, how could the ancients have known this if they had not traversed and measured the earth's surface?"

"Admittedly, you have a point there," observed Heron.

"Of course, the earliest Egyptians were knowledgeable about land measurements, too; and they practiced sophisticated surveying techniques. In fact, they understood enough to influence many other nations, in locating important cities and temples on meridians, all based on simple fractions of the earth's dimensions.

"It seems to me that this independent testimony from different races does back up Phil's evidence from the maps."

Perch smoothed his moustache. "Over breakfast, Jacob, you spoke of an ancient Chinese book."

"That I did, Charlie. I find it quite an astonishing document. I'm referring to the Fourth Book of *Shan Hai King* entitled 'The Classic of Eastern Mountains,' from 2250 BC. In it there are four sections describing mountains located 'beyond the Eastern Sea'—on the other side of the Pacific Ocean. Each section begins by describing the geographical features

31

of a particular mountain: its height, shape, mineral deposits, surrounding rivers and types of flora. Then it points the direction and distance to the next mountain, and so on.[4]

"It's like a road map. By following the clues, we've found that these sections describe in detail the topography of western and central North America.

'Each mountain can be identified—and each river.

"I tell you, this document is a geographical survey. But that's not all. It even gives the experiences of the surveyors—from picking up black opals and gold nuggets in Nevada, to watching seals frolic on the rocks in San Francisco Bay. They recorded their fascination at a strange animal that avoided danger by pretending to be dead (obviously the native opossum). You can read about their wonder at the Grand Canyon, 'a stream flowing in a bottomless ravine,' and a sunrise there. (That's in the Ninth and Fourteenth Books.)

'By the third century B.C., when many Chinese records were reevaluated and condensed, it was found that the geographical learning it contained did not correspond to any lands known at that time. So it was reclassified as a myth. Now we know better."

"Well, what do you know!" exclaimed Perch. "A detailed Chinese survey of North America 4,500 years ago!"

"Precisely. Part of the global survey, I dare say."

Denise Tagg sprang into action. "This is where my piece of the jigsaw comes in. I've done some detective work along many of the routes which those surveyors of North America took. Would you believe, some rock drawings still survive? Among these pictures on stone you can recognize carvings of the Chinese dragon.

"Stone-writers left their traces on every continent. A single system of signs was used.[5] They used 241 special sequences of particular geometric signs and symbols. The stone-writers were not barbaric hunters or nomads. They were intelligent people who were systematic in what they did. In their repetition and locations, the symbols had meaning and purpose.[6] I am certain the stone-writers left these guide signs to mark the way for others who would follow them. These surveyors left their traces in the form of maps, symbols and place names."

(Of course, symbols left on rocks and tablets presuppose communication by language. I recalled the biblical assertion that "the whole earth was of one language, and of one speech."[7] The evidence seemed now to support it.)

It was my turn to submit a piece of the jigsaw; I passed around copies.

"This is a report by the explorer Humboldt. In 1799, while wandering in Guiana and the upper Orinoco, Humboldt came across rock pictures and hieroglyphic signs high up on the mountains.

"The natives told him that their ancestors, *in the time of the great waters,* came to the tops of these mountains in canoes, and that the rocks were still so soft that a man could trace marks on them with his bare fingers."[8]

I paused to let this sink in.

"Go on," urged Heron.

"Can you see the significance?" I asked. "It tallies precisely with conditions that prevailed after the global Deluge. Great inland seas remained on all continents, often trapped at high levels, and not draining back into the ocean for centuries.

"The Deluge, as it reshaped continents, thrust sedimentary rubble mountain-high. This would have remained soft and impressionable for a considerable time."

Miss Tagg cut in. "That reminds me of picture writings elsewhere. From the highlands of Colombia to the gorge of the Xingu, on the eastern side of Brazil's Matto Grosso, they all have one feature in common: they are carved on high rocks, in gloomy canyons, impossible to climb. You know, some are up to seventy feet tall. It's the same in the Mexican mountain ranges; in Siberia too. The signs are found on impossible cliffs."

Perch cleared his throat. "So within centuries of the Flood, the new population undertook a resources survey of the whole earth. And they mapped every continent. Yeah, I see that.

"Now I think we can identify some of the men involved in this. Biblical chronology throws some light on it."

That was one out of the blue! Actual names?

"Yes, three, in fact. During the period 2800 to 2500 B.C.

"First there was a guy called *Peleg.* The Book of Genesis *(*10:25*)* states that 'in his day was the earth divided' (as in 'allotment,' 'marking off an area'). I've looked into this. A more accurate translation would be: 'In his day was the earth measured' (or 'surveyed')."

I noticed a murmur of surprise.

"Then there was *Mizraim,* according to the chronology a grandson of Noah, who is credited with founding Egypt. His name means 'to delineate,' 'to draw up a plan,' 'to make a representation' (especially in association with measuring distances). And sure enough, at least two old maps linked with the ancient past (the Piri Reis and Reinal) were based on a circular projection with the focal point in Egypt.

"Perhaps it is no accident that the Great Pyramid records in its dimensions the measurement of the earth on the scale of 1:43,200. Both the earth's circumference (including the equatorial bulge) and polar radius (with the flattening at the poles) were known with *an accuracy comparable to that recorded by satellite surveys from space.*"

Perch the detective was sparking now.

"There was also *Almodad* ('measurer'), the inventor of geometry, 'who measured the earth to its extremities.'[9] According to chronology, Almodad is the progenitor of the Southern Arabians. Many of these maps we've been studying reveal peculiarities of geography that were first noticed by the Arabs."

Wajsmann spoke now. "That's really something, Charlie. When did Almodad die?"

"About 2350 B.C. give or take a few."

"What a clincher! That Chinese *Shan Hai King* book was written only a century later!"

That evening the Jigsaw Team celebrated. Those isolated pieces—the maps, the traditional reports, the building survey methods, the rock signs and the chronology, all so different—were no longer a puzzle. They dovetailed.

AN
INCREDIBLE
ELECTRIC WEB
THAT GAVE
ONE CITY
WORLD CONTROL

Chapter 4

OPERATION SPIDER WEB

A chill blast whipped under her coat, as Rebecca stepped out.
It was a horrendous shock: the mud, the utter desolation, the floating bodies. But worse, an awful silence, the silence of universal death.

She turned with a heart-rending sob to her father-in-law. Here they were, eight people, the only living human beings in all the world. How indescribably lonely they must have felt and what a dread and fear must have come upon them!

As Noah and his family stepped down from their survival vessel, they gazed upon a world totally foreign to them. Gone was the enchanting, subtropic environment they knew. All the familiar landmarks had been swept away.

Instead, barren wastes, bleak and sterile hills and unbearable extremes of cold and heat confronted them. Great mountain ranges—high, forbidding, rocky walls—had been thrust up, destined to isolate areas into harsh climatic pockets.

The first generations were born and grew up in the foothills of Ararat. But in time their curiosity was to draw them out to stake new territories and to search for valuable resources.

They soon found a world reduced considerably in land area. The fertility of the soil and the natural resources necessary to human progress were now unequally distributed.

One resource was of particular concern. Antedeluvian scientists had unlocked a secret. They had discovered our spinning planet to be a giant generator, its land masses crisscrossed with energy lines.

These magnetic currents they had harnessed. But now all trace of the power network was gone.

OBJECT OF THE GLOBAL SURVEY

Within centuries the rapidly increasing population sent out exploratory expeditions. Soon almost every corner of the world was visited by a group of men who came with a particular task to accomplish.[1]

They were charged with relocating those energy springs and constructing a grid pattern to harness them. Today we might have called it—one imagines—Operation Spider Web, or some such thing.

To facilitate this, they employed units of measurement based on simple fractions of the earth's dimensions. They measured distances, as we have noticed, in degrees, minutes and seconds of latitude and longitude, just as we do today.[2]

Soon a "prehistoric" network of dead-straight alignments appeared. It seems to have sprung up everywhere at once. Planning took place on an almost unimaginably large scale.

Along these lines, (situated at terrestrial power points) arose temples, pillars, rocking stones, circles, crosses, mounds, pyramids, tunnels and platforms. Traces of these are dotted still throughout the world. You see them on every continent and even on remote islands.[3]

Sites had an exact geometric relationship to each other within a master worldwide pattern. For example, all ancient temples in Greece arose in relation to each other. Those in Greece were geometrically interlocked with those in Egypt.

Planetwide, the system constituted ONE GIANT SCIENTIFIC INSTRUMENT.

Today we all live within the ruins of this single vast ancient structure, whose sheer size has so far rendered it invisible. In the words of John Michell, "a great scientific instrument lies sprawled over the entire surface of the globe."[4] It is marked by these megaliths of all types, all aligned in a *single geometric pattern*—the remains of an ancient power network.

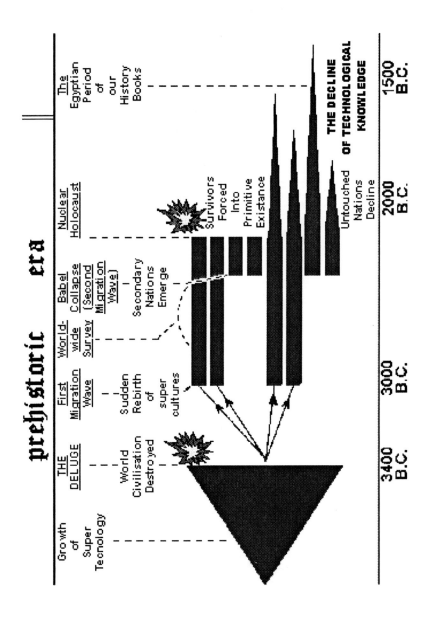

prehistoric era

Growth of Super Tecnology	THE DELUGE	First Migration Wave	World-wide Survey	Babel Collapse (Second Migration Wave)	Nuclear Holocaust	The Egyptian Period of our History Books
	World Civilisation Destroyed	Sudden Rebirth of super cultures		Secondary Nations Emerge	Survivors Forced Into Primitive Existance	

Untouched Nations Decline

THE DECLINE OF TECHNOLOGICAL KNOWLEDGE

3400 B.C.   3000 B.C.   2000 B.C.   1500 B.C.

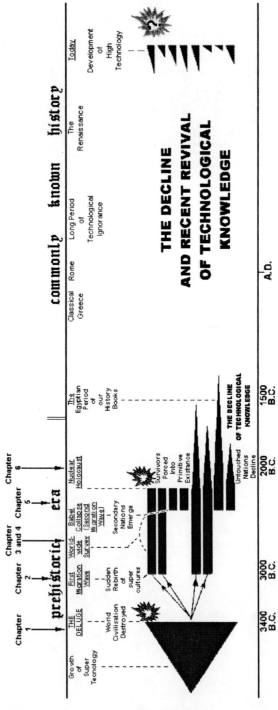

THE DECLINE
AND RECENT REVIVAL
OF TECHNOLOGICAL
KNOWLEDGE

In order for it to operate, many sites were aligned to favor certain astronomical phenomena. The planners were conversant with the introduction of solar or atmospheric energy into the terrestrial energy streams. They developed a technology to detect earth currents, and then to manipulate them to a predictable result.

Thus, all over the world, thousands upon thousands of pillars (called "menhirs") arose in symmetrical formation, their purpose to realign earth magnetism from its natural meandering paths to straight artificial lines.

At each pillar, the electric current of the atmosphere was attracted to combine with the terrestrial current to produce a fusion of power. (A secret we have not yet utilized.) Interestingly, the standing stones were all rich in quartz, a crystal similar to that used with the cat's whiskers in early radio receivers.

It has been suggested that megaliths were connected below ground by metal strips, although there is no conclusive proof for this position. Because the standing stones worked as cathodes, the corrosive current over the millennia would have most certainly dissolved the metal, leaving the grooves into which they were set. Such grooves are found below ground level in, for example, the Breton menhirs of France. That these grooves had some such functional purpose is a distinct possibility.

And something else. Researchers have detected an energy rising in spiral form from standing stones, gathering magnetic strength toward the top of the stone. Interestingly, photographs of the stones are sometimes marred by a mist of light surrounding their lower extremities.

The crucial factor was that from natural energy springs in the earth, the currents were ultimately directed to mounds—which focalized the energy fields.

There is overwhelming evidence for the reality of these forces, only rediscovered in modern times by Wilhelm Reich. He described how this energy could be trapped or accumulated by constructing a chamber lined with inorganic material and covered on the outside with alternate layers of organic and inorganic matter.

Is it not startling, then, to find that almost every ancient site has at least one such buried chamber—purposely lined with the same alternating layers! Often foreign stones and clay were used, selected for various magnetic properties. These submerged chambers were *energy accumulators.*

Finally, from these mounds, the currents were dissipated to the surrounding countryside.

Not only did standing stones, mounds and pyramids focus energy fields. *Across the whole world, the structures formed a gigantic power network.*

This provided the population with a source of energy and inspiration to which their whole civilization was tuned.

EARLY USES OF THE POWER NETWORK

It appears that a major effect of the energy lines was to *increase soil fertility and plant growth.*

Fig. 4-2. A spiral force has been sensed around ancient standing stones; this is derived from their positions above the crossing of earth's magnetic currents immediately underneath. (Francis Hitching.)

Fertility stones are no myth. (The phallic symbolism which later developed was a degenerative response to an earlier scientific truth.)

Modern experiments have shown that cosmic influences *do* affect magnetic currents at the earth's surface and that at certain seasons rocks become charged with energy which they release into the soil, stimulating seed germination and vegetable growth. Lightning flashes also are known to affect the nitrates of the earth, ensuring fertility.

Green tomatoes placed within a magnetic field have been shown to ripen four to six times faster; seeds placed in a current grew many times faster. Something new here?

The energy lines were also harnessed for *propulsion and transport,* if we are to believe Druid reports.

When a line became animated by a sunrise directly down a path, the currents were purposely directed so as to charge an object to such a degree that it could be levitated and made to travel. British flying vehicles so energized arc said to have flown to Greece.

Of course, an eclipse intervening could lead to disaster, by causing a sudden drop in the power of magnetic activity. This would shut down all of the society's machinery, an event comparable to modern-day electrical blackouts.

Thus, only by a constant computation of solar, lunar and planetary movements could the waxing and waning of the currents be measured and anticipated.

Here lies the answer to a riddle. We've long wondered why ancient astronomers seemed so obsessed—almost insanely so—by the need to predict eclipses with absolute certainty. Now you know.

Another use of the network was *power production and communication.* A word here on pyramids. The pyramid shape is known to accumulate and may even generate energy—provided that specific proportions and exact alignments are followed.

So somebody's told you that pyramids were tombs! In general, pyramids were not built as tombs (more on that later). Significantly, they were part of the worldwide network. For starters, eighty-five survive in Egypt; at least four in France (one radioactive); hundreds along coastal Peru; thousands in Mexico, Guatemala and Honduras; while still more survive in China, Tibet, Southern Russia, the Sudan, Brazil, Hawaii, Tahiti, the Marianas, Caroline Islands, Marquesas islands and Bermuda (submerged); as well as stone step-pyramids in Florida and pyramid-like temples in Southern India. Now, that's some list.

And there is evidence, quite considerable evidence, that the pyramids focused energy fields; that is, they produced power.

Additionally, *healing* probably resulted from this energy system. It has been observed that animals born over "springs" of favorable energy are always healthier than those born elsewhere.

A connection has been noticed between the incidence of ailments such as cancer and the location of dwellings over lines of earth current that have become sour.

Such "black streams" have been purified successfully by driving metal stakes into the earth above the cause. The effect, it seems, is to allow atmospheric forces to enter the flow of the earth current.

LATER USES

We know that the Chinese sited every building, stone, and planted tree to conform to the "dragon currents" that flowed along the lines.

The Incas utilized similar spirit lines with the Sun Temple at Cuzco as their hub.

The Romans built their famous straight roads along these already existing lines.

North African Bedouins use the line system marked out by standing stones and cairns to aid their crossing of today's desert wastes.

The Australian aborigines still use the "prehistoric" line system. At certain times of the year these "turingas" (lines) become revitalized, they say, by energies flowing through them, giving new life to the adjacent countryside. The natives paint the story on rocks, but claim it is not the pictures but the rocks themselves that release energy to fertilize plants and animals. The aborigines actually receive messages over vast distances and are forewarned of the approach of strangers—all through their system of magic lines. It's a residual legacy, you see, from a former global science.

THE BABEL CONNECTION

By its very nature, this network required that all terrestrial surface currents be accounted for, if it were to operate to its full potential.

Thus the stone monuments were strewn across the world, located on the crossings of the "ley lines."

This implies that *a single authority was directing a united world effort.*

Perhaps the biblical Tower of Babel was the receiving station for earth's ley line currents. At any rate, it was constructed as the result of a concerted effort on the part of the outspreading nations to remain together "lest we be scattered abroad upon the face of the whole earth."[5] The tower was a center of world communications, as well as of energy accumulation. The city of Babel (later to become Babylon) was a political center for world government.

By possessing such a global energy center, Babel effectively controlled the world. Old chronicles record that Nimrod, the egotistic founder of Babylon, "grew more and more wicked and mad until he thought in his heart that he was himself God." The arrogance of Babel became a scandal.

Then something happened—something significant enough to mark a break in world conditions and to bring the line system to an end.

Today we are left with but shadows and remnants of the former universal system.

Thanks to archaeological discoveries, much of what was classed as myth in the biblical account of the rise of nations is now being found true. It is becoming increasingly tenable to regard its "stories" as not religious fantasy but rather apt reporting of phenomena that actually occurred. The story of a former global unity which was broken into factions is now seen as real.

It might be said that the sudden breakup of the totalitarian world government was the catalyst. In the events which followed, most continents and island groups were to become so isolated, they would all but forget each other's existence.

Thus began the next stage of man's decline.

HOW
THE GLOBAL
TYRANNY
COLLAPSED-AND
WHY MANKIND
HAS BEEN
SLIPPING
SINCE

Chapter 5

SUDDEN FURY

The event was devastating. Shock waves from it are still being felt today. Until that moment, the plan to contain the fast-growing population under one central world authority, based at Babel, appeared to be working.

Then in one violent stroke, communications were destroyed.

In the resultant chaos, the world alliance collapsed.

A confused secondary migration began and many peoples lost contact (see map of prehistoric era in Chapter 4).

So now the world order was gone, but one thing lingered on—the memory of the technology they had once enjoyed.

SECONDARY CIVILIZATIONS ARISE

Traditions and biblical writings speak of a mass dispersion of peoples from the early Babel civilization about a thousand years after the Deluge.

It is significant that a number of archaeologists take the Tower of Babel record seriously and conjecture it to be in the period somewhat before 2000 B.C.

And sure enough, a surprising number of "new" civilizations that suddenly appear are dated to approximately 2000 B.C.

I'm wondering, could this be more than coincidence?

PROGRESSIVE DECLINE

Soon communications were reestablished among the now separate nations.

But all was not well.

Some of those who still retained the awesome knowledge, ultimately used it in a highly destructive war. In a succession of nuclear—yes, nuclear—holocausts, several advanced nations on three continents vanished. (The chilling story awaits us in Chapter 29.)

From their wreckage, "primitive" and agricultural economies emerged. Salvaging little but essentials, the survivors had to concentrate on bare survival.

Without technological facilities to repair what remained of the equipment and machinery, they soon fell into disuse. Only the vivid memory survived.

Of course there were civilization centers untouched by these disasters. These entered a period of decline.

Existing knowledge was fused with the cultures of later societies. But these civilizations lasted not many centuries past 2000 B.C.

There is some evidence that a brief period of revival was, over the centuries, experienced in each of the Middle Eastern countries, as remnants of earlier advanced technology resurfaced, although on a greatly diminished scale.

Sophisticated artifacts and records from their earlier past appear to have enriched both Babylonia and Egypt in later times.

Indeed, isolated elements of the old technology continued to resurface from time to time.

From about 250 B.C. to the time of Christ, there was a fragmentary technological rekindling among Mediterranean peoples. This, I might add, was brutally extinguished by the Roman invasion of the area.

Already for some time a privileged few had been the sole custodians of what knowledge remained. They had kept the secrets "safe" from abuse by the "unqualified."

Now, as the world began to slip into the Dark Ages, the few records that survived were jealously guarded by secret societies. Gradually these too passed into oblivion. And the world forgot its past.

Only in the last 300 years have we witnessed a cultural revival. And only now are we rediscovering that which used to be.

Doesn't it shake you up just a little to realize that *basically the way of history has been cultural regression?*

FROM SUPERIOR TO INFERIOR

Wherever we look, regression is evident. If there be any doubt, take these twenty-three examples. Skim through, if you wish. There's quite enough to prove it.

1. Digging to the lowest depths, archaeologists repeatedly come upon a *city complex* architecturally superior to later cities on the same site.
2. The *medicine* of ancient Egypt was, generally speaking, far superior to that practiced in Europe during the Middle Ages. Pre-Incan medical surgery was superior to that of the Peruvian Inca.
3. The *oceangoing vessels* employed by the ancient explorers were large, strong and immensely superior to the craft possessed by medieval Europeans.
4. The earliest ancient *maps* were drawn with the greatest precision—and superior to later navigational charts.
5. The old Maya *calendar* is superior to our own.
6. It can be demonstrated that many *languages* have suffered degeneration.
7. Ancient set *building stones* are much larger and more difficult to transport than those of subsequent cultures.
8. In dynamic realism, the masterpieces of the Cro-Magnon cave artists of Altamira (Spain) and Lascaux (France) were superior to the *paintings and sculptures* of later civilizations.
9. *Roads:* Britain's prehistoric Icknield Way (running 200 miles, in places as wide as a four-lane highway) is superior to any road constructed by the later Romans.
10. *Mathematics:* Whereas very ancient cultures knew about zero (the secret ingredient in advanced mathematics), frequently, as decadence occurred, they forgot it. The Babylonians, for example, wrote it as a blank space—a practice which eventually disappeared. The same retrograde process occurred in China.
11. *Astronomy:* Originally, constellations *took the form of* animals, making it easier to remember and identify them; however, as civilization retrogressed, they actually *became* animals, heroes or gods.
12. Scientific *compasses,* which pointed due north and south, were later preserved as magic, through which Chinese necromancers told fortunes.
13. *Crete:* The earliest Cretan empire was more culturally advanced than the empire which followed it (featuring running water, the most modem bathroom facilities, tinted-glass goblets, glazed dinnerware and elaborate dress styles).

14. *Canary Islands:* Considerable cultural deterioration operated until (by the time the Spaniards discovered them in the fourteenth century) warfare was being waged with stones and wooden weapons. They preserved the memory of a great civilization of cities, but were no longer capable of constructing anything more than simple huts.

15. *The Pacific:* On most islands of Polynesia and Micronesia are remains of cities, temples, harbors and statues, whose size and elaborate architecture indicate a civilization incomparably more advanced than exists there today.

16. *Pakistan:* The lowest strata of the remains of Mohenjo-Daro show a more developed art than the upper layers. Later the quality of the commercial seals fell off sadly. The soapstone was replaced by common clay; and crude geometric shapes replaced the lifelike engravings. Highly glazed ceramics were supplanted by plain clumsy pots. The city's systematic plan gave way to shabby structures and mere hovels at the topmost stratum. From a high early peak of technology, it then progressed no further. Everything, was done in imitation of the old techniques. Even the bricks were inferior.

17. *Central America:* The present-day descendants of what was once the greatest empire in the Americas (the Maya) are mere jungle savages, unable to read or write their ancestors' hieroglyphics; unable to construct large buildings, much less whole cities.

18. *Egypt* declined from technical sophistication to a vague shadow of its former glory. Earliest pyramid construction was superior to later pyramid construction; succeeding pyramids are clumsy imitations. Even construction methods changed (from levitation science to build the Great Pyramid in the Fourth Dynasty, to a balance of levers and pulleys a thousand years later in the Twelfth Dynasty). The workmanship level of jewelry as well as architecture was higher in earlier periods (everything being more perfectly made and more beautiful). On top of that, later generations suffered a decline in lifestyle.

19. *Sumeria,* extensive and all-encompassing, was in many respects more advanced than the cultures which followed it.

20. *Greece:* A city of the third millennium B.C. now at the bottom of Lake Copias (the legendary Copae destroyed by Hercules?) possesses a titanic complex of rock-hewn passages said to be beyond the capabilities of either classical or modern Greece.

21. *Bulgaria:* Grave excavations at Karanova have revealed an extraordinarily rich and complex technology of 3000 B.C. far in advance of later achievements in Europe.

22. *Peru:* Pre-Inca buildings and art were of a much higher level than those of the Incas. Furthermore, while more recent Spanish buildings collapse today in earthquakes, both the Inca and pre-Inca constructions survive them intact.

23. *Easter Island* statues of more recent times appear to be imperfect copies of the first creations. (And they have suffered most from erosion, whereas those from the archaic period have remained intact.) Again, the earliest settlement on the island was more remarkably developed than its two later successors.

Do you see? it is not at all obvious that mankind is progressing; historically, degeneration has been the trend.

PHYSICAL DEGENERATION ALSO

On the third day of our deliberations, the Jigsaw Team turned its attention to this question.

Perch set the pace. "I'll grant that culturally and morally we tend to retrogress," he said. "But let's look at the physical side. Surely in this sense we're improving, right?"

"Sorry, Charlie." It was Wajsmann speaking. "Here again, according to demonstrated science, the opposite appears to be true.

"For what it's worth, the skull capacity (with its inferred brain size) of Cro-Magnon man was at least equal to and sometimes superior to our own.

"Neanderthal ('Stone Age') man had an appreciably larger cranium (1,600 cubic centimeters) than that of modern man.

"The cranial capacity of ancient man in Morocco (called 'Mouillans' by anthropologists) measured an average 2,000 cubic centimeters, compared to modern man's cranial size of about 1,400 cubic centimeters.

"I suggest to you that the downward spiral of intellectual capacity began soon after the Deluge.

"Mankind today is no more intelligent than he was a thousand years ago, hut we have accumulated more technology. We have the accumulated knowledge of the past upon which we can draw and make improvements."

(I had to agree with Wajsmann. Most people would be shocked if they knew that a general regression is likewise evident in a good many species, both in the vegetable and animal kingdoms.)

"Ok, out with it," demanded Perch. "Where's the evidence?"

I proceeded. "Agassiz was one of the first to observe that in many instances the fish of extinct species were better developed and appeared

49

'more advanced' than later species, the modern included. Agassiz spoke as an authority in his field. Many better developed mammals likewise became extinct.[1] Similar observations have been made regarding practically all of today's life-forms.

"But there's more. While the fossil record presents better developed specimens than those now living, another feature—larger size—has been observed in association. Do you see what we have here?

"This is a blow to the evolutionary concept. 'Cope's Law' presumed that the evolutionary series would show increase in improvement and size as time went on.

"Darwin found himself at a loss to explain how 'now we find mere pigmies compared with the antecedent allied races.'"[2]

Perch leaned forward. "So you're saying that today's animals were once larger? Like sheep as big as horses?"

"Yes, Charlie. That's the evidence."

"What about man?"

At that moment, Corderoy shuffled a newspaper noisily, eliciting a frown from Denise. "How about this?" he crooned. "Just yesterday, October 19, in Nairobi, museum director Richard Leakey showed off an ancient skeleton of a twelve-year-old boy. Commenting on widely held scientific beliefs that man's ancestors were smaller than modern man, Leakey said: 'This specimen confirms early hints that Homo erectus individuals were fully as tall as modern people. We can now ask if many modern populat-ions are smaller than their early ancestors and if so why.'"[3]

I thanked Corderoy and continued. "We can go further and say with Dr. Louis Burkhatter that the 'existence of gigantic human beings (in the past) must be considered as a scientifically assured fact.'"[4]

"Did you know that on every continent are uncovered not only artifacts, but footprints, skulls and skeletons of humans who far exceeded us in stature?"

"Wasn't aware of that," said Perch.

"These are well documented. In fact, a fresh look at the fossils led Weidenreich, of Manhattan's American Museum of Natural History, to the belief that 'gigantism and massiveness may have been a *general or at least a widespread character of early mankind.*'"[5]

"That's staggering," gasped Perch. "But it does support the Genesis line that 'there were giants in the earth in those days.'[6] Yet surely, wouldn't large size be inefficient due to gravitational factors?"

"Not necessarily, Charlie. You see, the basic characteristics of gravity still elude analysis by modern physics. A number of scientists now believe that electromagnetic energy supersedes the orthodox laws of gravity.

"Larger size may have been to man's best advantage. There is scientific reason to believe that gigantic size and long life go together. The body cells become lighter, the blood moves more freely, there is less fatigue and the body wears out more slowly."[7]

Wajsmann broke in. "Let's not forget, the concept of an era when mankind lived longer does persist in the memory of most races. And scientific research in several countries suggests that life spans of several centuries are possible under certain conditions."[8]

"A combination of factors such as apparently obtained before the Deluge?" asked Heron. "Well, it appears settled then. Man was once a higher, superior being—certainly not a species of the monkey family. We are only a shade of the original man."

Denise had been scribbling madly. Just then her stomach rumbled and she glanced hastily at her Cartier. "Goodness, it's lunchtime!" she exclaimed. "Shall I sum up?"

We nodded.

"I suppose we must face it," she sighed. "We live today in a zoologically impoverished world. The fossil remains show that in the past plants and animals alike were (1) more widely distributed; (2) of greater variety; and (3) greater in both size and quality. Humans likewise were superior, even to living longer.

"That's it, guys. Physical degeneration, and not evolutionary improvement, is the story of life on this planet. You might say, like a clock once wound up, but now running down."

THE LAWS OF THERMODYNAMICS

We adjourned. "It's in the first two laws of thermodynamics," mused Wajsmann aloud as he pressed the elevator button.

"I beg your pardon, Jacob?" asked Perch.

"You must have heard of them. They're the two most basic and certain of all laws of modem physical science."

Perch looked blank.

"Well, the first is the law of energy conservation. You see, although energy can be converted from one form to another, the total amount remains unchanged—that is, energy is being neither created nor destroyed at present."

"The second is the law of decay. It affirms that although the total amount remains unchanged, there is always a tendency for it to become less available for useful work."

51

Just then the elevator door opened, and we filed in.

(Something flicked on in my cortex just then and I began to see what he was getting at. I recalled a statement by Harvard physicist, P.W. Bridgman. He had stressed the importance and universality of these laws:

"The two laws of thermodynamics are...accepted by physicists as perhaps the most secure generalisations from experience that we have," he had said. "The physicist does not hesitate to apply the two laws to any concrete physical situation in the confidence that nature will not let him down."[9]

(Significantly, these laws of thermodynamics applied not only in physics and chemistry but also in biology and geology. They had always proved valid wherever tested.)

Again the elevator door slid open. "Look," asked Perch, "would you care to explain the significance of this?"

"Very well, back in the room. Let's eat first."

"Better still," chirped Denise, "suppose we ride the cable car to the Peak and discuss it up there."

"Fine," beamed Heron.

An hour later, the heart-stopping vista of Hong Kong harbor sprawled far below us. A few nostalgic moments elapsed conversing on our favorite beauty spots. Then we settled with a dessert and resumed the subject of the morning.

Perch asked Wajsmann about the second law.

"Well," said Jacob, "it's quite simple. The second law of thermodynamics affirms that there is a universal tendency toward deterioration; a transition from a more orderly state, to a less orderly state, to deenergization.

"Left to themselves, things tend to fall apart and reach a state of chaos.

Consequently, where chromosome and gene mutations occur, they are almost always detrimental, rather than beneficial.

"I rather like the way Isaac Asimov puts it: 'As far as we know, all changes are in the direction of increasing entropy, of increasing disorder, of increasing randomness, of running down.'"[10]

Perch snapped his fingers. "I see! It predicts our research. Beginning at the top—culturally, intellectually and physically, the race has degenerated. But, is this not in conflict with the overall theory of evolution?"

"Yes, it is," Wajsmann responded. Let's not kid ourselves. Broadly speaking, evolution implies increasing organization and complexity in the universe and is in effect a doctrine of continuous creation. The first law of thermodynamics affirms, however, that creation is no longer occurring,

52

while the second law states that the original creation is decreasing in organization and complexity."

I was almost rendered immobile when I realized what Jacob was saying. Evolution is an absolute denial of the second law of thermodynamics.

Denise shuffled. "You mean, Jacob, that evolution requires a universal principle of upward change, whereas the second law is a universal principle of downward change?"

"Yes, put simply, Denise, *evolution and the second law cannot both be true.* As for the second law of thermodynamics, it has been confirmed by numerous and varied scientific tests, while evolution is—and always has been—a theoretical model not even capable of scientific test."

Corderoy nodded. "If one must choose, it would seem more rational to go with science."

"But don't all scientists believe in evolution?" queried Perch.

"No," said Wajsmann. "By no means is evolution universally accepted by scientists. Yet it is often mistaken for science. You'll be surprised, for example, how many people have accepted the myth that 'science has shown there is no God.'"

"Of course," Perch admitted. "Evolution is the kingpin of modern atheism and world communism."

"I'm telling you, however," said Wajsmann, "evolution is in trouble. No matter how enthusiastically it tries to sell its speculations, something in nature keeps standing up and saying No! The two great universal principles of thermodynamics—energy conservation and deterioration—bear witness to the scientific necessity of an original creation.

"Charlie, deep down you're still a detective. Pick the flaws in it!"

So the afternoon sped...as some cherished theories crumbled under a growing weight of evidence. All considered, it suggested the following conclusion:

Biblical statements as to the destiny of man throughout history appear to have more relevance than they have been given credit for.

For example: the Genesis assertion that God 'finished" creating and "rested" (i.e., ceased) from all His work of creation,[11] is a simple statement that the processes of creation no longer operate, a fact which is thoroughly verified by the two universal laws of thermodynamics.

And when the Bible claims that since man's severance of communication with the Infinite, this earth has become "subjected" to the "bondage of decay" for the present age,[12] it is telling us that creative processes have been replaced by deteriorative processes implicit in the second law of thermodynamics.

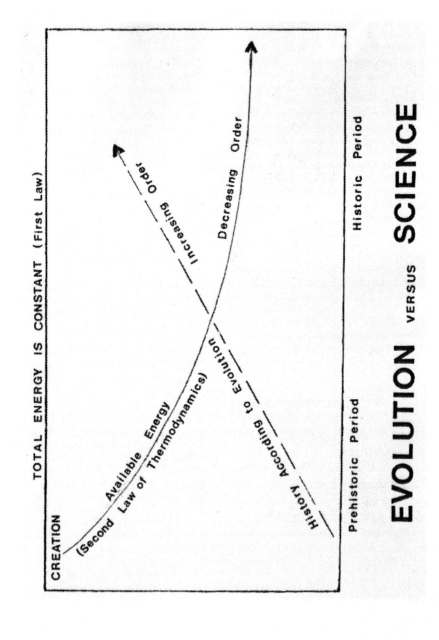

In short, the biblical record, once dismissed in favor of evolution, is now seen to rest upon scientific foundations.

At least since the time of Sir Isaac Newton, we have known that the universe is running down. British research scientist Dr. Alan Hayward, in his book *God Is,* put it this way:[13]

> So the universe is rather like a ship in mid-ocean, with its fuel tanks half full and its stores half consumed. In the case of the ship we know that somebody must have fuelled and provisioned it at the start of the voyage. But who originally filled up the 'fuel tanks' of the universe with hydrogen fuel, and provided all the necessary conditions for that fuel to be turned into heat at an appropriate rate?

There are still a great many scientists who answer that question the same way as Newton did: the Creator.

AFTER
RUINED
CITIES CAME
"STONE AGE"
MAN

Chapter 6

LOST SURVIVORS

"Say, would you repeat that?" sniffled the clerk. "It's this darned hay fever." The transmitter crackled: "Enemy eagle, approaching from the west."

The attendant reached for his Strategic Alert button…and paused. "A *single* aircraft? It's just a reconnaissance," he shrugged. It was *7:55* AM.

Four miles from town, a young hairdresser was serving scrambled eggs to her three-year-old. Mindful of an appointment, she glanced at the time— 8:20 AM.

That moment was to leave her shocked for life. Suddenly, a brilliant white flash lit up the room; seconds later a searing blast knocked her flat. As it subsided, she struggled, stunned, to the window.

An incandescent column of smoke and flame "as bright as ten thousand suns" rose in all its splendor. Transfixed, she watched as blood-colored clouds swept down onto the earth. Fierce winds began to blow.

Nearer the city, eyewitnesses wandered dazed. "Thousands of corpses burnt to ashes"…"in a few hours, all foodstuffs infected"…and shortly the nightmare symptoms of radiation sickness.

"Never before have we seen such an awful weapon, and never before have we heard of such a weapon."

The essence of this account I have drawn from an ancient document, a *document that couldn't possibly exist…but does.* I shall render details of it in Chapter 29. In pages now brown with time, the cold terror of the survivors still lives on.

The mutual collapse of the high civilization centers through nuclear warfare in the third millennium B.C. had come swiftly and without warning (see prehistoric era map in Chapter 4), leaving little time to salvage anything but essentials.

Small groups of survivors set out to begin life once more in the jungles and mountains that were untouched by radiation and ruin. Without industry, they were compelled to concentrate on producing their own essentials. The emphasis reverted to agricultural self-sufficiency.

Although their members had skills, there were too few of them to create a new civilization within the void they were forced to face. Every culture requires a certain density of population. This was no longer available, so they were forced into a more basic existence.

It happened all over the world at once. (And will historians please explain it?) All the world's major agricultural centers suddenly appeared in different places about the same time.

These new agricultural centers appeared in northeastern China, southeastern Asia, northeastern Mexico, Peru and Venezuela.

What is more, *they all sprang up in close proximity to areas which had been destroyed by some fiery holocaust* (that is, the Gobi and Indian civilization centers, the Death Valley ruins, the melted facade of Sacsahuaman and the vitrified ruins in the Brazilian jungle).

Were some of these new "primitive" communities survivors of man-made catastrophe?

In a downstairs lounge the next morning, we were approached by Reginald Stokes, a Canadian doctor who had overheard our conversation. He tossed up some lively questions to us.

"I saw this movie," said Stokes. *"20,000 B.C.* it was called. The film showed early humans as pitiful 'ape men' who devoured big chunks of rotten meat with savage grunts and dragged their women around by the hair.

"That's one piece of your jigsaw picture that doesn't fit. Just where do you slot cavemen and primitive societies? They were our ancestors, weren't they?"

Wajsmann flashed a reply. "I tell you, Reg. they were educated people just like us."

"What do you mean? Civilized?" His eyes narrowed.

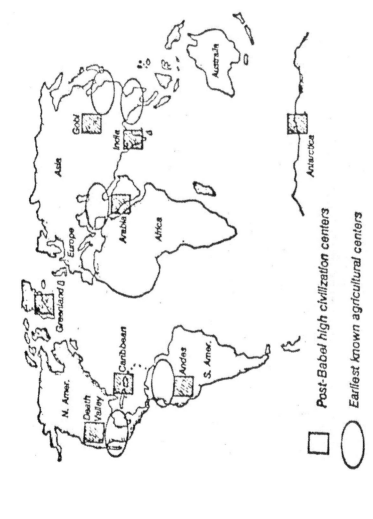

Post-Babel high civilization centers

Earliest known agricultural centers

Fig. 6-1. The Post-Babel civilization and earliest known agricultural centers. The close proximity of the agricultural centers to civilization centers supports the hypothesis that the two areas were somehow connected. (Map: Rene Noorbergen).

59

Wajsmann continued. "Archaeologists who have gone out to uncover *facts* know nothing of uncivilized cavemen.

"The point is, many of today's so-called primitives are not relics of a Stone Age. Rather, they are the wreckage of more highly developed societies, forced by various circumstances such as natural disasters to lead a much simpler, less developed way of life."

And who reached that conclusion?"

None other than a recent conference of anthropologists."

"Urrrh," grunted the doctor. "Look here, mind if I join you in your apartment this afternoon? There seems more to this caveman stunt than meets the eye."

We invited him to be there at three o'clock.

"Hurry, Jay. How much longer will you be? Breakfast will spoil." The refugee wife was well seasoned to this routine since settling into their makeshift hut in the hills. Her city life was now just a distant dream. This morning, you could hardly say the same for her husband. He had just cut his chin on an improvised razor.

"Ah, that's better. Nothing like a daub of clay to stop the bleeding." Jay dropped the offending razor onto a bench in the work cave and stumbled over the mossy rocks to join his family.

Now, did you notice something about this caveman? That's right. *He felt a compulsive need to shave!*

The telltale sign of his habit was left behind in the Lazzaretto Grottoes, near Nice, in France. A small deer-bone handle has since been found within the cave complex. The handle is skillfully split with scapula bones inserted—a prehistoric razor.

Here is evidence of men conscious of their civilized background, compelled to use all their technical skill in a savage and hostile environment; men able to make contact with other civilized people once, but afterwards isolated and forced to make use of crude implements for survival.

The story is the same on the other side of the world. In the Subis Mountains of West Borneo, a network of caves hollowed out on a cathedral-like scale contained *fabrics of extreme fineness and delicacy.* Here is further proof of a civilized background.

Charles Berlitz notes that many artifacts now found suggest a concern with ceremony, art and adornment, "as if they were trying to combine an art that was natural to them with a survival technique that had become necessary."[1]

60

...True to his word, at three sharp the doctor was rapping on our door. We seated Stokes with a tomato juice. He couldn't wait to begin.

"Now, how can you possibly know," asked Stokes, "that cavemen were anything but evolving savages?"

Wajsmann tossed a teaser. "They have told us, themselves."

"You're kidding, of course.

Wajsmann smiled. "For one thing, their art. It shows that their background was as developed as ours." Then taking a chalk to his portable blackboard, Wajsmann wrote:

QUALITY OF CAVEMAN ART

"There are six things I'd like you to note," he began.

1. The rock paintings of animals in the caves of Altamira, Lascaux, Ribadasella and others, I tell you, are masterpieces of art in any period. The realism and beauty of these cave paintings show artistic talent *immensely superior* to that of the animal paintings of Egypt, Babylon or Greece.

2. Paintings in the cave of Altamira (near Santander, Spain) are, from the aesthetic viewpoint, just *as good as modern paintings!*

3. Cave paintings in Algeria, Libya and Lascaux bear witness to a developed culture which used *perspective and freeness of form—an* amazingly sophisticated art. You realize that perspective was not used until the fifteenth century!

4. And do you know that cave drawings followed *a planned pattern* of figurative arrangement that is remarkably constant *throughout western Europe?* In each case the decorated cave was divided up according to some unknown metaphysical system.

5. Not only that, but cave paintings (as to motifs and themes) have *a common style worldwide.* It's as though they came from a common school.

6. The original caves of Montignac-Lascaux (now closed to the public) have been called "the Sistine Chapel of prehistory" for the beauty of their paintings. The artists achieved a remarkable *three-dimensional effect* by using the natural contours of rock. This is what they did: small holes became the glaring eyes of a bison; cracks became the wounds of a stricken deer; odd-shaped bulges were incorporated into the painting as a head or back hump. Even today, light and shadow contrasts using the natural rock shapes make the animals

61

appear to be alive and breathing. *Here is a technique and effect unique in the history of art.*

"I tell you, these cavemen scaled heights not reached again until late in our era.

Stokes stared at the six points. "Incredible!" he gasped. "Simply incredible!" Wajsmann continued. "We probably have to admit that our artistic capabilities are no higher today than they were in the 'caveman' period. One thing is sure. Their painting culture was more advanced than that of the average European country dweller today."

(Robert Charroux had pointed out that even to manufacture the ferric oxide or manganese sticks to paint with required a complex, sophisticated technique.)[2]

Wajsmann summed up. "Are we to believe that these were dim-witted savages, incapable of putting two stones together to build a wall?"

Stokes sat silent.

Paul Heron rose, sidled to the blackboard, and wrote:

CAVEMEN LIVED IN HOUSES

"This is my special interest," said Heron. "Looks like a paradox, doesn't it? But note this:

1. The Lascaux artists did not live in their caves but fashioned them into an art gallery. Listen. Do you know how they managed to paint those pictures up to twelve feet above the floor? The answer is, they used *scaffolds—and* the holes in the rock, where they put in crossbeams for planks, are still there. Now scaffolding cannot precede the knowledge of masonry; it follows from the development of masonry. Therefore we can he sure that 'cavemen' knew how to construct houses.
2. And what shall we do about the "Stone Age" oven found at Noailles, France? It was built by using stones *shaped like bricks and mortared with cement.*
3. At Charroux (a large prehistoric tool centre where you can still pick up stone axes) there are caves within three miles, but excavations have found so sign that these were ever inhabited by men.
4. In Czechoslovakia and Yugoslavia, "Stone Age" houses have actually been unearthed. These reveal sophisticated construction

techniques which called for a knowledge of mathematics and geometry.

"So we can conclude that all 'cave men' did not live in caves (except in rare cases as still occur today). Most stone tool sites (including the largest in the world of ten thousand acres) were nowhere near caves. 'Cave men lived in houses.

"All right, Paul, that's enough," said Denise. "Give me a chance."

Stokes eyed this smartly dressed lady with curiosity. "What do you know about all this?" he queried.

"What do I know? I know what they wore, that's what!" she exclaimed. "Yes, they wore clothes—and how! Here, let me show you." She started writing:

CAVEMAN'S SOPHISTICATED CLOTHING

1. Prehistoric cave paintings in the Kalahari Desert of southwest Africa depict light-skinned men in elaborate garments. Men with blond beards and well-styled hair are wearing boots, tight-fitting pants, multicolored shirts, coats and gloves. A woman is wearing a short-sleeved pullover, closely-fitting breeches, and gloves, garters and slippers.
2. Engraved stones of the Magdalenian period unearthed in a cave at Lussac, France, show modern-looking people in casual poses wearing robes, belts, boots, coats and hats. A seated young lady wears a pantsuit with a short-sleeved jacket, a pair of small boots, and a decorated hat that flops down over her right ear to her shoulder. On her lap is a square, flat object with a flap that folds down the front, like a modern purse. Men wear well-tailored pants, broad belts with clasps, and clipped beards and moustaches.

"Why, that's sensational!" exclaimed Stokes.

"But I'll tell you something," said Miss Tagg, almost in a whisper. "It's highly significant that when I went to photograph these engraved drawings, I was blocked. Just as others before me. This is very embarrassing material. And it's decidedly not open to public inspection."[3]

"Understandably," said Stokes. "It refutes all that we've been told to believe."

Perch cut in. "There's a vested interest at stake, here. So many people's careers are bound up in it now. Lifetime reputations. It's not just big business; many of the theorists are totally sincere. They believe they have

63

found the answer, and they don't want someone to come along and tell them it's all made up."

"I haven't finished yet," cried Denise.

"We're all ears," sighed Corderoy.

"There're a couple of points remaining."

3. Ancient cave paintings in the Honan Mountains of China show hunters in modern jackets and long trousers.
4. In Vladimir, Russia, actual remains of a "Stone Age" man were dug up. He was wearing trousers made of fur, an embroidered shirt, mind you, and a very practical jacket, with ivory badges and clasps. How about that?

"Great Scott!" exclaimed the doctor. "This is dynamite!" Corderoy arose. "There's more yet. Just catch this." He took the chalk and wrote for all to see.

THEIR CIVILIZED ORIGIN
OTHER EVIDENCE

1. *Community cooperation* was highly developed. We see this in (a) their clusters of habitations; (b) the specialization of both labor and sites of labor; and (c) in the sharing of construction and design ideas over a wide area.
2. Another thing. *They were familiar with sea travel.* At Montgaudier, France, and Nerja, Spain, 'caveman' discoveries comprise (a) engravings of a spouting sperm whale and two seals so detailed they can be recognized as male and female; and (b) cavern paintings of three dolphins (two males and a female) in a face-to-face encounter. Their creators, from caves up to a hundred miles inland, would have had to journey far out on the open sea in order to witness and record their story.
3. As further evidence of ocean travel, tools have been found from the same "Stone Age" people on both sides of the Atlantic, together with skeletal remains.
4. Then there is the remarkable coincidence of writing symbols between the "primitive" American Indian and the cave cultures of Europe.
5. "Stone Age" peoples and those of the ancient civilizations must have directly inherited *a lunar calendar system* from a civilization older than them both. Thousands of notational sequences—such as vertical markings, lines and dots, painted and engraved on stone or bone—are scattered from Spain to the Ukraine. These are now known to be

records of observations of the moon, made for calendric purposes—a complex memoranda of lunar studies.

Stokes interrupted. "Excuse me, Phil. But isn't it generally conceded that prehistoric men had only stone with which to work? If, as you say, they came from a highly civilized background, why could they only work with stone?"

"Very good, Reg, murmured Corderoy. "I was getting to that." He scratched across the blackboard the following words:

"STONE AGE" MEN MINED METALS

1. The truth is, many prehistoric mines have been located *throughout the world.* The same form of *iron ore* mined in Swaziland—hematite—has been found among remains in France, Tasmania and Tierra del Fuego— always in coastal areas. It is possible that the use of hematite (bloodstone), used in cosmetics, may have been exported worldwide.
2. They certainly had methods of *transporting ore* a thousand miles from Michigan, U.S.A., for not one ounce of the ore was ever uncovered for use within 1,000 miles of the mine sites.
3. As to their intelligence, the prehistoric miners *used mathematics and kept records* of what they produced (witness bone etchings, Border Cave, South Africa). They had *writing* (witness engraved tablets, Glozel).
4. At a depth of eighteen feet within one prehistoric mine (actually, near the Ontonagon River, Michigan), there was discovered a detached mass of *copper* weighing six tons. The mass had been raised on timbers and wedges to about five feet above its break-off point and pounded smooth to facilitate easier transportation. In the shaft lay a stone hammer weighing thirty-six pounds.
5. Another mine at Isle Royal, Lake Superior, had been worked to a depth of nine feet through solid rock before a copper vein eighteen inches thick was uncovered at the bottom. Excavations are connected underground and drainage cut. At one point, a tunnel extends for two miles in an almost straight line.

"Just a moment, Phil." It was Stokes again. "If these people were refugees from a high technology, then why have no metal tools been found among Stone Age relics?"

WHY ONLY STONE TOOLS?

Corderoy smiled. "The truth is, metal will barely survive when exposed to the weathering processes of time. Most objects will decay, rust, scatter and become unrecognizable in time. Only stone survives.

"However we know that prehistoric man worked metals from the discovery of these gigantic mines.

"Now notice this. In caves near Odessa. U.S.S.R., were found prehistoric animal bones skillfully cut with perfectly circular holes and regular grooves. Experts declare that these bones were *cut with a metal tool,* then polished.

"It is significant that in regions particularly rich in iron ore, such as Alsace-Lorraine, there is no trace of a culture using stone tools! Yet those regions certainly were inhabited."

Stokes sighed. "Well, that does make sense."

That reminded me of a statement by Robert Charroux. He argued that our ancestors never used flint knives, axes and other tools, except for a few outcasts who lived at a more primitive level. If the use of flint tools had been the general rule, we ought to find billions and billions of them. The fact is that, relatively speaking, practically none have been found: only a few hundred thousand axes (the main tool). not enough to justify the assumption of more than twenty inhabitants of the globe per generation.[4]

He added: "The Paleolithic and the Neolithic have never existed except in the imagination of the prehistorians."[5]

Surely, he reasoned, it is erroneous to define a whole period by the insignificant percentage of the total population.

By the same logic, we could say that the twentieth century is part of the Stone Age, since people in New Guinea and Borneo still use flint tools; or the Caviar Age or the Chewing Gum Age, since a few people eat caviar or chew gum.[6]

Indeed, you might well ask, was there ever a *Stone Age?* The answer is, NO! Have there been *stone cultures?* Yes.

But, I hear you say, are not some of these stone cultures tens of thousands of years old? Yet the Great Flood wiped the whole earth clean 5,400 years ago. How can this be?

Now you're talking. Let's investigate.

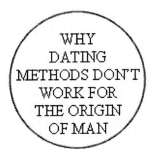

WHY
DATING
METHODS DON'T
WORK FOR
THE ORIGIN
OF MAN

Chapter 7

SOMEBODY'S MISREADING THE TIME

"**G**entlemen," she enquired, "would you please tell me how old these are?"

The veteran Maori guide, Rangi, was conducting a party of Australian geologists around one of New Zealand's thermal attractions. She led them to a volcanically formed protuberance and paused.

One learned member of the group gave the site a cursory examination and stated that in his opinion the rocks were 50 millions years old.

"Are you sure?" she asked.

"That figure would be close."

"What do you other gentlemen say?" queried the guide with a twinkle in her eye that evidently passed unnoticed.

"Ten million years"…"No, nearer to twenty million," came the replies. Whereupon the genial lady straightened herself, beamed at the three sages in her inimitable style and said: "Thank you, gentlemen. Now let me tell you something. I stood on this very spot just ten years ago and watched these rocks being formed."

MISREADING THE TIME can be downright embarrassing. Particularly for a man professing to know so much.

Misreading the time concerning our own origin might even be considered dangerous. Especially if it sets us on a false trail as to who we are, our sense of purpose and what's in store for us.

You will have noticed in the events of earlier chapters a time factor.

1. An original super civilization was annihilated and our planet swept totally clean by a Deluge, about 3400 B.C.
2. The earliest postdeluvian nations sprang into existence ready made, about 3,000 B.C.
3. Primitive cultures were offshoots from the civilized world of 3400 B.C. and later; all societies had degenerated more or less.

Now, some dear person will refer me to "Stone Age" tribes like Aborigines who have been in Australia for 20,000 years.

Have they???

The time factor is so important, that if we can go back without interruption 20,000 years, then you can toss out almost everything we have so far discussed.

The question is, *HOW FAR BACK WITH ABSOLUTE CERTAINTY CAN WE GO?* As far as dates are concerned, where does fact end and speculation begin?

The answer is, ABOUT 3,000 B.C. And the reasons for my stating this are compelling.

Yes, I know that much older dates have been suggested by historians. For example we're told that man already had a brain larger than ours 60,000 years ago and left drawings in 30,000 B.C. that would do justice to a modern painter.

Now think about it. If this is so, then why would man have waited so long to develop cities and the type of agriculture associated with them? We should expect that those isolated civilizations which developed independently would be somewhat spread out over this period. Even one civilization from 20,000 B.C. would be strong proof against my account of the worldwide Flood. But, I repeat, the oldest cultures on earth all go back to about the same time—3,000 B.C.

What does the evidence show?

For one thing, the written records of no nation on earth are older than about 3,000 B.C. That is generally agreed by historians.

But get this. Even modern dating techniques cannot take us back further than about 3,000 B.C. Dr. W.F. Libby, a foremost authority on modern dating methods, who won the Nobel Prize for his research on carbon- dating, was shocked to discover this limitation:

"You read statements in books that such and such society or archaeological site is 20,000 years old," he noted. "We learned rather abruptly that these numbers, these ancient ages, are not known accurately; in fact, it is at about the time of the First Dynasty of Egypt that the first historical date of any real certainty has been established."[1]

Does that shock you?

Consider the much acclaimed carbon - 14 dating method. This is based on the radioactive decay rate in organic matter. It is a fact that every living thing absorbs cosmic radioactive carbon-14 from the atmosphere. At death, this intake ceases and the radiocarbon in the organism begins to disintegrate. The amount of remaining C-14 is used to calculate how long ago the organism died.

The accuracy of this dating method has come under some criticism lately. For example, a living mollusk from salt water can show age dates of 3,000 years (as though it had been dead for 3,000 years).

Under normal conditions, radiocarbon dating is reliable to about 4,000 years ago. Then the disparity runs wild. You see, this dating method depends on the assumption that atmospheric radiation has remained constant.

The trouble is that any traumatic environmental change occurring in the past would have accelerated the decay rate, adding to "apparent age," if calculated on the assumption of uniformity.

Thus an upheaval like the Deluge would play *immeasurable havoc upon readings prior to about 3,000 B.C.* It's as simple as that.

Let's not underestimate the impact of the Deluge. The thing to remember is that this event was a universal catastrophe. It encompassed epic changes: mountains rising and falling, tidal waves rushing faster than the speed of sound, as well as thousands of Krakatoas belching out dust to darken the atmosphere for centuries. Anything that could happen did happen. Seismic and atmospheric distortions persisted for hundreds of years.

Get this. The earliest *civilized* cultures that can be dated go back no further than the post-Deluge period.

CAVE CULTURES CONTEMPORANEOUS
WITH CITY CULTURES

And the same can be said for *primitive* men. Here are some bones found in caves near Rochebertier, in France. How old are they? "Twelve thousand years," we're told. But notice these script characters on them. What nags at me is this. They resemble and in some cases are identical to the script of Tartessus (of the period 2500 to 2000 B.C.). Are we to believe that a script, once developed, would remain relatively unchanged for 10,000 years? It does not happen. So what do the two scripts really demonstrate? Just this—that the cultures must have been *of the same period.* Do you see?

The same is true of Paleolithic antler bones found at Le Mas d'Azil and La Madelaine. These are inscribed with signs identical to Phoenician script from about 2000 B.C.

And painted pebbles from Le Mas d'Azil are marked with signs and symbols that were once predominant throughout the Mediterranean—again, between 3000 and 2000 B.C.

What does this all mean? Simply that "Stone Age" and "civilized" cultures existed at the same time! And, by the way, *not* 12,000 years ago.

Yet we are still asked to believe in a long progression, first from caveman to Stone Age, thence to wandering hunters, to settled farmers, and later to cities and civilization.

I feel sorry for the evolutionist, but that will not do.

There is enough evidence now to show that these groups existed simultaneously, each aware of the other. On this point, ancient literature agrees with the latest archaeological findings.

Just as even in today's "Space Age", there live "Stone Age" tribes on all continents except Europe.

Concerning primitive people, Thor Heyerdahl, the "Kon-Tiki" explorer, observed correctly that their intelligence is "exactly like our own "[2]

In other words, 'stone culture" implies neither "dim-witted" nor "prehistoric." There's no 20,000 B.C. here.

DOES "APE-LIKE" MEAN "ANCIENT"?

I hear somebody asking, "But didn't the first men look like apes?" Surely the transition to our present appearance must have required hundreds of thousands of years?

It is time for the truth. One thing you should know about discovered specimens of the earliest men is that they look remarkably like us.

Here's a short checklist:

Perfectly preserved bodies of "ancient" cavemen found near the Bay of Biscay were almost identical to those of present-day man.

Fossil skulls characteristic of "modern" man have been found in "ancient" strata in Britain, France, Germany, Hungary, Ethiopia, Tanzania

70

and the Middle East. In some places, fragments of modern man have been found in strata below (hence "older than") bones of "Stone Age" man.

Regarding a skull found in Kenya, evolutionist Richard Leakey wrote in the June 1973 issue of *National Geographic,* "Either we toss out this skull or we toss out our theories of early man…It simply fits no previous models of human beginnings." This skull "leaves in ruins the notion that all early fossils can be arranged in an orderly sequence of evolutionary change." You have to admire the man for his honesty.

In Australia, an excavation produced modern man and Neanderthal ("Stone Age") man in a contemporary environment. "This raised the disturbing possibility that there may have been no ancestor of man—that he appeared fully formed." The comment on this occasion came from A.A. Abbie, at the time Professor of Anatomy and Histology at Adelaide University. He added, "A Neanderthal man in modern dress would not attract much attention today. It appeared that geologists and anthropologists have wasted time looking for a 'missing link' between man and his ape-like ancestors, which probably did not exist."[3]

But haven't there been "ape men"?
Yes, and quite simply, these were degenerates from the main stock, the result of interbreeding from isolation. With such a limited gene pool, the appearance of bad genetic traits increased considerably, producing birth defects and physical mutations.
As to physical deformities, Harold G. Coffin, of the Geoscience Research Institute in Berrien Springs, Michigan, U.S.A., has a point to make. He refers to "the recent discovery that the classic descriptions of Neanderthal man were based in large part on the (skeletal) remains of…a man suffering from severe osteoarthritis."[4]
Researchers Straus and Cove agree that this "arthritic old man…has his counterparts in modern man similarly afflicted with spinal osteoarthritis. He cannot…be used to provide us with a reliable picture of a healthy, normal Neanderthalian."[5]
Sir Ambrose Fleming asks: "Even if these fragments are of humans and show unusual features, why should they not be examples of deterioration rather than evolution?"[6]
Monkey-faced men? Today I saw one driving a bus. Arthritic spines? The bottom line is, you cannot time-slot a man by his posture or by the shape of his head. "Long aeons" ago has nothing to do with it.

71

WHY THE "LONG AGES" SYNDROME?

Most of us have seen those elaborate charts in books which show geological ages, from the first simple life form to the emergence of man. Millions of years are postulated. You have to admit, they look very convincing to the point of being overwhelming.

Once again, I have news for you. With all due respect, these charts, so painstakingly prepared, cannot be further from the truth. They are largely hypothetical, you see; they assume the theory of evolution to be correct— and build on that. They assume that the earth's strata was deposited in a uniform, steady fashion over a tremendously long period of time. They assume that the uniform action of nature has never been interrupted by catastrophe.

This assumption is called "uniformitarianism."

Let me tell you how Dr. Henry M. Morris put *these standard evolutionary assumptions* to the test. Dr. Morris set out to calculate the age of the earth from various natural processes such as the uniform decay of the earth's magnetic field, the erosion of lands, and the gradual influx of chemicals into the ocean. In fact, he compiled *a table of seventy separate natural processes of worldwide change.* And do you know, the majority of these chronometers yielded a young age. More importantly, the processes showed *extreme van-ability* ranging all the way from 100 years to 500,000,000 years for the age of the earth.[7]

You realize what this means? Quite simply, it proves there is something wrong with the basic premise of uniformity. Evidently nature has *not* always behaved as it does now.

The other day my neighbor assured me that an orderly evolutionary sequence spanning millions of years was indicated by the rock strata with its "ascending" fossils. For example, coal beds were laid down 340 million years ago, dinosaurs ruled from 130 to 65 million years B.C., and man appeared just a million or so years ago.

I'll tell you something. In most parts of the world this theoretical sequence never occurs. Remains of marine and land animals arc mixed up in every possible sequence. Human relics are found even inside coal beds. As if that were not tricky enough, these remains of human origin sometimes occur with or beneath the bones of dinosaurs. Can you see what's wrong? The evidence shows they were deposited at the same time—not millions of years apart. The man and the dinosaur died together, you see. (And before the coal was formed!)

Figure out what this does to the theory of evolution. For one thing, it does not allow for the vast periods of time needed for the organic evolutionary process.

The truth is, each successive layer of sediment with its dead bodies was deposited wave upon wave by the Deluge and sorted further by local currents.

Remains all over the world—often perfectly preserved—attest that countless billions of creatures were buried suddenly and violently in a water-borne disaster. Animals from different geographical zones and all climatic areas of the world are found heaped together in one common graveyard.

Sometimes lower strata contain fossils of smaller creatures, while in the higher strata larger animals are found. This is a logical consequence of an advancing global flood. Often the first to be engulfed were the smaller, less mobile creatures, whereas larger animals escaped to higher ground, to be overtaken later. These successive burials were accomplished within a year. Think it through.

I'm not talking about the raw material of our planet, which is possibly some 5 billion years of age. Life on earth is quite a different matter; this is a recent event.

(Moreover, if we are totally honest about this, we should not ignore the substantial new scientific evidence suggesting that even the earth's raw materials may be measured in terms of only thousands of years of age.)

In an interview with *Science and Mechanics,* July 1968, Immanuel Velikovsky expressed surprise that the body, brain and mind of man, a tremendously sophisticated biological apparatus supposedly spanning millions of years of time, was able to produce a recorded history of only a few thousand years.

Doesn't it make you wonder? Could it be that man is *not* so old, after all?

We speak of millions of years for terrestrial life only because evolution demands that it be so. It needs the time. In other words, evolution has an answer it likes, and is trying to make the questions, and the facts, fit its answer.

The exaggerated time element must be rejected.

WE MUST REVISE PREHISTORY

Constant media bombardment has moulded our attitudes, until we accept the evolutionary time viewpoint almost without question. Those who influence us try hard to ignore the real nature of their proffered sacred cow. It is 100 percent speculation.

It is not within the scope of this work to present the growing mass of scientific evidence for a dramatically 'recent" time scale; this is reserved for a subsequent book.

Does it really matter what we believe concerning our roots? It does, very much.

By having lost our historical links to our early ancestors, we have lost much of our heritage; and in rediscovering these links, we may begin to find ourselves. As William Fix observes:

The question of our origin is of supreme importance: it is the basis of our identity and destiny. The models with which we identify profoundly influence our behavior: the man who believes he came from a beast may be more inclined to behave like a beast. The image is not only degrading; it is dangerous.[8]

So now, having swept aside the false, conventional view of prehistory, with its idea of a lowly form of man living in caves, using stone tools and incapable of producing the wonders of the past, we at last see a door opening to us.

Now we are ready to conceive of that past as awesome and fantastic—as it really was.

Well, almost. Two loose ends remain. One is the "space gods" theory. Could intelligent man's sudden appearance conceivably be the result of a visit by galactic astronauts? Let's see.

DID WE
ORIGINATE ON
EARTH OR IN
SOME OTHER
GALAXY?

Chapter 8

DID SPACE GIANTS EXPERIMENT WITH US?

Erich von Danicken caused a sensation in the seventies when he claimed that sophisticated ancient relics were the result of a space visit to earth. Now it is time for the truth.

Von Danicken, like others, assumed that early man struggled for endless millions of years as a primitive dumb and stupid creature, unable to accomplish anything on his own.

Then we find man quite suddenly (in the last few thousand years) nurturing a technology so intricate, so sophisticated, that it suggests intellectual maturity from the start.

You don't have to be smart to sense there is something wrong here. So, faced with the new evidence of high technology in ancient times, and realizing that man could not have obtained such advanced thinking capabilities and complex technology simply by evolving from nothing, Von Danicken's camp suggested that maybe galactic visitors were responsible. These alien giants crossbred with primates to produce modern man, then left behind artifacts from their visit.

Did they? You have to admit, it's an interesting theory. Of the following facts we can be sure:

1. None of the out-of-place artifacts is composed of material unknown to earth.
2. Their technological makeup conforms with the development of our own modern civilization.

3. Interbreeding would have been—we must face it—a virtual impossibility. That's right. Aliens, you see, would need a carbon-based physiology. Not only that. These giants would need to be physically adapted for entering the human female. But wait. Their chromosomes would have to be interchangeable, even for artificial insemination. Chromosomes and genes must *both* match up, which is extremely unlikely and does not happen even between animals and humans of the same planet!

4. And of course you realize that if these were to match, they would already be of the same or closely related species—and man would be already intelligent.

5. Still unresolved, the problem of the origin of intelligence is only removed to another planet. You have to account for civilizations on two worlds now, instead of one, and you still have to find out how the first began. Now naturally, if evolution cannot account for it on this planet, it is equally impossible to explain a more highly intelligent man evolving on some other planet.

6. Memories of "gods" from the skies are explainable as the recollection by primitive people of visits from contemporary civilizations who had aircraft. Similar reactions have occurred in our day.

With whatever good intentions, the "space gods" theory was born in careless research; since then it has been perpetuated through the use of faulty reasoning and sensationalism.

Its promoters are correct, however, on one point: Human intelligence cannot be the product of chance evolution. Man did appear suddenly—at the top, not at the bottom. Man is a created artifact, far more wonderful than any computer. He was carefully planned and endowed with the gift of language and the most amazing intellect, as well as a feeling for handcrafts and technology.

And something else was implanted within man: both the capacity and the need to communicate with his Maker, the prime Intelligence. Consequently, there is a part of every person which is restless, seeking unattainable goals, yet experiencing futility and emptiness until it finds identity and peace with the Creator. And that makes all the difference.

One remaining question deserves an answer. If the early world was so advanced, then why is there such a paucity of physical evidence?

Four reasons coming up: stay tuned.

THE CASE
OF THE
DISAPPEARING
CLUES

Chapter 9

VANISHING EVIDENCE

Consider, for a moment, the awful possibility that your hometown was forever wiped out. Can you imagine what future generations might find?

Has it occurred to you that our noblest buildings today are scarcely more than facades supported by thin tendons of steel?

Even with no disaster, our main cities would be little more than rubble in a thousand years. Our motorways would be crumpled pieces of hardness beneath vegetation. Our once complex railway network would be red dust blowing in the wind.

Make no mistake about it. Few house chattels would survive the corrosion of time. Generally, paper books cannot last more than a few centuries (hence the need to recopy). Plastics will eventually disintegrate when exposed for long periods outside. The same goes for everything metallic. Yes, that's right. Hair dryers, automobiles and carpets would be reduced to dust, along with photographic plates and film.

What is more, all iron and steel buildings would rust and crumble to earth. Nothing would be left except a few stone structures downtown and maybe a few statues. Stone is the only indestructible material; it will survive a dead civilization. Isn't it ironic? Nature allows dressed blocks of stone to survive, but not thick iron girders.

Probably there would not be one item left in the suburbs to show that they even existed—except for the odd stone axe-head.

In the event of a total catastrophe, the survivors would be driven to the countryside, to live primitively. They might, for a time, be able to salvage and use certain elements of their civilized technology.

Eventually the last machine would break down, with nobody remembering how to repair it. The transistors, toasters and x-ray machines, though revered, would be useless.

To the grandchildren and their descendants they would become legends. The "magic mirror" that could see events far away; the metal bird that could fly above the clouds; the room that could move up and down inside big houses—these would become "magical" myths of a people whose survival instinct would direct them back into the rapidly encroaching forests.

Archaeologists 4,000 years later could claim that twentieth century man was not yet familiar with iron. (If they found cassettes with tapes, these would be a meaningless puzzle to them.) What do you think of that?

Texts speaking of gigantic cities with houses several hundred feet high would be classed as myths.

Do you begin to see the picture? It is this very situation of meagre clues that confronts us in relation to the original super world. I can think of four reasons for this.

1. MOST PHYSICAL REMAINS WERE WIPED OUT

Numerous ancient cities now lie below ground level; many are *covered* by desert sands or swallowed by dense jungle; while others still may lie intact under the mile-deep ice of Antarctica.

On the other hand, *exposed* remains can disappear so fast. Take, for example, the 4,000-year-old ruins of Tiahuanaco, in Bolivia. As recently as the sixteenth century there still stood immense walls with massive rivets of silver in the stonework as well as lifelike statues of men and women in a thousand animated poses. Even until last century, travellers could admire and sketch imposing colonnades. Of these there is no trace today. The Spaniards and more recently the Bolivian government plundered them for building materials.

Again, many *scale replicas* of ancient apparatuses probably perished when the Spanish conquistadors melted down all the gold artifacts they could find in Central and South America.

The scale of destruction over the centuries will never be known.

2. *MOST ANCIENT RECORDS HAVE ALSO BEEN DESTROYED*

The destruction of printed records has been much greater than was originally thought.

The great library of *Alexandria* once contained one million volumes in which the entire science, philosophy and mysteries of the ancient world were recorded (including a complete catalogue of authors in 120 volumes, with a brief biography of each author). In a single act of vandalism, Julius Caesar destroyed 700,000 priceless scrolls. In the seventh century, the Arabs completed the wipeout. Do you know how they did it? They used the books as a fuel supply to heat the city's 400 public baths for six months.

Totally destroyed also were the papyri of the library of Ptah in *Memphis. Carthage,* with a library of 500,000 volumes, was razed in a seventeen-day fire by the Romans in 146 B.C.

The library of *Pergamos* in Asia Minor (with 200,000 volumes) likewise perished.

When the famous collection of Pisistratus in *Athens* was wiped out (in the sixth century). surprisingly Homer's writings escaped.

In the eighth century, Leo Isaurus burned 300,000 books in *Constantinople.* In *China,* Emperor Tam Shi Hwang-ti issued an edict (213 B.C.) to destroy innumerable books.

Thousands of Druidic scrolls in *Autun,* France, on philosophy, medicine, astronomy and other sciences, were obliterated by Julius Caesar. Not one survived.

Much *classical* literature was systematically destroyed by the papal Inquisition.

Spanish conquerors searched out and destroyed *the entire Mayan literature* (except for four documents now in European museums). It was related that Mayan scholars screamed in agony as they saw their life's purpose go up in flames. Some committed suicide.

The Council of Lima (1583) decreed the burning of the knotted cords ("quipas") on which the *Incas* had recorded their history and that of their predecessors.

What a story of carnage, in which the greatest depositories of knowledge from the ancient world are lost forever! (Yet somehow the Indian books escaped.) Did you know that even of the Greek and Roman literature, *less than 1 percent* has come down to us?

Is it any wonder we are ignorant of our early heritage? I agree with Andrew Tomas that "we have to depend on disconnected fragments, casual passages and meagre accounts. Our distant past is a vacuum filled at random with tablets, parchments, statues, paintings and various artifacts. The history of science would appear totally different were the book collection of Alexandria intact today."[1]

3. EVEN WHERE NOT LOST, MUCH REMAINS A MYSTERY

Undeciphered still are writings at Easter Island, tablets at Mohenjo-Daro in Pakistan, and Mayan scripts. Some finds will remain unsolved forever. There are no inscriptions awaiting us at Tiahuanaco or Machu Picchu.

Then there are many museum relics, whose significance may have eluded us.

A methodical reexamination of pieces labelled "art objects," "cult objects" and "unidentified objects" would yield much new data. So would a systematic exploration of museum vaults.

It is a well-known fact that museums are in the habit of "burying" objects that do not coincide with current theories, or that are not beautiful to look at. The vaults of the Smithsonian Institution and the Museum of Prehistory of Saint Germain-en-Laye are full of crates of incomprehensible objects that nobody is studying.[2]

Could it be that many objects we have discovered had a purpose that we do not yet understand? The ancients may have achieved results similar to ours by quite different processes. (For instance, look at what happened to German technology. It diverged tremendously from that of other countries in just twelve years, from 1933 to 1945, when Germany was progressively isolated from the rest of the world.)

Then again, is it possible that some of the antedeluvian artifacts we have found cannot yet be identified, simply because they are ahead of our technology?

A point to remember. As any technology advances, its methods and equipment do not become more complex; they become simplified. (Take, for example, printed circuits, silicon chips.) Such equipment may not be recognizable to a civilization of inferior knowledge.

The point is we may be looking at objects—quite exciting objects—without recognizing them. Who would have expected that items in Baghdad Museum, long labelled as "ritual objects," would prove to be components of batteries? Do you see what I mean?

4. OTHER RELICS STILL AWAIT DISCOVERY

Here is a tantalizing thought. Some authentic and incredibly ancient documents are known to be safely locked away. We may never see them. These forbidden treasures are known to be concealed in four places:

1. Catacombs beneath the Potala in Llasa, Tibet
2. Vaults in the Vatican Library, to which even the pope does not have access
3. Morocco, where Moslem leaders are fiercely opposed to making them public
4. A secret place known to a few initiated rabbis (believed to be in Spain)

But this is not all. There must be numerous lost cities undiscovered. Hold it, I hear you say. That's overdoing things, isn't it? An occasional ruin, maybe, but *numerous* lost cities? There aren't any unknown areas *in this day and age!*

On the contrary, there are many totally unexplored areas left about. Quite a lot of things occur in out-of-the-way corners of the world—and some not so out-of-the-way—that most persons never hear of.

Still not explored from the ground are immense expanses of the interior of Central and South America, New Guinea, Asia and Australia.

Although Europeans have lived and worked in India for some centuries, building bridges, railways and modern cities, the jungles have scarcely been investigated. There are remote villages that have never seen a white man.

In the trackless Central Australian desert, a structure from an unknown civilization was discovered when vehicles from a nearby atomic test site drove into it purely by accident.[3]

What you shall see in Part Two is *just a hint* of what still awaits us in desert, jungle and ocean.

The largest unexplored jungle area in the world is the Amazon Basin. This region is so little known that a river tributary *200 miles long* was only recently discovered—and then only by satellite. The Amazon system comprises 50,000 miles of navigable "trunk rivers" and an estimated 16,000 tributaries. The jungle on each side of the rivers is almost totally impenetrable, at least for a European. I know of settlers who have lived on riverbank clearings for forty years and never ventured more than a mile back into the jungle.

The Amazon contains some of the most solid jungles and hostile environments to be found anywhere. Surprisingly, this now mysterious region was once the center of a very intense and highly active population. Large cities flourished here, with high volume commercial traffic to the Andes.

Despite satellite technology, we face almost insurmountable problems in locating any remains.

A pilot over the Amazon may spy towers, villages or ruins, pinpoint them and report them. A few days later, someone setting out to verify the data will find they have already vanished—swallowed again by the jungle since that forest fire or whim of weather that exposed them.

Karl Brugger mentions that the "Transamazonica spur of the road between Manaus and Barcellos on the lower Rio Negro, built in 1971, was overgrown by tropical vegetation within a year. The technicians even had difficulties locating the approximate direction of the road. It is not surprising therefore that there are no more signs of 'white cities.'"[4]

Again, there are vast stretches where the fog never lifts, and in others it doesn't clear until late afternoon.

There is an area in Eastern Ecuador from which natives have been carrying out thousands of artifacts belonging to what they describe as giant pyramids and immense deserted cities. But don't get carried away. This is a forbidden region; local Indians still massacre inquisitive outsiders.

Intruders in the Matto Grosso region of Brazil can expect a similar welcome. Yes, believe it! Documented accounts are numerous. Once an entire patrol of 1,400 vanished in the jungle without trace. This trackless, unexplored "green hell" swallows visitors. The ruins clasp their secret.

Think of it. Five thousand years ago (when our forefathers were supposed to be existing in caves or crude settlements) a highly advanced culture reached over the whole globe—from Siberia to Antarctica, from Greenland to Africa.

This super world vanished so completely we thought it never existed. It is not unlikely a whole empire could disappear like this. The more advanced the culture, the more easily it could vanish without a trace. If it were so advanced, then its powers of destruction must also have been enormous. More on that later.

What an epic! The wonder is that despite wholesale obliteration of evidence, many thousands of pieces do survive—written records, oral traditions and physical remains.

Fig. 9-1. Recently discovered "Temple of the Thousand Steps" in the southernmost state of Mexico is now covered with growth. Artist's conception shows how the complex originally appeared.

83

There now follow about one thousand of the more interesting exhibits. Yet these can never be more than a tantalizing peep at this astonishing, unknown world, shrouded in opaque clouds of mystery.

PART TWO

CLUES THEY LEFT BEHIND

In this section, each "island" paragraph clue is coded as follows:

O -An Oral tradition

W -A Written or pictorial record

S -A currently or recently Surviving object

Chapter 10

Geographical—THE DISAPPEARANCE OF ADMIRAL OT

From the coffin came life...after 2,100 years!

It was May 1985. Chinese archaeologists had just cracked open a Han Dynasty tomb in the Fenghuang Mountains. Beside the corpse were containers of ancient seeds. "Let's cover these with a damp cloth," motioned one of the men to his colleague. "We don't want them to crack."

For some days the partners excavated further, unaware that something peculiar was happening. Until the lifting of the cloth; that's when the shock came. Still alive, would you believe, after 2,100 years, forty seeds had sprouted into tomato plants.

But the implications went deeper. Until now, the tomato was held to have been discovered, together with its native South America, only four centuries ago—concomitant with the development of ocean travel. We must now reexamine history.

Dead men do tell tales, you see. Tales of journeys long forgotten.

Stand by for adventure...—gigantic adventure.

Come with me now, far back into the center of the Great Unknown. Our destination: a strange planet (albeit our own), 5,000 years in the past.

What is our purpose, our main objective? To unravel some geographical mysteries:

1. Did ancient races have luxury ocean vessels equipped with sophisticated instruments to travel the earth's surface?

2. Could there have been global communication in the distant past which equalled that of modem times?

Now I realize that an affirmative answer to either of these questions will throw the whole of prehistory into confusion.

Ought we not to ask such questions? It seems to me that the classical method of research into antiquity has gotten bogged down and therefore cannot come to the right unassailable kind of conclusions.

I set before you a *mere sampling* of known discoveries. Make no mistake. The implications arc dynamite.

SHIPPING SOPHISTICATION

ITALY

1 (S): Two Roman ships were found in the 1920s at the bottom of Lake Nemi, and between 1927 and 1932 were restored, only to be destroyed by German bombers toward the end of World War II.

These *luxury cruisers* contained accommodation for 120 passengers in 30 cabins of 4 berths each, plus crew's quarters; were richly decorated with mosaic-tiled floors; walls of cypress panelling; metal columns, marble statues; and paintings in the lounge. There was a library; a ceiling sundial; a salon where a small orchestra entertained the passengers; a large restaurant and kitchen; copper heaters which provided hot water for the baths; and modern plumbing, with bronze pipes and taps.

The underwater part of the hull was sheathed with lead, fastened with copper nails.

EGYPT

2 (W): Egyptian open-sea ships were up to 350 feet long and 60 feet wide, with as many as four decks.

GREECE
CHINA

3 (W): Ancient vessels from 250 to 600 feet long and capable of carrying a crew of up to 600 were far larger than anything built by later European explorers.[1]

GREECE
ROME
4 (W): Large luxury ocean liners over 500 feet long contained temples and swimming pools; also dining halls of marble and alabaster.

SUMERIA
5 (W): An Akkadian dictionary of the Sumerian language contained *a whole section on shipping.* It catalogued *as many as 105* Sumerian terms for various ships, by size, destination or purpose. A further 69 Sumerian terms connected with the manning and construction of ships were translated into the Akkadian.

UGARIT, SYRIA, 1400 B. C
6 (W): *A catalogue* of ships details the types and uses of cargo vessels, passenger ships, fishing smacks, racing boats, troop transports and warships.

SUMERIA
7 (W): Ancient texts refer constantly to a type of ship used by the "gods" called "elippu tebiti" ("sunken ship"—what we would today call a *submarine).*

INDIA
8 (W): A 3,000-year-old document contains eight chapters of plans for craft that could travel in the air, on water or *under the sea.*[2]

BRITAIN
CHINA
9 (W): Legends of sophisticated *flying water craft* come to us from Britain and China.

NAVIGATIONAL ABILITY

GREECE
10 (S): Maritime computer: On Easter Day, 1901, divers working in a very old shipwreck on the seabed off Antikithera Island, Greece, brought up, among other relics (mostly statues), a metal artifact fused by the sea into a lump.

The object collected dust for 50 years, until restored by acid baths.

It proved to be a bronze machine with complex dials, moveable pointers, inscribed plates and a sophisticated system of interlocking gears (more than twenty gear wheels, a differential gear and a crown wheel).

On one side was a spindle that set all the dials in motion at varying speeds as soon as it was turned.

The pointers were protected by bronze covers on which long inscriptions could be read.

It could work out and exhibit the motions of the sun, moon and planets, calculate their positions, the movement of tides and the time of day. Signs of the zodiac were included.

To use the computer, one could set a particular planet on the scale, turn the gears for so many months or years and a number would show through a hole in the case, telling you where the planet would be.

Here is first-class precision mechanics, as accurate as any that can be made today.

This computer was used for navigation purposes; a mechanism for checking one's position at night. First century B.C., but doubtless of a much older technology.[3]

As Dr. Derek Price, a Cambridge scientist, observed, "finding something like this is like finding a jet plane in the tomb of Tutankhamen!"[4]

NORWAY

11 (W): Early sea travellers used a *"magic stone" for all-weather navigation,* which was able to "find the sun, even when behind clouds and fog."

Pilots today have compasses with crystal polarization, capable of finding the exact position of the sun when it is not directly visible. This legendary "stone" was based on the same principles.

It was probably cordierite (from the magnetic rocks of Italy, Finland and Norway), whose fine, clear crystals are better known as water sapphires.

Its most important quality is change of color, varying from yellow to blue when the natural alignment of its molecules forms an angle of 90 degrees with the plane of polarization of sunlight.

These items of equipment were simply the result of a much earlier technology—one anteceding both the Vikings and the Greeks.

CHINA
OLMECS, MEXICO
PHOENICIA
12 (W,S): Compasses.

EXTENT OF ANCIENT TRAVEL

That's right!

There was a time when the whole world was known. Travel around it was regular, safe and profitable.

Then most nations lapsed into a subsistence economy, the trade routes dead and forgotten.

TRAVEL TO NORTH AMERICA

RECORDS OF OTHER NATIONS

13 (W): A *Tibetan* record of at least 300 B.C. contains a map of "a green land lying far across the eastern sea" (i.e., the Pacific).

14 (W): *Greek* navigators spoke of islands in the "western sea" (i.e., the Atlantic) with a great mainland beyond (America); also regions where "for 30 days on end, the sun sets for little more than an hour, and for several months the night is faintly illuminated by the western twilight" (the Polar regions); and "countries where there was a day for 6 months and night for 6 months."

15 (W): *Egyptian* priests told the Greek Solon that the Atlantic "is a real sea and the surrounding land may be most truly called a continent" (i.e., America).

16 (W): According to interpretations of texts by Plato and Diodorus, *Phoenicians* traded with America around 1000 B.C.

17 (W): Seneca (first century) speaks of lands between the east coast of Asia and the west coast of Europe (e.g., the Americas); he says that "one day, vast new lands will offer themselves to human view."

18 (W): Strabo (born c. 60 B.C.) writes of "other inhabited lands" and says that "a huge continent will be discovered one day."

MASSACHUSETTS

19 (S): An underwater rock carving in Lake Assawompset, Massachusetts, was temporarily exposed when the waterline receded during a drought in 1957. It clearly portrayed a ship of ancient *Phoenician* or

Minoan style (suggesting it was incised when the sea level was lower, and the level of in-shore waters corresponded).

TENNESSEE
20 (S): A stone found in 1885 near Morganton, Tennessee, bore an inscription speculated to be recent Indian. However, when the stone is turned upside down the letters spell a message in ancient Canaanite: "For Jehu"—an example of an inscription having been looked at upside down for almost a century![5]

CANADA
21 (W): The Micmac clan of the Algonquian nation wrote in 2,000 characters of pure Egyptian hieroglyphics.

GENERAL
22 (S): Arab remains in America are fairly numerous.

NEW HAMPSHIRE
23 (S): A stone labyrinth with *Minoan-like* inscriptions and of a similar construction to that of 3,500 years ago, stands at Mystery Hill, New Hampshire.

IOWA
24 (S): An American "Rosetta Stone" called the Davenport Stele (found 1874, in the lower levels of an Indian burial mound) contains inscriptions in three languages: *hieratic Egyptian, Iberian Punic and Libyan.*

Harvard professor Barry Fell, in *America B.C.*, remarks that this stele is genuine because neither the Iberian nor the Libyan scripts had been deciphered at the time it was discovered.[6]

GREAT LAKES REGION
25 (S): Two-way trans-Atlantic trade around 2500 B.C. is indicated by woodworking tools and fishing gear found in the Great Lakes area, and in ground slate knives found in *Scandinavia and the Baltic countries.*

GENERAL
26 (S): Distinctive pottery of North America (1000 B.C.) closely matches *Baltic pottery of the same age.*

GEORGIA
27 (S): Manfred Metcalf found a stone which bears a *Phoenician* script used around 2000 B.C. (Columbus, Georgia).[7]

TENNESSEE
28 (S): In 1970, the Batcreek Stone from Tennessee was positively identified as being of *Hebrew* origin; so was an amulet recovered from a very old tomb.

Caches of coins dating from the Hebrew Bar Kokhbar rebellion against Rome in AD. 132—135 have been unearthed in Kentucky and Tennessee.

GEORGIA
29 (S): In 1973, Mrs. Joe Hearn was digging in her backyard when she unearthed a metal tablet containing a cuneiform script called *Classic Ur II,* which was in use in the *Middle East* 4,000 years ago.[8]

Similar authenticated finds are common all through the United States; inscriptions on buried temples, on tablets, on gravestones and on cliff faces.

CENTRAL AMERICA

GUATEMALA
30 (W): The ancient Popul Vuh of the Maya speaks of a land *"where whites and blacks dwelt together in peace"* (an unusual statement for a land whose people are neither white nor black!)

MEXICO
31 (S): Sculpted heads dated from as early as 1500 B.C. show unequivocally *bearded Jews, African Negroes and other distinctive racial types.*

GUATEMALA
32 (W): In both the Mayan calendar and the *Near Eastern* calendar, the same sequence of animal types is used in the same order to represent each month. Even the origination date for these calendars is the same— approximately 3000 B.C.

MEXICO
PERU
33 (S): Many finds in Mexico and Peru display *Chinese* and/or *Buddhist* features.

MEXICO
34 (W): There are *"oriental"* aspects to Aztec religion and astronomy.

PANAMA35 (W): Asian-sounding names are inscribed on an ancient tomb.

MEXICO
36 (S): Similarly complicated rules were worked out for a board game known as "pachisi" in *Asia* and "patolli" in Mexico.

SOUTH AMERICA

GENERAL
37 (S): Thousands of inscriptions on South American standing stones and dolmens contain letters from early *European* and *Mediterranean* alphabets.
(The same is true of weapons, implements and crockery found in South America.)

ECUADOR
38 (S) Pottery 5,000 years old is almost certainly *Japanese* in origin.[9]

ECUADOR
39 (S): During my 1967 expedition to remote jungle villages in the Amazon headwaters, I came upon *Egyptian* hieroglyphics on metal plates.

ECUADOR
40 (S): *Every race* in the world is represented in statuettes found in a very ancient city on the seabed, just off shore, near Guayaquil. There are Aryans, Semites, Caucasians and a race looking remarkably like modern Japanese.

ECUADOR
41 (S): Artifacts found in caves deep in the jungle near Tayos include:[10]

- Several superb wood statues carved in the *Pacific Oceanic* island style and depicting *Negroid* men and women
- A mahogany Adam and Eve with definite *Semitic* features
- Bronze images of *Egyptian* princesses and *Assyrian* gods
- A plaque of a *Caucasian* man writing with a quill pen
- *Phoenician* bronze calendars
- A large aluminum sheet depicting the *Greek* goddess Athena.

AMAZON JUNGLE (ECUADOR)
42 (S): A plaque found in the Amazon jungle was carved in pure *Libyan—which* was also spoken by the Zuni Indians of *southwestern U.S.A.!*

PERU
43 (S): An inscription discovered 150 miles from Cuzco relates that its authors (from the era of Egypt's first king Menes) had arrived from the Indus Valley *(Pakistan).*

PERU
44 (S): Images of symbolic white, yellow and black men, as well as a fourth race (unidentified); also animals from other parts of the world and several figures resembling *Egyptian* sculptures, stand on the Plateau of Marcahuasi.

PERU
45 (S): A piece of pottery found at Nazca bears the faces of five girls— one white, one red, one black, one brown and one yellow. This indicates that the Nazcans had knowledge of *every racial group* around the world, and possibly even models to work from.

PERU
EGYPT
46 (S): Cotton-weaving looms in *Peru* and *Egypt* were almost identical, even to the point of each having eleven working parts.

BOLIVIA
CANARY ISLANDS
SAHARA
ETHIOPIA
PHOENICIA
47 (S): Ideograms of the Aymara Indians of the Lake Titicaca region exactly correspond to ancient signs in the *Canary Islands,* in the *North African Sahara,* in *Ethiopia,* and among the *Phoenicians,* halfway around the world.

BOLIVIA
48 (S): A row of stone sculptures embedded along a surviving wall at the ruined city of Tiahuanaco, portray heads of virtually *every known race* on earth, and some that are not identifiable.

BOLIVIA
EGYPT
49 (S): Copper trepanning instruments of Tiahuanaco (for opening the brain) were *identical* to those used by the *Egyptians—as* were the methods used!

PARAGUAY
EGYPT
EUROPE
50 (S): Inscriptions relating to *Egypt* have been found in some caves at Teyucare. At Villarrica (further south) are carvings resembling *Germanic* and *Scandinavian* runes.

ARGENTINA
51 (S): At the mouth of the Rio de la Plata, a dagger and helmet were found with inscriptions from the time of *Alexander the Great.*

ARGENTINA
52 (S): The old *Irish* (according to their legends) maintained a very early connection with a "golden civilized race across the Western Ocean"— and in the cordilleras of the Argentine, today, there is actually an Indian tribe speaking pure Gaelic or Erse!

BRAZIL
53 (S): Near Manaus, over 600 miles inland, was found a pot buried with an Arab inscription "sakad-bahar" ("riversea"), dated at 4,000 years old.

BRAZIL
54 (S) Over 2,800 graffiti, some very ancient, have been found in Brazil, many in the heart of the jungle or on mountaintops. There are "pre-Egyptian," *Phoenician* and *Sumerian* scripts and hieroglyphics. (At least 2,000 photographs of these have been taken.) The earlier Indians had many ancient traditions of an advanced civilization that flourished thousands of years ago to the north and west of the central highlands.

BRAZIL
55 (S): *Phoenician* inscriptions have been found which give the names and dates of the rulers of Tyre and Sidon.

BRAZIL
56 (S): In the province of Amazonas, the French engineer Apollinaire Frot came upon an ancient carved rock hidden by dense jungle close to a river, which recorded the journey of a *proto-Egyptian* priest to what is now Bolivia. The inscription gave directions to silver and gold mines. Stage by stage, such markers ran across central Brazil.

BRAZIL
57 (S): In the dead cities of the Matto Grosso are found the same names of the zodiacal constellations that we use today!

BRAZIL
58 (S): Ceramics and ornaments found on the island of Marajo, at the mouth of the lower Amazon, depict human faces from *every race* in the world, and identical inscription symbols to those in ancient *Mexico, China, Egypt* and *India.*

ASIA

KAZAKHSTAN
FRANCE
59 (S): Petroglyphs in Kazakhstan (over 3,000 years old) portray a sorcerer casting a spell over a circle of beasts—remarkably similar to one in the "Three Brothers" cave of *France.*

SIBERIA
MANCHURIA
INDIA
AFRICA
60 (S): Carvings resembling *Scandinavian* and *Germanic* runes have been found.

INDONESIA
61 (S): Cloves from the Moluccas have been excavated in *Syrian* rubble of 2500 B.C.

INDIA
62 (S): Artifacts and records show that the *Sumerians* sailed to both Britain and India.

CHINA
63 (S): Peanuts (native to *South America)* have been dug up from sites in China dated 2335 B.C.

GERMANY
CHINA
64 (S): Richly patterned clothing embroidered in *Chinese* silk has been recovered from a "Bronze Age" Celtic grave near Hochdorf.

SOUTHEAST ASIA
65 (S): *African Negro, Armenian, Phoenician, Egyptian* and *Greek* facial features are still identified among the indigenous populations of Southeast Asia, Indonesia and the Pacific Islands.

SOUTHEAST ASIA
66 (S): Headdresses worn by chiefs and warriors of the same region bear great similarities to the helmets of the classical *Greek* warriors of Alexander's time.

PACIFIC—ANTARCTICA

PACIFIC ISLANDS
AFRICA

67 (S): Rock engravings in the *Southern Sahara area of Africa* show females wearing clothes and exhibiting tattoos similar to those 15,600 miles away as the crow flies, in the South Pacific.

EASTER ISLAND

68 (S): An early stone carving clearly shows an ancient ship with three masts—much larger than anything used by the islanders.

EASTER ISLAND
INDUS VALLEY, PAKISTAN

69 (S): Wooden tablets bear hieroglyphics in detail similar to that used in the *Caroline Islands* and also to the archaic *Indian* writing of the Indus Valley, on exactly the opposite side of the world.

EASTER ISLAND

70 (O): Polynesians were aware of the treacherous passage beyond the southern extremity of *Cape Horn* and of the *Antarctic,* "once inhabited by several nations"; they remembered also that in the midst of Antarctica was a mighty cliff of red rock.

(Remarkably, an identical landmark was recently discovered in Antarctica's heart; several hundred miles inland, it could not have been observed from the coast. Nor could any Polynesian have traversed the white continent in its present state to see that red cliff and tell about it.)

HAWAII

71 (O): Numerous striking similarities exist between the languages of Hawaii and ancient *Greece.*

What happened to the records of such world-circling by ancient fleets?

FIJI
CAPE YORK, AUSTRALIA

72 (S): Cave art of a Mayan (Central American) character has been found.

NORTHERN NEW GUINEA
PHILIPPINE ISLANDS
CHINA
73 (S): *Mayan jade artifacts have been discovered.*

GILBERT ISLANDS
74 (S): *Mayan blood groups and racial features exist.*

NEW GUINEA
75 (S): *Egyptian* influence at least 2,000 years old is seen in many of the native philosophies, rites and wooden carvings.

NEW GUINEA
76 (S): Five structures identical to 3,000-year-old step pyramids in the *Middle East,* exist in the eastern Sepik district.

OFF THE TIP OF NEW IRELAND
77 (S): Remains of an ancient sun worshipper's temple of *Egyptian* style, and an idol facing the rising sun, with features half-man half-bird, were discovered in 1964 on New Hanover Island.

POLYNESIA
SOUTH AMERICA
78 (S): *South American* sweet potatoes called "kamar" were grown and called "kumara" throughout Polynesia.

NEW ZEALAND
NORTH AMERICA
79 (S): The sailing vessels, lodges and totem poles of the Indians of *British Columbia and Alaska* closely resemble those of the Maori.

SOLOMON ISLANDS
GREECE
SOUTH AMERICA
80 (S): A reed musical instrument of ancient *Greece* is virtually the same as one played in the Solomon Islands and the Andes highlands of South America. It possesses an almost identical structure; even the pitch is the same.

AUSTRALIA

GENERAL
81 (W): In 338 B.C., Shi Tzu recorded the presence of pouched animals, which were introduced to *China* about the time that Emperor Chao despatched ships to a southern land called Chui Hiao to collect these same creatures.

GENERAL
82 (W): *Chinese* records prior to 338 B.C. mention a great southern continent on which dwelt fierce black people who used a strange weapon (the boomerang).

GENERAL
83 (S): Archaeologists have unearthed carved stones in *Persia* depicting world maps, including one describing a southern continent, dating back to 3000 B.C.

GENERAL
84 (W): The *Egyptian* explorer Knemhotep returned with a wild report of a "vast continent" where animals carried their young in pouches and the natives threw a weapon that came back to the hand.

GENERAL
85 (S): Eucalyptus resin (obtainable only from Australia) was found in the embalming of a woman of 1000 B.C. in the *Jordan Valley*.

GENERAL
86 (S): Chemical analysis of some *Egyptian* mummies has revealed the presence of eucalyptus oil—indicating contact with Australia in the days of the Pharaohs.

NORTHERN TERRITORY
87 (W): Confucius, the *Chinese* philosopher, wrote in his *Spring and Summer Annals* (481 B.C.) of the observation of two solar eclipses, one on April 17, 592 B.C. and the second on August 11, 553 B.C., on what appears to have been the coast of Darwin, Australia.

AUSTRALIAN EAST COAST
TAIWAN
88 (W): A map in *Taiwan* Museum shows the southern coastline of New Guinea, and Australia's east coast to Victoria and Tasmania. It is 2,000 years old.

WESTERN AUSTRALIA
89 (S): Aborigines of the Kimberleys of northwestern Australia greeted the first white man with ancient secret Masonic hand signs; they also had customs, religious features and words clearly of *Egyptian* origin, as well as *Middle East* blood groups and racial features.

WESTERN AUSTRALIA
90 (S): The Wandjina cave art of the Kimberleys shows people clothed in garments unknown to primitive tribesmen, but like those worn by *Egyptian* and *Phoenician* seafarers of 3,000 years ago. (The tribesmen say that the people in the artwork came over the Indian Ocean.)

WESTERN AUSTRALIA
91 (S): An inscribed bronze plate of *Phoenician* origin (dated from 600 B.C.) was found preserved in the tidal mud off the coast of northwestern Australia, near Derby and close to a very ancient mine.

CENTRAL AUSTRALIA
92 (S): A non-Australian man appears in rock images on a cliff west of Alice Springs, Central Australia, wearing a miter of Babylonian or Egyptian style.

NORTHERN TERRITORY
93 (O): Aborigines claim that an uninhabited secret city called Burrungu (once inhabited by gigantic *white men)* is even now concealed in the northern hinterlands. It was a vibrant "place of much activity."

NORTHERN TERRITORY
94 (S): *Egyptian* death beliefs and rites (including mummification) are held by Arnhem Land and Torres Strait natives; the incisions and method of embalming are identical to the practice of 2,900 years ago in Egypt.

SOUTH AUSTRALIA
95 (S): The name Ot appears on what may be *Phoenician* carvings, found near Adelaide in 1931. (Was this the same Babylonian admiral Ot who went off to South-East Asia in 636 B.C. and disappeared?)

NEW SOUTH WALES
96 (S): Many strange symbols, ships and figures, of *Egyptian, Phoenician* and *Syrian* style have been found carved on rocks along the Hawkesbury River, New South Wales.

NEW SOUTH WALES
97 (S): A small axe blade of *Middle East* style, widely used by shipbuilders 2,500 years ago, was found near Penrith, New South Wales.

QUEENSLAND
98 (S): *Phoenician-style* engravings were discovered on a marble slab in North Queensland.

QUEENSLAND
99 (S): Also unearthed were:* A *Ptolemy IV* bronze coin (of 221 to 204 B.C.), near Baron Falls, North Queensland, 2 feet below ground in a rain forest (c. 1910)* In the same district, a large rock of sandstone carved in the form of a scarab beetle, a religious object of ancient *Egypt.*

QUEENSLAND
100 (S): In 1977, museum curator Rex Gilroy found in a mountain cave on the Atherton Tableland, Queensland, some Aboriginal paintings which included 3,000-year-old *Egyptian* Masonic signs. (The identical detail of the symbology could not possibly have been invented by the Aborigines themselves.)

QUEENSLAND
101 (S): A statue of the *Egyptian* god Thoth in the ape form of pre-2000 B.C. with the papyrus flower, was found at Gympie, Queensland, in 1966. Over the last century, this location has yielded a *Middle Eastern* spoon, an Egyptian scarab beetle pendant, as well as numerous *Phoenician* and Egyptian pottery fragments and drawings.

QUEENSLAND
102 (S): In the same district, a stepped pyramidal structure constructed of crude lumps of stone, rises in bushland in eighteen terraces to a height of

100 feet. Another twice the size stands in dense scrubland near Sydney, New South Wales. (As with the five similar structures in New Guinea, these are identical to 3,000-year-old step pyramids in the *Middle East.)*

QUEENSLAND
103 (S): Ancient Aboriginal legends tell how people in large ships like birds (the bird-headed prows of the old *Phoenician* triremes?) sailed into Gympie (now 34 miles inland), dug holes in the hills, erected the "sacred mountain" and interbred with local inhabitants. Interestingly, evidence of ancient mining and smelting was recently found here.

****

Fiction couldn't challenge your imagination more. And yet here it all is, fact after fact, story after story, about the lives and discoveries of a people thousands of years ago.

Now naturally these exhibits will *not* be popular with some people. The majority of the scientific community has greeted them *with deathly silence* because of early indoctrination in evolution. It tries to ignore them for the sole reason that it cannot explain them.

However, in this chapter we have begun to tie up the apparently disconnected threads which stare us in the face—and make sense of them. Undeniably, we are confronted with an incredible past, of which there remains but an imperfect and diminishing echo.

Chapter 11

Astronomical—SECRET PLANET—ARE WE IN FOR MORE SURPRISES?

A s I first researched this, Earth's unmanned spacecraft *Voyager II* was hurtling beyond Uranus toward the planet Neptune for a rendezvous in 1989. On August 24 that year (yes, the exact day was known), it was calculated to swing around past Neptune, then head off out of the solar system forever, into unknown deep space.

Was it *as recently as the nineteenth century* that most people thought the earth we live on was flat, center of the universe, surrounded by a distant vault of fixed stars? And that the planets and sun moved around us? That's right! "The earth cannot be a ball," said one prominent scientist, "otherwise the people on the lower half would fall into the void." Even the great Kepler not so much earlier had said there were only 1,005 stars.

So long did ignorance prevail that we assume it was always so.

Now enjoy the taste of a surprise! Contrary to history as we know it, in that remote period we call "prehistory," there subsisted an embarrassing wealth of astronomical knowledge. And may I suggest that the more one looks into it, the more one feels that a race of scientific giants has preceded us.

The conclusion is unavoidable that the astronomers of Babylon, India and Egypt either possessed sophisticated instruments themselves, or they were the custodians of a prehistoric science—that of a Mother Civilization.

Even later, among the classical Greeks and Romans, there were sages who still had access to a body of knowledge extending back into the dim past.

The nations with particular knowledge cited below were not alone is possessing this. Such a science must have been universal at first, but remember, the surviving evidence is fragmentary.

THE EARTH

EGYPT
CHINA
ENGLAND
GUATEMALA
TIAHUANACO, BOLIVIA
GREECE
INDIA
SUMERIA
BABYLON
ASSYRIA
HITTITE
SASIA MINOR
THE BIBLE[1]
1 (W): The earth is a *sphere,* surrounded by the heavens.

The Sumerians, for example, identified, named, and grouped the constellations of both the northern and southern skies to the South Pole (i.e., the complete skies of a global, not a flat earth). Egypt's pyramid builders could project maps from spherical to flat surfaces, which shows they knew the earth to be round. They calculated the shape and size of the earth far more accurately than anybody before the mid-nineteenth century.

CHINA
GREECE
2 (W): The earth is *slightly egg- or pear-shaped.* (And modern science agrees. Our distorted sphere is a little pear-shaped, with a bulge in the Southern Hemisphere.)

106

INDIA
CHINA, 1600 B.C.
GREECE
ROME
THE BIBLE[2]
3 (W): The earth *floats in space.*

EGYPT
GREECE
CHINA
INDIA
THE BIBLE[3]
4 (W): Earth spins on its axis in 24 hours.
    • "The circuit of the earth"; "the earth in its courses" (Nesi-Khonsu Papyrus, Egypt—1000 B.C.)
    • "The seeming rotation of the stars is due to earth's revolving on its axis." (Greece—2000 B.C.)

BABYLON
EGYPT
INDIA
GREECE
5 (W): Earth revolves around the sun.

GREECE
6 (W): The orbit of the earth is elliptical (oval-shaped). "The earth revolves in an oblique circle while it rotates at the same time about its own axis."[4]

EGYPT
INDIA
GUATEMALA
CHALDEA
ENGLAND
GREECE
7 (W): Size of the earth:
• A circumference difference from our modern calculation of only 225 miles—Egypt
• Diameter computed to be 7,840 miles, compared to our calculation of 7,926.7 miles—India[5]

GUATEMALA
8 (W): The weight of the earth
BABYLON
EGYPT
9 (W): Exact length of the year:
- Earth's solar year is 365.2420 days—Guatemala (whereas we know it to be 365.2422 days)
- The annual movement of the sun and moon determined to an error of less than 9 seconds of an arc—Babylon
- The exact length of the solar year, the siderial year, and the anomalistic year, seems likely to have been clearly understood—Egypt[6]

GREECE, 2000 B.C.
10 (W): The seasons are caused by the earth's rotation around the sun along the ecliptic.

GREECE
11 (W): An awareness of the torrid, temperate and frigid zones existing on our planet.

THE MOON

INDIA
12 (W): The distance to the moon is 253,000 miles.

(By comparison, we calculate the maximum distance to be 252,710 miles.)[7]

GREECE
CHALDEA
INDIA
CHINA
13 (W): *The moon's light is reflected.* "The moon illuminates the nights with borrowed light."[8]

GREECE
14 (W): The moon circles about the earth.[9]

ENGLAND
THE ARABS
15 (W): *The path of the moon is an ellipse, varying closer or further from the earth.*

ENGLAND
THE ARABS
16 (W): *A variation exists in the moon's motion* (an irregularity caused by differences in the sun's pull at various points of the moon's orbit).
(This was "discovered" only by precision instruments in the seventeenth century!)

MEXICO
17 (W): *The length of the moon's cycle calculated accurately to within 4/10,000 of a day!*
(Duration of the lunar month is 29.53020 days, according to the Copan Maya; or 29.53086 days, according to the Palenque Maya. Actually, we calculate it *at* 29.53059 days.)

GREECE
18 (W): *Eclipses (solar): "It is the moon that darkens the sun."*[10]

GREECE
CHALDEA
19 (W): *Lunar eclipses: "it is the earth's shadow that falls on the moon.*[11]

BABYLON
ENGLAND
20 (W): *Accurate forecasting of eclipses to fractions of a second of an arc:*
- The present methods of calculation established in 1857, included an error of 7/10 second of an arc in estimating the movement of the sun. Babylon's calculation was 2/10 second nearer the truth.
- The maximum amplitude of the moon's wobble, which occurs immediately before the season of lunar eclipses, was observed— England 2000 B.C.

(To predict an eclipse, however, three checkpoints at 120 degrees longitude distant from each other must first be established, and information communicated from each of them.)

ENGLAND, 2000 B.C.
21 (W): There is a 56-year cycle to moon eclipse patterns.[12]

BABYLON
CHINA
GREECE
ROME
22 (W): *The moon exerts an attraction on earth's tides.*
(Only 300 years ago, Kepler was criticized for this same conclusion.)

PYTHAGORAS, GREECE
23 (W): *The moon has a 2-week-long day* (fifteen times longer than ours).

CHINA, 1700 B.C.
24 (W): *The lunar month has a precise length of 29.5305106 days.* (Our modern calendars are only 8/100,000 more accurate.)

GREECE, 500 B.C.
25 (W): *"The markings on the moon are shadows from high mountains and deep valleys."*

CHINA
SUMERIA [13]
PLUTARCH
26 (W): *The moon is dreary and cold wastelands.*

THE SUN

PLUTARCH
27 (W): *The distance to the sun is 804 million stadia* (91.4 million miles—almost the figure we accept today).

CHINA, 1st cent B.C.
28 (W): *The stars, sun and moon all float in empty space.*

GREECE
29 (W): The relative sizes of the sun and moon understood.

GUATEMALA
30 (W): Our sun is moving through space, carrying our family of planets along. It is circumnavigating a Central Fire ("Mya") near the Pleiades.

GREECE
31 (W): *Solar parallax* (the apparent displacement of the sun amid the stars because of the movement of the earth on its orbit) *understood*. (This was not noticed again until 1670.)

THE PLANETS

MEXICO
32 (S): The planets are globular in shape. (The Aztecs had a ball game to simulate this.)

GREECE
EGYPT
33 (W): The order of the planets in distance from the sun, listed correctly.

BABYLON
SUMERIA
ASSYRIA
GREECE
34 (W): The planets revolve around the sun.
• "those that are shepherded" (by the sun)—Sumeria.

ASSYRIA
35 (W): Mercury:
• Is the fastest-moving planet.
• Its orbit is warped.
• Its surface is mercilously baked by the sun.

BABYLON
36 (W): *Venus:* A knowledge of Venus' moonlike crescent phases ("the horns of Venus"), similar to those of the moon. (However, this is invisible to the naked eye!)

GUATEMALA
37 (W): The transit of Venus across the solar disk.

GUATEMALA
38 (W): *Venus'* "evening star" pattern is repeated in an 8-year cycle. (It is true that Venus makes 13 revolutions of the sun for every 8 that our earth makes.)

GUATEMALA
39 (W): A year on *Venus* is 584 days long. (Our modern computers agree—placing it at 583.82 days!)

ASSYRIA
40 (W): *Venus:*
- Has a diaphanous gown of clouds
- Its surface is hellish. (True. We know today that there is sulfuric acid in its atmosphere.)
- Though beautiful with its clouds, it is very destructive. (In fact, the atmosphere is so dense it has easily crushed every earth probe sent to the surface.)

GUATEMALA
41 (W): Mars: The length of its year accurately predicted.

SUMERIA
GREECE
42 (W): Mars' two moons and their distance from that planet.

ASSYRIA
43 (W): *Mars:*
- After long hope, it is a disappointment, with no life as on earth
- Its surface is broken
- There are four great volcanic "boils" present
- These "boils" caused the nearby valley "tears"

GUATEMALA
44 (W): *Jupiter:* An accurate awareness of the number of years and days it takes Jupiter to circle once around the zodiac.

MAORIS, NEW ZEALAND
45 (W): *Jupiter's* bands (invisible, except by telescope).

ASSYRIA
46 (W): *Jupiter* has a ring, like Saturn, but not nearly as spectacular as those of Saturn. (And yes, a single faint ring around Jupiter was confirmed by the *Voyager I* fly-past in 1979!)

ASSYRIA
47 (W): *Jupiter "rages," like the sun.*

We have now found that Jupiter's interior is much hotter than had been estimated, and it spews deadly radiation out into space. Jupiter wallows in a seething mass of hydrogen and helium gas clouds, forming a turbulent atmosphere. Some planet!

"Tornadoes and cyclones whirled across its surface. Perhaps they've *raged* non-stop for thousands of years." So reported the *Australasian Post* of May 10, 1979, concerning *Voyager I's* discoveries in March of that year (emphasis is mine).

"The first sensation was when *Voyager 1* detected and reported a blinding light above it—so strong that it *appeared to sensors to be even brighter than the sun* as seen from earth...it is an aurora which engulfs the whole of Jupiter."

Jupiter sends out ray particles. "Jupiter is the largest producer of rays in our system." (The same *Australasian Post* article)

BABYLON
DOGONS, MALI
48 (O,W): *Jupiter's moons* (again, invisible without a telescope).

DOGONS, AFRICA
MAORIS, NEW ZEALAND
ASSYRIA
49 (O,W): *Saturn* has glorious rings.

BABYLONASSYRIA
50 (W): *Saturn's moons.*

ASSYRIA
51 (W): Saturn:

- Is very large
- It is squat (with a smaller diameter from pole to pole than across the equator)
- It gives off more heat than it absorbs from the sun and thus keeps its moons warm
- Saturn's chief moon will give up "treasures to all"; it is a "blessed" place

In the Talda Makan Desert of Western China, Dr. Irwin Wilson came upon tablets in the Assyrian script. When translated, these were found to contain an ode to the planets. And what a shocker it is!

A published copy of this translation came to my attention in May 1980.[14]

At that very time the *Voyager I* space probe, having left the vicinity of Jupiter, was now racing toward Saturn, nearly a billion miles from earth.

The tablets gave information which, if correct, should see some startling discoveries when the spacecraft arrived six months later.

Among other things, we should expect to find heat radiating from Saturn and a moon offering treasures. Not until *Voyager I* reached Saturn in November, could the incredible accuracy of these ancient claims become apparent.

Within the space of a few dramatic hours, discoveries were made that shattered numerous modern theories. "Voyager had something for everyone" (Melbourne *Age*, November 17, 1980), and the main moon Titan unexpectedly revealed a nitrogen-dense atmosphere, like earth's.[15]

Suddenly watching the twentieth century catch up with this document was exciting.

SUMERIA
ASSYRIA
GREECE
52 (W): There are *further planets* beyond Saturn.

Zecharia Sitchin refers to a Sumerian celestial map with the comment: "If this...had been discovered and studied two centuries ago, astronomers would have deemed the Sumerians totally uninformed, foolishly imagining more planets beyond Saturn. Now, however, we know that Uranus and

114

Neptune and Pluto are really there. Did the Sumerians imagine the other discrepancies, or were they properly informed?"[16]

ASSYRIA
53 (W): *Uranus* (the next planet out from Saturn):
- Is tipped on its axis.
- Presents the poles to the sun.
- Has a set of rings, but lightl.

Absolutely correct! The Uranian axis, unlike that of any other planet, is tilted an exceptional 82 degrees, so that it lies very nearly in the plane of the planet's orbit. Thus, and only on Uranus, each pole in turn faces toward the sun.

And on January 24, 1986, *Voyager II* confirmed that there were, indeed, eleven faint, dark rings around Uranus.

SOUTHERN AFRICA
GREECE
54 (W): *Uranus* regularly covers (i.e. eclipses) its moons in its course around the sun.

ASSYRIA
55 (W): *Neptune* (the next planet out from Uranus) is eclipsed by another planet.

(And it is a fact that during its revolution around the sun, Pluto actually comes closer to the sun than Neptune, eclipsing it!)

SUMERIA
56 (W): *There is one more planet beyond Pluto.* (An old map showed the sun and eleven planets, counting the moon, all by size.)

There is now good reason to believe that this "secret" planet does exist. [17] On December 31, 1983, scientists announced their belief that they have located a body in orbit beyond Pluto.

DOGONS, MALI
57 (O): Our solar system is part of the Milky Way.

COMETS AND METEORS

BABYLON
GREECE
58 (W): *Comets* move in orbits, like the planets.   (Magnificent reasoning, since comets do not carry identification plates.)

GREECE
59 (W): *Meteors* frequently fall to earth.[18]
(This was considered nonsense until modern times.)

BEYOND OUR SOLAR SYSTEM

CHINA
60 (W): *The blue of the sky* is merely an optical illusion.

INDIA
GREECE
61 (W): The universe is infinite. The distance to and between the stars is "immeasurable."

DOGONS, MALI
62 (O): The stars are much more distant than the planets.

INDIA
GREECE, 5th cent. B. C
THE BIBLE[19]
63 (W): The stars cannot be numbered.

GREECE
64 (W)*: The stars are blazing suns like our sun, and some of them are larger than our sun.*

SUMERIA
GREECE
65 (W): Each star is the center of a *planetary system.*

On June 13, 1984, Dr. Hartmut Aumann announced to the American Astronomical Society that forty nearby stars show excess infrared emission, suggesting that they may be orbited by solid material, or even planets.

Six months later, Professors Donald McCarthy and Frank Low from the University of Arizona claimed to have actually discovered a planet moving around the Van Biesbroeck 8 star in the Ophicius constellation some 21 light-years (125,000 billion miles) from earth. It had a mass thirty to eighty times that of our Jupiter.

Credit for this first-discovered planet outside our solar system was counterclaimed by Professor Robert Harrington, of the Washington Naval Observatory, who said he saw the planet eighteen months earlier, with two other astronomers.

GREECE
66 (W): Each star rotates on its axis.

INDIA
GREECE
THE BIBLE[20]
67 (W): There exist "other earths" with inhabitants.

GREECE
68 (W): *The Milky Way* is a huge number of very distant stars scattered throughout space. (And we reached this conclusion less than two centuries ago!)

DOGONS, MALI
69 (O): *The Milky Way* is of a spiral-like shape. (A fact not known to astronomers until well into this century.)

MEDITERRANEAN AREA
70 (W): The "tenth star" of the Pleiades constellation (not visible to the naked eye) was known.

BABYLON
GUATEMALA
71 (W): The "Scorpion" constellation was so called because it has a "tail," a comet within the constellation. (But this can be seen only with a powerful telescope!)

EGYPT, 1000 B.C.
SUMERIA
DOGONS, MALI
ITURI PYGMIES, ZAIRE
72 (O): Details concerning the "dark" companion of the star Sirius A:
- Digitaria is a white star, but invisible
- It has an elliptical orbit around Sirius A
- Even the position of Sirius A within this ellipse was known
- It revolves around brightly shining Sirius once every 50 years
- It is also the heaviest star (i.e., very dense)

Powerful telescopes and calculations have confirmed every detail as true.

Sirius B, as we call it, is totally invisible to the human eye. It orbits Sirius A, the brightest star in the sky.

It was not seen through a telescope until 1862, and it was not possible to capture it on a photograph until 1970. This dark star has a gravity 100 million times greater than that of earth. Its density is so great that a cubic meter weighs around 20,000 tons.

Thus the Dogons, though today an illiterate and primitive society, preserve a remarkable body of astronomical learning.

INSTRUMENTS

ENGLAND
73 (S): *Astronomical clocks:* The central axis of Stonehenge was constructed to correlate exactly with sunrise in midsummer. It is a 56-year stone calendar, as well as an observatory—a giant astronomical calculator. (Eclipses were predicted by moving three black and three white stones around certain six holes yearly in the 56-hole Aubrey Circle.) At least 600 sites operated in similar fashion throughout the country.

TIAHUANACO, BOLIVIA
74 (S): *A calendar* which gives the equinoxes, the astronomical seasons, the positions of the moon for every hour, as well as the moon's movements, taking the rotation of the earth into account.

SOMERSET, DORSET AND OTHER SITES IN ENGLAND
75 (S): Mysterious labyrinths which took the form of *astronomical maps.*

EGYPT
76 (S): Many early Arab writers claimed that the Great Pyramid was built as an *observatory.* The gallery designs could have enabled the recording of the precise movements of heavenly bodies and the compilation of a comprehensive star map, since all the major stars in an 80-degree arc passed the end of the gallery opening.

GUATEMALA
77 (S): *Domed observatories* with a more exact orientation than those of seventeenth century Paris.

MEDZAMOR, ARMENIA
78 (S): *A three-story observatory* oriented to the south, where the stars are most numerous.

GUATEMALA
79 (W): *Calendars more accurate than ours:* The Maya calculated 365.2420 days to a year; our Gregorian calendar calculates 365.2425 days to a year; actual, is 365.2422 days to a year.

(The Mayan year was accurate to nearly 1/10,000 of a day.)

PLANETARIUMS (IMMENSE AND SMALL, MECHANICALLY REVOLVING)

SICILY
80 (W): *Machines imitated the universe,* following a star in its orbit and making eclipse prediction possible.

CHINA
81 (W): *A globe with metal rings* representing the paths of the sun and other bodies, was powered by a water clock.

CHINA
82 (W): *A three-foot high device* with stars, sun, moon and planets fulfilling their periods. The stars were luminous in the dark and faded in the

light. The central earth globe was continually revolving by a mechanical device and was accurate.

PERSIA
GREECE
ROME
83 (W): *Other devices* in Persia, Greece,and Rome.

GREECE
84 (S): *A complex astronomical computer* embodying precision mechanics, as accurate as anything that can be made today.[21]

WRITTEN RECORDS OF TELESCOPES

Galileo conceded that the ancient world had scientific instruments such as telescopes, but today's conventional science will not hear of the suggestion. Very well, then. But how shall we regard the following?

SICILY
85 (W): Instruments "to manifest to the eye the largeness of the sun" were used by the inventor-scientist Archimedes.[22]

GREECE
86 (W): "For studying sky details."[23]

ALEXANDRIA, EGYPT
87 (W): A device "to detect distant ships."[24]

PERU
88 (W): The word "quilpi" in the Quiche (Inca) language had the meaning of concave or convex mirrors or glass pieces, spy glasses or spectacles; in summary, "an optical instrument for looking into the distance."

GUATEMALA
89 (W): The Popol Vuh records that the ancients could "see the large and the small in the sky and the earth."[25]

ICA, PERU
90 (W): An engraved stone shows Indians squat, gazing at the heavens through telescopes.

BRITAIN
91 (W): Telescopes were used.

ROME
92 (W): Nero used a telescope made of emerald lenses to watch the Roman games.

Is that enough?

In Chapter 15 I shall detail for you some actual discoveries of machine-cut lenses and reflectors of the utmost precision (which are the elements of the astronomical telescope).

That is the ultimate proof.

Chapter 12

Cosmology—TRAVEL FAST AND LIVE LONGER

A merican scientists spent two weeks flying around the world in jets equipped with atomic clocks.

Their object was to confirm a prediction of Einstein's special theory of relativity that time on a moving object slows down the faster the object moves. They did. And it does.

This time dilation effect is now an accepted scientific fact. Astronauts flying at close to the speed of light would age more slowly than their friends on earth. The reason is that the space traveller's heartbeat, the decay of the cells of his body and his other physiological processes would slow down.

Scientists can calculate accurately the extent to which time would slow down on a spaceship travelling at close to the speed of light. Time would appear to pass normally, yet in just a few years the travellers would reach the most distant stars.

After twenty-one years on the spaceship, they could be in the heart of the Milky Way—while on earth 75,000 light years had passed!

But notice. The theory of relativity (of space and time) was apparently known to our early forefathers.

Lucretius, Heraclitis and Zeno each postulated aspects of this principle. It was also known in India.

A Japanese love story incorporates the fact of time dilation in space travel. The Island Child went into the skies for 3 years, but found on his return to his earthly home that 300 years had passed there.[1]

The Slavic version of the Book of Enoch (reflecting very ancient origins) narrates the story of a space trip which for the hero lasted only a few days, while on earth whole centuries passed.[2]

The Vision of Isiah (second to third century A.D.) speaks of a space trip to heaven. When told it was time to return to earth, the traveller asked in surprise. "Why so soon? I have been here only two hours." The angel replied. "Not two hours but 32 years." Isiah now feared he would suffer old age and death if he returned, but he was assured that upon his return to earth he would not have aged.[3]

These ancient people were not hallucinating. If our astronauts could travel close to the speed of light, they would experience a comparable shrinkage of time. This we now accept as scientifically valid.

Modern science is today stumbling upon discoveries known to an ancient forgotten science. Take these, for example:

INDIA
1 (W): *The law of gravity.*[4]

WORLDWIDE
2 *(S): Terrestrial magnetism.*

PYTHAGORAS, GREECE
3 (W): *The law of the force of attraction.*

INDIA
4 (W): *Cosmic rays.*[5]

INDIA
5 (W): *Radiation of atomic particles.*[6]

INDIA
6 (W): *The kinetic nature of energy.*[7]

PHILOLAUS, 5th cent. B.C.
7 (W): *Antimatter.*

LUCRETIUS, 1st cent. B. C
8 (W): *The uniform speed of bodies falling in a vacuum.*

CELTS, BRITAIN
9 (S): Perishables are preservable in a vacuum.

INDIA
10 (W): Fractions of seconds (the measurement of 1/300 millionth of a second).

THE MAYA, GUATEMALA
INDIA
11 (W): *The use of astronomically enormous multiples of numbers:*
- Units were devised to incorporate unwieldy numbers into simple terms. A kinchiltun equalled 57,600,000. An alautun equalled 23,040,000,000 days, or 63,123,000 years.
- The kalpa is a period of 4.32 billion years.[8] (Similarly, today's astronomers have developed a numeral system to cope with the vastness of space. The distance between stars is measured in light-years, and the distance between galaxies is frequently measured in parsecs, a unit composed of 3.26 light-years.)

EMPEDOCLES, 5th cent. B.C.
12 (W): Light requires time to travel.

EGYPT
13 (S): "The word 'pyramid' has the literal meaning of 'measure of light.'" Is it coincidence that "the vertical height of the Great Pyramid, when the structure was intact, was 483 grid feet, which is the square of the reciprocal of the angular velocity of light"?[9]

EUCLID, 3rd cent. B.C.
14 (W) *The principles of light refraction and magnification.*

KANADA, OF INDIA
15 (W) *Light and heat only different forms of the same basic substance.*
It is worth noting that current scientific concepts of the universe are literally atheistic, that is, without a God In contrast, the sophisticated cosmology of all ancient nations recognized a Creator at the center.

Chapter 13

Mathematical—WHO BEAT OUR COMPUTERS?

At a brisk four miles per hour, what distance can you stride in one second? Precisely seventy inches. In that same second, you can blink your eyes six times. All considered, little can be achieved in a mere second.

Then what, possibly, could a man do in three one-hundred millionths of one second? And why on earth should one wish to measure it? Our predecessors did, indeed, measure something that occured in that brief fraction of time. They recorded it.

Let's say that the accuracy of the ancients to the point of infinitesimal fractions is enough to make even the most die-hard skeptic stop and think.

The construction of the Great Pyramid was perfectly square to within 3/10,000 percent. The enormous blocks were fitted together with an accuracy of 1/100 inch.

The solar year in Mexico was pinpointed to an accuracy of 1/20,000 day. The lunar month was calculated to as close as .00027 day.

Indian measurements of time spoke of the "kashta," equivalent to 0.00000003 of a second.

But more astonishing was the discovery on the mound of ancient Nineveh in Assyria of numbers with fifteen digits—something that cannot be registered by any computer—a calculation with the final result in our notation of 195,955,200,000,000. (Even the oft-quoted Greeks never arose above the figure 10,000. Anything beyond was considered infinite.)

The gap between rich knowledge and poor instruments in antiquity has baffled many a scientist.

How is anyone going to explain these and many other puzzles to us?

Behind this mathematical knowledge can be dimly discerned a distant epoch in which a vanished race might have attained a high degree of technology.

And after the instruments had gone, the knowledge lingered.

Even the fragmentary records at our disposal firmly establish that the ancients possessed advanced mathematical skills.

INDIA
MEXICO
BABYLONIA
CHINA
PERU

1 (W): *The use of zero,* upon which all mathematics and science operates.

For the purpose of advanced mathematics, zero is the secret ingredient. Without zero, involved calculations are difficult. The most ancient cultures utilized it, yet often, as cultural decadence occurred, they forgot it.

MEXICO
EGYPT
PERU

2 (W): *Decimal system.*

BABYLONIA
UR, CHALDEA

3 (W): Geometry: Euclid's classic triangle problems were studied 1,700 years before Euclid was born, as was Pythagoras' theorem (on an inscribed tablet) 1,500 years before Pythagoras.

ENGLAND, 2000 B. C.
CARNAC, FRANCE

4 (S): Geometric harmony in buildings embodied near-perfect Pythagorean triangles.

EGYPT

5 (S): The dimensions of the Great Pyramid's "King's chamber" incorporate the 3 by 4 by 5 and 2 by 5 by 3 triangles commonly ascribed to the Greek mathematician Pythagoras, who lived 2,000 years later.

EGYPT

6 (S): Egyptian art and architecture point to the fact that they understood *the phi ratio.* Apart from the natural aesthetic quality of the phi proportion, it *"allowed the builders to construct a scale model of the Northern Hemisphere."*[1]

BABYLONIA
INDIA

7 (W): Algebra: Exact tables in algebra helped astronomers work out the position of celestial bodies at any time.

EGYPT

8 (S): The Great Pyramid's proportions incorporate a value, accurate to several decimal places, for *the sophisticated concept of* π

(Pi π is the fractional figure by which a circle's diameter is multiplied to determine its circumference.)

ENGLAND
Also known in GREECE 2nd cent. B.C.

9 (S): Knowlege of *trigonometry* is reflected in the construction of the exact correlations of Stonehenge.

INDIA

10 (W): *Square roots* used.

UR, CHALDEA, 2500 B.C.

11 (W): The *cube root* known and utilized.

MEXICO

12 (W): *Logarithms.*

EGYPT

13 (W): A special hieroglyphic sign for *a million.* (Not until the seventeenth century did the modern world gain any conception of millions in mathematics.)

EGYPT
MEXICO
INDIA

14 (W): *Calculations in microfractions.*

BABYLONIA
GUATEMALA
15 (W): *Large numbers manipulated by the use of reckoning tables.*

BABYLONIA
EGYPT
CHINA
16 (S): One of the world's first calculating machines, the *abacus,* was a manually operated digital *calculating device with extreme precision (embodying 15 digits).*

Chapter 14

Metallurgy—THE SAD FATE OF THE GOLD GARDENS

W hen the Spanish conquerors entered Peru, they came upon an island near Puna on which was a royal garden so astonishing it might have come out of a fairy tale.

Every living thing was reproduced in gold and silver models. Trees, even to the roots, and lesser plants with leaves, flowers and fruit fashioned in natural size and style; some ready to sprout, others half-grown or in full blossom.

Golden birds sat perched on silver trees, as if singing, while others were flying and sucking honey from flowers.

Whole fields of maize were imitated—roots, stalk, flowers and cob; the beard of the husk in gold, the rest in silver.

Other plants were similarly treated—a flower or anything of a yellow tint in real life was done in gold, the other parts in silver. From the trees hung nuggets of fruit.

Nothing remained uncopied: rabbits, foxes, mice, lizards, lions, tigers, stags, snakes. All were set in their natural surroundings to enhance reality. And as if that were not enough, golden butterflies flitted around in the breeze.

Life-size fish, ropes, hampers, baskets, bins and even woodpiles for burning were all fashioned in gold and silver, soldered together.

Such gardens, would you believe, graced all royal residences throughout the land.

The others were disassembled before the treasure-lusting invaders could reach them. So carefully were these artifacts hidden, that they have never been found.

Regretfully, most of that upon which the invaders did lay their hands was melted down for shipment to Europe.

So vanished an unbelievably precise metal technology.

But the Incas were heirs to a much earlier culture...As I see it, the evidence for an advanced knowledge of metallurgy in the remote past is irrefutable.

The following examples are but representative.

Wait for the surprises...

COLUMBIA, 2000 years ago
EZION-GEBER, ISRAEL, 3000 years ago
NORTHEAST SIBERIA, 3000 years ago
TIAHUANACO, BOLIVIA
SPAIN, 3000 B.C.
1 (S): Smelting of metals (blast furnaces).

USA—9000 degrees C.
PERU—1773 degrees C.
2 (S): Other super-heat furnaces.

STEEL

MEDZAMOR, ARMENIA, 2500 B. C
3 (S): *A steel mill* with 200 furnaces (about the oldest factory known): The workers wore gloves and covered their mouths with protective filters—just as they do today.

VARIOUS PLACES
4 (S): *Steel objects* found:
- Cube: Austria (pre-Flood)
- Ingot: India, 4th cent. B.C.
- Nails: Britain (pre-Flood)
- Tweezers: Armenia, 2500 B.C.
- Reinforced concrete: U.S.A.
- Shield: Ecuador
- Wheel rim: England, 100 B.C.

BRONZE

SUMERIA
EGYPT
CENTRAL AMERICA
SOUTH AMERICA
THAILAND, 3000 B.C.
5 (S): Bronze *at the start.*

Bronze is a hard alloy made of copper with the addition of 1/10 part tin.[1]
It *should* have taken ages to discover that the addition of 1/10 part of tin to
copper creates a better metal. But copper artifacts in our museums are few.
Bronze seems to have appeared *suddenly* and spread *far and wide* in great
profusion. Everywhere—including the Americas—the alloy appears quite
suddenly.

CHINA
CANAANITES
6 (S): Hardening of bronze to the strength of high-grade steel (harder
than we can produce)—we still do not understand this technique.

IRAN
7 (S): Bronze works of art containing arsenic (a complicated procedure).

ROME
8 (S): Valves (up to 80 lb) made of a zinc-free, lead-rich anticorrosion,
antifriction tin bronze.

ALUMINUM AND PLATINUM

CHINA, 297 AD.
9 (S): An aluminum belt (85 percent pure); aluminum metal ornaments
(almost pure).[2]

PAKISTAN
10 (S): An aluminum cup and thimble.

ECUADOR
11 (S): An aluminum harp, box and other objects.[3]

ECUADOR
12 (S): Rolls of intricately figured sheet metal in rolls 15 to 30 feet long, composed of smaller 4-foot sheets artfully riveted together (of gold, a unique untarnished silver, and an unknown alloy with the appearance of shiny aluminum).[4]
All of these are ancient aluminum artifacts.

However, aluminium was supposedly not discovered until 1803 and not obtained successfully in pure form until 1854. It is very difficult to isolate, from bauxite, as a pure metal without using a lot of electric power.

PERU
ECUADOR
13 (S): Ornaments and other objects of *platinum.*

ECUADOR
14 (S): Alloyed platinum and gold objects.

PERU
15 (S): A 25-foot-long sheet of "white gold" (an alloy of platinum, gold and silver) was found by the Spaniards.

Europeans did not learn how to alloy this hard, very high melting (1773.5 degrees C.) mineral until 1804.
It requires either a high-heat furnace and forced-air pumps or, alternatively, powder technology only used in space technology since about 1966!

OTHER METALS

BACTRIA, AFGHANISTAN, 2nd cent. B. C
16 (S): *Nickel-content coins* (of a metal which can only be extracted from its ore *by complicated procedures!).*

EGYPT

17 (W): *Noncorrosive iron ("arms* which did not rust"): Such instruments were reported by the Arab historian Ibn Abd Hokm to have been buried in vaults.

Fig. 14-1 Sheet metal wall-covering in rolls, twenty to thirty feet long. This aluminum-like metal is artfully fabricated from four-feet-wide sheets jointed with rivets. Excavated in Ecuador. (Photo Richard Wingate.)

CHINA
18 (S): Iron farm implements that were not rusty after 2,000 years in wet soil, were recently dug up.[5]

MEHAULI, near DELHI, INDIA
19 (S): *Ancient castings of LARGE pieces:* The Ashoka Pillar (1,500 years old) is a column of cast iron 6 tons and 23 feet 8 inches high—a huge casting job, with *hardly a trace of rust.*

Here is testimony to a sophisticated unknown science. (Iron that was 1,500 years under tropical heat and monsoon should have corroded and long ago.) This is pure iron, which *can be produced today only in tiny quantities and by electrolysis.*

KOTTENFORST, W. GERMANY
20 (S): An iron pillar much older, likewise weathered, but with very little trace of rust.

MOCHICAS, PERU
21(S): Alloys of gold, silver and copper *worked by processes not yet discovered.*

ECUADOR
22 (S): A steel-hard copper wheel
Numerous artifacts recovered from ancient mounds in Michigan, U.S. A were likewise made from chilled, or hardened copper by a method long lost to mankind.

CENTRAL AMERICA
23 (S): Metal thread manufactured by extrusion.

EGYPT
24 (S): Jewel-headed drills that required tremendous pressure.

PERU
25 (S): Precision-drilled quartz jewelry, requiring a complicated process, possible today only with high-speed drills.

CATAL HUYAK, TURKEY
26 (S): Drills capable of boring a hole finer than the thinnest needle.[6]

EGYPT
27 (S): Copper-headed chisels that were tempered in some manner unknown today.

IRAQ
EGYPT
28 (S): Bronze or copper saws hardened with silica set with jewelled teeth.

CENTRAL AMERICA
PERU
INDIA
TIAHUANACO, BOLIVIA
IRAQ
29 (S): Soldering and welding (including soldering with a 60:40 lead-tin alloy, comparable to the best solder we have today).

GOLD AND SILVER

TIAHUANACO, BOLIVIA
30 (S): Silver plating, embossing, filigree, damascening.

U.S.A.
31 (S): A silver inlaid floral-pattern jar (pre-Flood).[7]

ECUADOR
32 (S): Silver that does not tarnish, even to this day.

EGYPT
PERU
BULGARIA, 3000 B.C.
33 (S): Gold or copper wire.

MYCENAE, GREECE
CRIMEA
EGYPT
GUATEMALA
34 (S): Gold death masks, reproducing precisely the wearer's features.

COSTA RICA TO PERU
35 (S): A gold plating technique that required fewer operations than our present-day method.

EGYPT
36 (S): Gold hammered into leaves so thin that 367,000 made a pile only 1 inch high.

PERU
CHINA
37 (S): Thread of gold and silver, used in stitching.

PERU
38 (S): A fine net of gold; also cloth made of gold *CRETE, 1500 B.C.*

CRETE, 1500 B.C.
39 (W): An intricate honeycomb of gold.

EGYPT
40 (S): Tiny objects of gold—so light in weight that one might suspect they were made by the ultramodern process of galvanoplasty.

ECUADOR
CRETE
GREECE
TROJANS, GREECE
SUMERI
ETRUSCANS, ITALY
41 (S): *Granulation of gold:*
- Ornaments made from tiny grains of gold half the size of a pin head, sometimes interspersed with even smaller, hollowed out granules
- The same technique for the mane of a lion barely half an inch long; and the feathers and wings of a duck 1-1/4 inches
- And for the wings of a screech owl and the warts of a toad about 1 inch long
- The same technique for tiny purses and earrings
- And for other objects

These can be appreciated only by studying them through a strong magnifying glass.

COLOMBIA
BABYLON
PERU
TIBET
42 (S,W): Statues and monoliths (up to 90 feet tall) totally covered with gold or silver.

PERU
MEXICO
43 (S): Solid gold and silver life-size statues.

(One image of solid gold inlaid with emeralds and other gems covered a total wall of 50 feet! When struck by the rays of the real sun, this false sun brilliantly illuminated the interior of the building. It also caught the moonlight.)

LIMA, PERU
44 (S): The temples of Pachacamak were fastened with gold nails that were found to weigh a ton.

An abundance of precious metals in earlier times enabled many items in common use to bear an aesthetic superiority to our own. Thus we see finely worked gold and silver furniture, eating utensils, garden tools and even footwear. There were bathtubs of gold and silver, fed by water pipes of silver and gold.

The early Greeks recorded that ships calling at Tartessus found silver so plentiful that on the return journey they substituted silver anchors for their leaden ones. Montezuma of the Aztecs never ate twice from the same gold or silver plate! The value of the gold used in the construction of Solomon's Temple and its contents was, at current exchange rates, in excess of 3 billion dollars! Whatever happened to all the gold?

Perhaps some of it may yet be found. Two ancient copper alloy scrolls discovered in a Jordan Valley cave have become a focal point of suspense. It is now confirmed that they constitute a treasure list, hastily prepared thousands of years ago when Jerusalem with its temple was under siege. Sixty-one hiding places are listed. The scrolls not only itemize in detail the temple vessels concealed in a given location, but provide detailed descriptions of those locations. Of course the passage of time has served to obliterate many of the old landmarks.

However, our concern has been more with the high technology of our early ancestors. Did you notice several particulars in which ancient metallurgy remains in advance of our own? (Item nos. 6, 17—21, 27, 32 and 35)

It seems certain that metallurgy declined and became forgotten; we are still attempting to rediscover its secrets.

Chapter 15

Glasswork—MICROSCOPE ON A SEXY SPIDER

"**L**eaping lizards! What do you make of that? Shall we bank for another run?"

The Peruvian fliers could scarcely believe their eyes.

Spread out below all over the desolate Nazca plateau was a mass of geometric patterns and giant pictures of birds, animals and people as far as the eye could see.

These ground-drawn objects were so enormous that they could be seen only from a plane. Small wonder that they were not discovered until that day in 1939.

Fashioned by an unknown pre-Inca culture, and covering an area of thirty square miles, they are still unexplained.

We have no idea how, working from the ground, anybody could execute such figures in perfect proportion. They can be observed successfully only from a thousand feet in the air.

One of the drawings depicts a spider; it has one leg deliberately lengthened and extended, and at the tip there is a small cleared area.

Only one spider known uses the tip of its third leg in the precise manner shown in the drawing—the Ricinulei. It inhabits caves deep in the Amazon jungle.

This spider is recognized by scientists for its unique method of copulation for which it uses that extended leg in the described manner. It is an extremely rare species.

Now for the incredible aspect: this spider's mode of reproduction can be observed *only with the aid of a microscope!*

The question is, how were these artists able to find and then observe their tiny model—unless we concede that they inherited a knowledge of science equalling our own? Including the use of the ground optical lens microscope?

Turning, therefore, to glasswork, we find ourselves treated to more surprises from the ancient world.

Yet NOTHING is incredible any longer. The word "impossible" should have become literally impossible for us.

CHINA before 2500 B.C.
ASSYRIA (IRAQ), 2700 B.C.
MEDZAMOR, ARMENIA, 2500 B.C.
1 (S): Making of glass.

HAIFA, ISRAEL
2 (S): A glass block weighing 88 tons.

There are only two masses of glass larger than this. Both are the casts for the huge mirrors of the Mount Palomar telescopes.

We're told, of course, that ancient man was "backward".

I hope my curiosity will be pardoned: I have a question. How did those early races develop the enormous amount of heat necessary to melt the ingredients into this enormous mass of glass?

Obviously, this block is inexplicable except with reference to a super technology.

POMPEII, ITALY
3 (S): Shatterproof glass in sheets.

ATHENS, GREECE
4 (W): Spheres of glass.

ROMAN EMPIRE, 1st cent. A.D.
5 (W): Pliable, unbreakable glass.

EGYPT

6 (W): References to unbreakable glass appear constantly in Arab legends of the secrets of antiquity, as well as a mention that the Pharos lighthouse (44 stories high) was set on solid blocks of glass.

ROME, ITALY

7 (W): A theater with *a whole floor of glass.*

ROME

8 (S): Glass vases, goblets, and the like, and "chalises of gold" *(a thin sheet of gold covered in glass).*

CRETE

9 (S): *Tinted glass goblets and glazed dinnerware.*

EGYPT, 3000 B.C.

10 (S): *Glass miniatures,* which are among the most astounding achievements in the history of glassmaking.

ZIMBABWE
AYMARAS, PERU

11 (S): *Crystal birds* made with exquisite workmanship.

THE USE OF OPTICAL LENSES IMPLIED

MEDZAMOR, ARMENIA, 2500 B.C.

12 (S): Steel tweezers have been found, like eyebrow tweezers, that enable chemists and watchmakers to handle microobjects which they cannot manipulate by hand. The manipulation of such *microobjects* implies the use of microscopic lenses.

EGYPT
ROME
ECUADOR

13 (W,S):
- A version of the *Iliad* written on parchment so small that it could be rolled into a ball and stored in a walnut
- An ivory-carved chariot which could be covered by a fly's wings
- A seal containing fifteen figures in an area of 1/3-inch (7 millimeters) radius
- Rings still existing (Khufu, from 500 *B.C.;* and one acquired by Michaelangelo, about 2,000 years old), bearing *inscriptions too small to be seen with the naked eye*

- Minute bead particles, each smaller than the head of a pin, and many elaborately engraved, chased, welded together and pierced

(No artist without an optical lens could have produced any of these.)

ECUADOR
14 (S): Wood carvings, baked brick tablets and metal plates, each showing male sperm cells—which can be seen only by a *microscope*.[1]

GROUND OPTICAL LENSES AND MIRRORS DISCOVERED

MYSORE, INDIA
15 (S): Mirrors with two reflections.

MEXICO
16 (S): Highly polished circular magnetic mirrors, ground to the precision of optical lenses.

OLMECS, MEXICO
17 (S): Miniscule concave mirrors.

SEABED, ECUADOR
18 (S): A convex obsidian lens 2 inches in diameter, which functions as a mirror and reduces but does not distort the reflection—so precisely made that the reflection of the face shows the tiniest hairs.

PERU
19 (S): Concave mirrors.

LIBYA
20 (S): Lenses found in tombs.

BRAZIL
TIAHUANACO, BOLIVIA

CRETE
21 (S): Lenses and reflectors have been found also in South America and Crete.

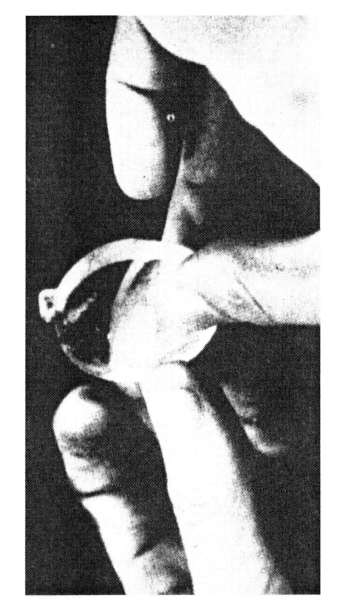

Fig. 15-1. This crystal lens was found in an Egyptian tomb and shows that this early civilization had mastered a technique which was only discovered in Europe in the late Middle Ages.

NILE VALLEY, EGYPT
CENTRAL AUSTRALIA
NINEVEH, ASSYRIA

22 (S): Spherical crystal lenses of the utmost precision (obviously machine-cut).

CARTHAGE, TUNISIA

23(S): A convex lense the size of a button, of perfectly cut rock crystal.

BRITISH HONDURAS

24 (S): A crystal skull recovered in 1924 from jungle ruins possesses eye sockets with ground lenses. Light is ingeniously channelled from the base of the skull by means of "light pipes", then concentrated through a set of concave and convex lenses, which focus the light rays directly into the excavated eye sockets—evidence of an advanced understanding of the use of light. (More on this in Chapter 23.)

Chapter 16

Large-size construction—STRANGE RUINS ON THE SEABED

A startling surprise awaited Captain Don Henry. On that particular day in 1976 he was forty miles off the southern coast of Florida directing sonar soundings of the ocean floor.

Suddenly an immense, pyramid-shaped structure showed up. It was 300 feet below the surface. Subsequent underwater closed-circuit TV was to show the pyramid to be about 420 feet high—a veritable skyscraper—nearly the size of the great pyramids of Egypt.

When twelve other pyramids turned up on a NASA satellite photograph of the Amazon jungle, noted author Charles Berlitz and Dr. Manson Valentine, curator of the Miami Science Museum, excitedly organized a major scientific expedition to the underwater pyramid—the first of its kind—which set out with a crack team of fifteen archaeologists, researchers and divers, early in August 1978.

At the same time, a NASA-supported expedition led by Florida explorer Phillip Miller set out for the Amazon jungles of Peru, accompanied by a documentary film team, to investigate the foliage-covered pyramids found there.[1]

I am intrigued by an apparent relationship here. HUGE RUINS THROUGHOUT THE WORLD generally resemble each other in construction, as well as in geographical and astronomical alignment.

What is more, constructions which are technologically "impossible" face us. PRECISE CONSTRUCTION AND COLOSSAL SIZE indicate that the builders had unknown techniques and energy sources at their disposal.

One feels that these magnificent, time-defying ruins that still exist after 4,000 years can hardly be the work of primitive barbarians. Surely they are the scientific instruments of an advanced universal civilization.

Join me on a Grand Tour and you'll see what I mean.

1 (S): TIAHUANACO, BOLIVIA

Things that can't happen have happened here.

The site is built 12,000 feet above sea level. This is oxygen-poor air, in which the slightest exertion can cause nausea and worse. Yet blocks of up to 200 tons were maneuvered over distances up to 90 miles. In rarified air this is not possible by muscular strength.

This grand complex was built with a technical skill embarrassing to us and by a method unknown to us.

Here was a city of startling dimensions.

Acres and acres lie covered with truncated pyramids, artificial hills, lines of monoliths, platforms, underground rooms and giant gates which incorporate *architecture beyond our technical scope at the present day:*

- Many large *gateways* were built from a single stone. The Gate of the Sun is the biggest carved monolith in the world, a single block 10 feet high and 6 feet wide.
- *The size of some of the buildings* is astounding. The Fortress of Akapana, 650 by 496 feet, was once a pyramid 167 feet high. The "Sun Temple" was on a platform 440 feet long by 390 feet wide, composed of blocks 100 to 200 tons each. Walls of the temple complex itself had blocks 60 tons each. Steps of the stone stairway were 50 tons apiece. Here were terraced temples like those of faraway Babylon and Nineveh. The walls of the Palace were 220 feet long by 180 feet wide. Its throne room was 160 feet long by 130 feet wide. The steps from the palace entrance were washed by the lake (now receding and 15 miles away). The paved court under our feet is 80 feet square, with a covered gallery 45 feet on one side. Court and hall are one single block of dressed stone.
- *Building blocks:* One is 36 feet long and 7 feet wide, fitted without lime or mortar and without any joint showing. Nearly every stone is microaccurately cut and polished, nicked, mortised, and occasionally even bevelled.

150

- *Water conduits* have a completely modem shape with smooth cross-sections, polished inner and outer surfaces and accurate edges. See these half-pipes? They have grooves and corresponding protrusions that fit together.

Plundered: Spanish invaders stole the interlocking copper or silver keys which secured the stonework from earthquake damage; until then they had survived for thousands of years. Subsequent earthquakes levelled the structures. As late as the nineteenth century there were imposing colonnades to admire, of which, sadly, there is now no trace. Many of the great buildings were dynamited and untold treasures disappeared. One 24-foot statue remains.

2 (S): SACSAYHUAMAN, PERU

The ruined mountaintop "fortress" of Sacsayhuaman (pronounced "sexy woman") overlooks the ancient capital of Cuzco. Its terrace walls are 1,500 feet long and 54 feet wide.

- *Enormous blocks* (up to 25 feet wide and of 50 to 200 tons) are so intricately flush one to the other, it is impossible to pass a knife blade between them.
    One block in an outer wall has *faces cut to fit perfectly with twelve other blocks.* There are other blocks cut with as many as ten, twelve and even *thirty-six sides—and* with no mortar between them. Take notice how each fits exactly to the next touching stones, from every side, *including the inner surfaces!* It defies belief. The whole system interlocks and dovetails, making the chance fitting of each block, or the grinding back and forth in situ for a perfect fit impossible. Even if it had been possible, the power required to do this would be sufficient to supply the needs of a modern city. Do you see the problem?
- Within a few hundred yards of the complex, an abandoned *single block the size of a 5-story house* weighs an estimated 20,000 tons! Yes, 20,000 tons. It is impeccably cut and dressed. *We have no combination of machinery today that could dislodge such a weight,* let alone move it any distance. This indicates mastery of a technology which we have as yet not attained.

- The *quarries* are 20 miles away, *on the other side of a mountain range and a deep river gorge.* How the gigantic stones were moved across such hopeless terrain is anyone's guess.

Fig. 16—1. The massive Gate of the Sun, in Tiahuanaco, Bolivia, is fashioned from a single block of stone. It is similar to other megalithic structures found widely distributed throughout the world.

3 (S): EL ENLADRILLADO, CHILE

We visit another site high on a plateau.
- A total of 233 stone blocks are placed geometrically in an amphitheater arrangement; some as large as 12 to 16 feet high, 20 to 30 feet long, and weighing several hundred tons.

And just look at those huge chairs of stone! Each weighs a massive 10 tons.

4 (S): OLLANTAYTAMBO, PERU

Fortress walls of tightly fitted blocks weighing 150 to 250 tons each are of very hard andesite. Special tools are required to penetrate such *hard* rock.
- The quarry is on a mountaintop 7 miles away. At a 10,000-feet altitude, would you believe, the builders carved and dressed the hard stone, lowered the 200-ton blocks down the mountainside, crossed a river canyon with 1,000-foot sheer rock walls, and then raised the blocks up another mountainside to fit them in place.
- Wall mirrors composed of six gigantic masses of roseate porphyry each weigh at least 20 tons—and one is 40 tons.

The more one studies these buildings, the more one feels that a race of scientific giants built them.

5 (S): CHAN-CHAN, PERU

This city of the Chimu Empire has walls up to 40 feet thick. Buildings were richly decorated with stylized animals, flowers and geometric designs.

6 (S): MACHU PICCHU, PERU

Perched in the Andes on a razorback high above a horseshoe canyon, this is a breathtakingly beautiful site. These fabled ruins offer romance and mystery.
- But just notice those squared blocks—they're 16 feet long! And look above these doors—each granite lintel weighs 3 tons.

- We enter a room. Each wall is composed of a single solid megalith, carved into thirty-two angles which join it to the neighboring blocks perfectly. Such walls astound modern architects.

7 (S): PACHACAMAK, PERU

Here the temples were fastened with gold nails that weighed a ton each.

8 (S): AMAZON JUNGLE, BRAZIL

Numerous remote cities lie between Goyaz and the Roosevelt; one has a triple arch formed of stone slabs weighing at least 50 tons apiece. How did they do it?

9 (S): PARAIBA, BRAZIL

A huge ruined fortress with walls over 80 feet high and 16 feet thick, and with an inner wall which once measured 492 feet long by 150 feet wide. (South America is full of stupendous ruins of this kind.)

10 (W): COLOSSUS OF RHODES, GREECE

An iron-reinforced bronze statue of the sun-god Helios towered for 100 feet beside the Rhodes harbor.

11 (S): MYCENAE, GREECE

- A stone gateway 18 feet high supported a stone crosspiece which weighed 240,000 pounds, was 30 feet long, 16 feet wide and over 3 feet thick. It was carved from a single piece of limestone. (This crosspiece was larger than any single piece used in Egyptian pyramids.)
- Ramparts up to 30 feet thick.

12 (S): TIRYNS, GREECE

- Walls, more than 50 feet thick in places, had corners so neat that they bore comparison with Egypt's pyramids.
- The palace contained a 1,300-square-foot hall of slate with a painted stone floor.

13 (S): TONGA

- A huge, single stone arch of 95 tons (once a gateway to a complex of buildings) was brought 250 miles from the nearest quarry—over the ocean.
- A stone tomb weighs 170 tons!

14 (S): VANUA LEVU ISLAND, FIJI

A monolith bearing an unknown script weighs 40 tons.

15 (S): RIMATORA, MARIANA ISLANDS

Columns up to 66 feet (equal to 6 stories) in height.

16 (S): PONAPE I., CAROLINE ISLANDS

Here stands the mysterious city of Non Madol (or Metalanim). Shall we explore it by boat? Notice these features:

- Over ninety walled artificial islands, square or rectangular, covering 11 square miles of buildings, and intersected by canals that are also artificial. A gigantic abandoned Venice of the Pacific.
- Walls of buildings are up to 15 feet thick and 33 feet high, rising above watery "streets." (And some of these buildings were once 60 feet high.)
- Enormous stone slabs of 5 to 25 tons were transported, take note, from 25 miles away; then they were lifted to the tops of massive walls several stories up.

- A huge temple complex built over a network of cellars and crypts connected to one of the canals, has at its center a room in the shape of a pyramid. Encircled by other ruins and a labyrinth of canals and terraces, this complex is large enough to seat 2,000,000 people! No, that's not a misprint.

17 (S): EASTER ISLAND

We are now on a most isolated island.
- Here hundreds of mysterious stone faces, each weighing 35 to 50 tons, jut from the soil and stare out to sea. They once wore red hats. The hats alone weighed 10 tons apiece, had a circumference of 25 feet, a height of 7 feet 2 inches—and were put on *after* the statues were erected.
- The statues were carved near the crater top, and then lowered 300 feet over the heads of other statues. This was accomplished without leaving as much as a mark. Then they were moved up and down cliff walls and on for 5 miles to their present resting place.
- On a dangerously windy sheer rock face plunging 1,000 feet straight into the sea, is a ledge—400 feet down. On this precarious ledge, 25-ton statues were lowered to stand.

The question is, how did the builders cut, move and erect the gigantic heads, including those which approach *the size of a 7-story building?*[2]

18 (S): BAALBEK, LEBANON

Baalbek conceals a mystery that may never be solved. Two magnificent Roman temples were built upon an already existing, immense, prehistoric dressed platform. These temples, the greatest in the Roman world, were dwarfed by the platform. The platform is a *feat of engineering that has never been equalled in history:*

- Here are individual stones as big as a bus. Up to 82 feet long and 15 feet high and thick, they are estimated to weigh 1,200 to 1,500 tons each. One block weighs 2,000 tons—4 million pounds of solid rock! It contains enough material to build a house 60 feet square and 40 feet high with walls a foot thick.

- And you notice that they are raised into the building as much as 20 feet above ground.
- There are tunnels in the walling large enough for a train to go through.

Fig. 16-2. Baalbek,Lebanon. The gigantic stone blocks of the prehistoric dressed platform are raised up to 20 feet above the ground. (Photo: Popperfoto)

- Even with the tools of modern technology, we could not move these building blocks intact. Our largest railway cars are too puny. There are no cranes or other lifting apparatus in the world today that can budge, let alone lift, these titanic blocks—yet they are fitted together with such precision that no knife blade can be inserted between the blocks.
- It would take three of our largest overhead cranes (hoisting 400 tons each) to lift one of them—even if it could be done without damaging the block by the stress of its own tremendous weight. At freight-train speed, the largest freight car can transport just 110 tons.   Supposing that somehow a block could be maneuvered onto a wheeled vehicle, the enormous load would drive the wheels into the ground or grind them to pieces on the rock surface.
- One individual block still lying prepared in the quarry is 12 feet high by 12 feet thick and over 60 feet long. To move it by brute force to join the others would have taken the combined efforts of 40,000 men. (But then how could so many have had access to the slab, in order to raise it?)

19 (S): STONEHENGE, ENGLAND

This was erected in stages during the period 2800 to 1700 B.C., as a celestial observatory and calculator.

- Forty blue stones, each weighing 5 tons, were transported 240 miles over land and water.
- Other blocks are 25 and 50 tons—and came from a quarry 20 miles distant.
- These 18-foot sandstone pillars were erected in a circular colonnade, and then connected by horizontal slabs atop them. Holes in the slabs fitted exactly onto projections from the flat-top uprights. Somebody had to lift these 20 feet, and (if we accept their astronomical purpose) *it all had to be fitted to the nearest inch.* (Even today this would not be easy.)

Historical legend asserts that some form of prehistoric machinery provided the lift needed, thus enabling the stones to be laid lightly.

Somehow, by a technology unknown, the Stonehengers *figured out beforehand the depth of hole required to match up exactly—working out results in advance that would need the help of a computer today.*

Certainly they required tools and instruments of exactitude those in present use.

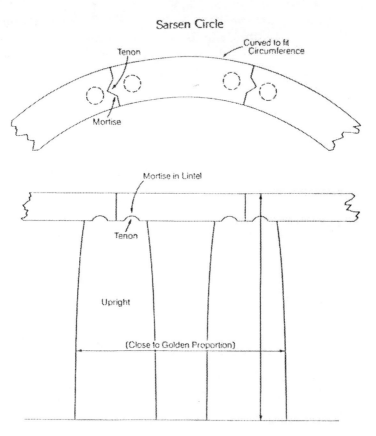

Fig. 16—3. The huge masonry of Stonehenge was interlocked with scientific precision

Such difficult calculations presuppose the existence of writing. The tenons and mortices on the raised stones indicate architectural skills sufficient to build stone houses. The whole demands a high level of intellectual attainment—a veritable Newton or Einstein must have been at work.

Do you see what this means? Yet Stonehenge is only part of an extensive complex of giant circles, monuments, and streets as broad as motorways, throughout Britain.

20 (S): AVEBURY, ENGLAND

A temple here is claimed to have been larger than Stonehenge. It once had 650 mammoth stones forming a huge circle around an artificial hill. For centuries the breaking up of the stones for building has left only twenty still standing.

21 (S): 600 SITES ALL OVER BRITAIN

- These sites were laid out with a precision that today can be measured only by a highly qualified team of surveyors—with a scientific exactitude (in some cases) of 1 in 1,500.
- And get this. Many of the stones have cup and ring markings carved to a diameter accuracy within a few thousandths of an inch!
- The builders all worked to an exact unit of length measure from one end of Britain to the other—the "megalithic yard" (2,720 feet). Such uniformity suggests that one central authority sent out the standard rods and planned and directed the construction of all the sites.
- Some are not in circles but enormous ellipses—planned to observe the bobs and weaves of the moon before the eclipses. (This setting out was only possible with complex theorems based on Pythagorean triangles.)
- What is more, the differences and strategy of locations made possible a knowledge of the curvature and size of the earth.
- All sites appear to be aligned in a single geometric pattern. A check of more than 3,000 prehistoric stone circles and single-standing stones shows that every one is aligned to neighbors up to 20 miles away at an angle of 23-1/2 degrees, or a multiple of that angle. (This is most significant, because it is the angle of the inclination of the earth's axis.)

22 (S): ALSO IN BRITAIN

- West Kennet Long Barrow (constructed long before 2000 B.C.) was a burial mound 350 feet long and up to 75 feet wide, terminating in a sepulchre blocked by enormous stones. One stone weighed 20 tons. Probably the oldest in Britain, it exhibits building skills of the highest order.

Silbury Hill (the largest artificial earth mound in Europe) covers 5.5 acres and rises to 130 feet. It was carefully built with internal radial walls for stability and shows insight into the problems of soil engineering. The list grows.

23 (S): BRITTANY, FRANCE

- The megalithic monument of Ile-Melon originally weighed 90 tons.
- The Locmariaquer monolith once stood 67 feet high and weighed over 380 tons; it was clearly visible 10 miles across the sea.
- At Louden is the gigantic Bournand dolmen, 56 feet long, whose largest slab weighs 350,000 pounds.

24 (S): ALTIN TEPE, TURKEY

This is near the mountains of Ararat, the landing place of the Flood survivors.
- The walls of the precinct and the citadel were more than 30 feet thick, built with great skill.
- Engineers raised granite blocks weighing 40 tons to a height of 200 feet, or 20 stories up, before fitting them together.

25 (S): DERINKUYU, TURKEY

- Here was an underground city, burrowing thirteen stories deep into the earth. There were shops and numerous amenities, including a sophisticated

- air-conditioning system to every corner of the city at every level.
- Can you visualize it? Some rooms could hold 60,000 people—that's the capacity of a large sports stadium!
- But there's more. Connecting routes linked at least fourteen underground cities, housing no less than 1,200,000 people.

26 (S): KLAGENFURT, AUSTRIA

This metropolis of 2,500 years ago had walls 23 feet thick. Actually, its stone blocks were brought to the summit of the mountain and riveted with huge slabs of marble.

27 (W): CLUSIUM, ITALY

Here a sepulchre stretching 300 feet on each side contained an extensive labyrinth, rose 50 feet high and was surmounted by three series of towers; the total height of the structure was 350 feet. Some tomb.

28 (S): MALTA

- Here titanic monuments confront us, as well as innumerable tunnels with 3-story underground chambers.
- Temple stone pillars exceeding 16 feet in height; a stone more than 26 feet long and 13 feet wide; a slab 23 feet long and 10 feet high (and what is visible may weigh nearly 70 tons).

With a history of earthquakes, the Maltese temples have survived thousands of years.

29 (W): TYRE, LEBANON

Walls 165 feet (or 16 stories) in height.

30 (W): NINEVEH, IRAQ

Surrounded by a 60-mile wall 100 feet in height, Nineveh was defended from 1500 towers.

31 (S): UR, IRAQ

Massive brick buildings and a city wall 80 feet thick!
Is your head in a whirl? Perhaps this is a good time to take three long, deep breaths. I want you to stay alert; the most astonishing information is yet to come.

32 (W): BABYLON, IRAQ

- One of the most magnificent and powerful cities ever built, Babel (Babylon) covered an area of some 150 square miles. All this was encircled by a wall 30 feet thick and 100 feet high.
- The Marduk Tower, consisting of seven stages (each a different color) and surmounted by a temple in blue glaze, rose a 30-story height into the sky. (It took Alexander the Great 600,000 working days just to remove the debris!)

33 (W): RUB EL KHALI DESERT, SAUDI ARABIA

This area of Arabia, known as the Empty Quarter, is a dangerous and forbidden land, impossible of entry. Thus it remains one of the world's great unexplored areas.

Here there once flourished five kingdoms, whose cities boasted enormous building blocks comparable to those of Baalbek, as well as tall skyscrapers.

The structures that still exist in cities that can be visited have nine stories. Arab texts say that these buildings are reduced-scale imitations of those in the lost cities of the Empty Quarter. Multiple records agree concerning a super-skyscraper with twenty floors.

34 (S). BAMIAN, AFGHANISTAN

Five statues carved out of the cliff face include one 180 feet tall and another 125 feet high.

35 (S): INDIA

A slab lying atop a 228-foot pagoda weighs 2,000 tons!

36 (S): QUEENSLAND, AUSTRALIA

A number of mysterious pyramidal structures here are claimed by geologists to be natural formations.

These pyramids (often measuring 400 feet high, with four sides each 400 feet long at the base), when arranged on a grid, are found to connect with one another over distances of some hundreds of square miles.

37 (S): BATHURST (New South Wales), AUSTRALIA

Stone alignments covering several square miles incorporate stones up to 15 feet tall.

38 (S): U.S.A.

- Thousands of giant, geometric earthwork constructions (platforms for vanished building complexes or cities) are found throughout the United States. Individually and collectively, these involved organized labor on a scale even greater than that needed to build the pyramids or Stonehenge.
- The Cahokia Mound in Illinois (10 stories high) covered 16 acres.
- A mound at Poverty Point, Louisiana (1300 B.C.) is over thirty-five times the cubage of the Great Pyramid.
- In Texas, walls 49 feet high, in a buried city of over 4 square miles, were built in the manner a fine stone mason would use

today. The stones appeared to have been bevelled around the edges.

39 (S): BAHAMAS AREA

A submerged pyramid on the ocean floor has a base 540 feet wide and a height of about 420 feet.

40 (S): ROCKING STONES, U.S.A.

Believed to have been artificially placed in at least eight locations, these weigh from 15 to 60 tons.
- One is 45 feet in circumference and 7 feet thick.
- Another, 31 feet around, can be moved by the hand, but six men with iron bars were unable to throw it off its pedestal.

41 (S). MEXICO

About 1500 B.C., stone blocks of 20 to 50 tons were brought by the Olmecs 80 miles across a lake.

42 (S): MEXICO (MAYA RUINS)

- Up to eighty geometric stone cities with some buildings 200 feet high.
- Stones of public buildings sometimes weighing up to 40 tons.
- Carved basalt heads weighing 24 tons.

43 (S): CHOLULA, MEXICO

The pyramid of Quetzalcoatl was 210 feet tall; its 1,150-foot base covers
30 acres. (That's almost equal to 16 city blocks.)

44 (S): TIKAL, GUATEMALA

166

Here one of the steep pyramids, with walls up to 40 feet thick, rises 230 feet in height.

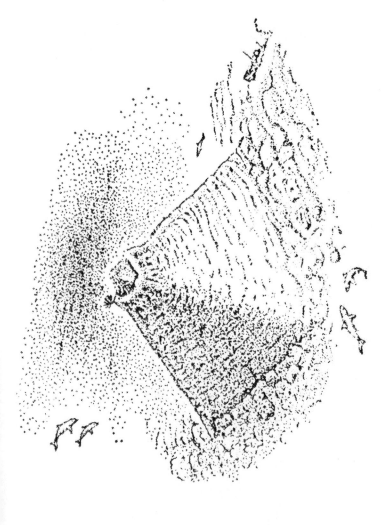

Fig. 16–4. Concept by Dr. Valentine of the undersea pyramid formation (based on sonor readings and closed circuit TV), located off the coast of Florida. This is but one of many archaeological sites under the water from the Bahamas to Yucatan.

45 (S): AXUM, ETHIOPIA

In this ancient capital, reputed to have been founded by one of Noah's grandsons, enormous monoliths (some standing) can still be seen. The largest, 500 tons in weight, stood 110 feet tall before it collapsed.

46 (S): THEBES, EGYPT

- The temple of Amen, as it stands today, is over one-fifth of a mile long. (The entire Notre Dame cathedral could fit within one of its halls.)
- Here rise 78-foot-tall pillars, each as much as 10 feet thick.
- The statue of Rameses II weighed a monstrous 900 tons. It was 57 feet high, with an across-the-shoulders span of 22 feet, while its big toe was a yard long. Just the toe!
- Two giant statues, each weighing more than 1,500 tons, were transported from the Red Mountain, a 438-mile distance. Originally 65 feet high, each was carved from a single block.
- Two obelisks transported 133 miles *from* Aswan by Queen Hatshepsut were later broken up by her successor. Each was a single piece of stone 185 feet (18 stories) tall and weighed 2,400 tons.

47 (W): THE PHAROS, ALEXANDRIA, EGYPT

The 440-foot lighthouse on the island of Pharos (constructed of white marble) projected its light to a viewing distance of 25 miles.

48 (S): PYRAMIDS, GIZA, EGYPT

The largest structure is the Cheops pyramid.

Size
- The Cheops pyramid is 476 feet high, with a base 764 feet, and covers thirteen acres (an area almost equal to seven city blocks). The polished limestone facings (now removed) covered 22 acres.

- It is still larger than any modern building. New York's Empire State Building is among the very highest erected by modern man, yet it is only about 2/5 the volume of the Cheops pyramid.

Weight

- The building comprises 2,300,000 blocks, totalling 6,250,000 tons in weight (each stone is 2-1/2 tons). This amounts to more stone than has been used in all of England's churches, cathedrals and chapels built since the time of Christ.
- Covering the "King's Chamber" are granite slabs of 60 to 70 tons each, brought from a quarry 600 miles away.
- The casing stones (which are still in place on the north face near the base) each weigh 15 tons.

Accuracy of Construction

- The pyramid is perfectly square to within 3/10,000 percent.
- Although it is constructed of 2,300,000 great blocks put together without any cement, you still can't get the thinnest blade of a knife between them. The joints of the original limestone casings are "barely perceptible, not wider than the thickness of silver paper."[3] One of today's biggest U.S. contractors has stated that we do not possess any machine capable of making equally smooth surfaces as those connecting the stones of the pyramids. They were fitted to an accuracy of 1/100 inch.
- The pyramid is *level* over an area of 13 acres to within half an inch.
- It is the world's most accurately aligned building, true north.

Beauty

- Originally this pyramid had a beautiful covering of glistening white marble (polished to a mirror like finish) and could he seen for 50 miles, reflecting the light. It was capped by a golden point that shot shafts of light back at the sun.

Measurements in its Design

- The pyramid incorporates higher mathematics in its very design, and advanced scientific knowledge in its measurements. The relationship of the pyramid's height to the perimeter of its base is the same as that between the radius and circumference of a circle. It thus incorporates the mathematical value known as pi (the constant by which the diameter of a circle may be multiplied to calculate its circumference)—and it does so accurately to several decimal places. Its main chamber made use of several Pythagorean functions not "discovered" supposedly until thousands of years later.

- It served also as a calendar by which the length of the year can be measured to the exact minute. And it was as an observatory from which maps of the stellar hemisphere could be accurately drawn.
- It is so finely aligned to the North Pole that modern compasses can be adjusted to it.
- "The measurements of its sides and angles accurately reflect the geographic measurements of the northern hemisphere, such as the degree of latitude and longitude, the circumference and radius of the earth—even accounting for polar flattening. All this data was not 'discovered' until the seventeenth century."[4]
- (In the International Geophysical Year in 1958, the exact dimensions of the earth were determined by satellite, and the French meter—which is our own standard system of measurement, supposedly based on the dimensions of the earth—was found to be incorrect. But more amazingly, the Egyptian cubit—the unit of measurement used in the pyramid—was found to be exact. In other words, the cubit fits into the dimensions of the earth within five decimal places—a rather startling coincidence.)

Energy Fields
- *Cosmic radiation inside the pyramid contradicts every known law of science and electronics—it* implies an advanced knowledge of electromagnetic forces.
- *An energy field radiates from the apex,* which prompts us to wonder *why* it was built. The mass of evidence suggests that the major pyramids were *not* intended to be tombs.[5]

Speed of Construction
- The pyramid was *erected at an incredible speed.* Recent evidence suggests that this enormous structure may have been built in a fraction of the time generally assumed. It may have been built in 4 years by just 4,000 workers, laboring only 3 months a year![6] This is a technological feat beyond comparison

171

in the modern world. The supposition that enormous manpower, inclined planes and rollers were used, must be discarded. [7]To handle or move one of the blocks might require a thousand hands (500 men), for whom there would not have been room around the stone. (Assuming the use of primitive methods, the block must still be handled, even if only to pass ropes under it, or to load it onto a barge.) Furthermore, engineers have estimated that a ramp to service the Cheops pyramid would finally have had to be a mile long, with a volume of masonry four times greater than the pyramid itself. No, that's not how they built it. I shall reveal the method to you later in this book.

Almost Indestructible

- In a search for hidden powers and riches, Melik al Aziz, in 1196, employed thousands of workers to pull down the three Giza pyramids stone by stone. They went at the smallest pyramid for 8 exhausting months, after which he gave the order to suspend all work when he saw that the building had scarcely been touched.
- The pyramids are as strong today as when they were built. Scientists have conceded that modern man cannot build a great pyramid that would retain its shape for thousands of years without sagging under its own weight.

49 (S): THE SPHINX, GIZA, EGYPT

Shaped as a lion with a human face, the mysterious Sphinx was carved from one piece of solid rock 164 feet long by 75 feet high. Its proportions are indeed staggering: a 33-foot head, a 7-foot-long mouth, a 6-foot nose and ears 5 feet long. Bear in mind that the Sphinx was transported here in one piece!

50 (S): ABU SIMBEL, EGYPT

Far up the Nile, these beautiful isolated twin temples were carved from the pinkish sandstone cliff.

- They are majestically flanked by four colossal, 67-foot-high figures, also carved out of the cliff.
- Tunnelling 200 feet inside the cliff, the builders then hollowed out enormous halls guarded by rows of lesser statues 3 stories high.
- In chamber after chamber are walls adorned with carvings of jewel-like beauty.

At any time this is an awesome sight, but at the moment of dawn it is incredible. When the rising sun tops the mountains across the Nile and flashes full on the temple frontage, the figure of the sun god seems animated by sudden light, as though to step forward to greet the morning.

51 (W): THE LABYRINTH, EGYPT

This greatest labyrinth in the world (under the village of Hawara, east of Lake Moeris) no longer exists. It was designed to baffle and confuse.
- An immense palace 650 by 500 feet contained 12 large apartments and 3,000 other rooms. "The Labyrinth excels even the pyramids," reported Herodotus, in the fifth century B.C.
- Here was an inextricable maze of rooms and passages, in which one could easily get tired of walking and no stranger could find his way alone.
- Some of the temples in the complex were so arranged that as soon as the doors opened a fearful clap of thunder was heard inside.

52 (S): ALSO IN EGYPT

- At the Serapeum are mighty 65-ton coffins.
- At Tanis lie the remains of a statue 89 feet high. Other pieces of sculpture found here include an eye over 1 foot 4-1/2 inches long, and a foot with a big toe 1 foot 11 inches long. "They thought in terms of men 100 feet tall" (Champollion).[8]

53 (S): ANGKOR WAT, KAMPUCHEA

173

An imposing pyramidal temple, so huge that several dozen Greek temples and the imperial palaces of Rome could all have fit within it, rises terrace upon terrace by sweeping stone staircases to a sanctuary 200 feet high, and five watchtowers.

54 (S): GREAT WALL, CHINA

This longest wall ever built (2,200 years old and 1,448 miles) rises 18 to 50 feet above the ground, is wide enough to allow a lane of cars in each direction.

55 (S): SHENSI PROVINCE, CHINA

The tallest building in the world until this century (and still the most massive structure on earth) is an ancient pyramid 120 stories high! It stands on a long, desolate, flat stretch of land about 40 miles west of the ancient capital Sian-fu, on an old dirt-road caravan trail that crosses from Peking to the Mediterranean. *About 2,000 feet at the base, it rises some 1,200 feet high.*

- There are actually seven pyramids, flat-topped, with three carved giants resting along the outer edges.
- The four faces of the pyramids are, like so many ancient structures, aligned to the compass points.
- Traces of color remain on the sides, indicating the colors that were given to each side: east—aqua green; south—red; west—black; north—white; and on the flat tops—traces of yellow.

A pair of American adventurers who roamed Asia between the two world wars, R.C. Anderson and Frank Shearer, were shown these pyramids. (Anderson visited Egypt's pyramids in 1970 and believed himself to be the only man living to have seen both the Chinese and the Egyptian pyramids.) In 1946, a U.S. Army airplane crew rediscovered and photographed these pyramids from the air.

Place 26 skyscrapers the size of the Empire State Building and you have the volume of the largest Shensi pyramid.

56 (S): QUITO, ECUADOR

The Panecillo, a big hill within the city limits of Quito, is of such size that it was always considered to be natural. Recent investigation, however, has revealed it to be a giant, unstratified artificial mound 600 feet (or equal to 60 stories) in height. Already some surprising constructions are coming to light here.

57 (S,W): SOME SKYSCRAPER-HEIGHT CONSTRUCTIONS

In China equivalent to 120 stories; Ecuador 60 stories; Egypt 48; Bermuda seabed 42; Italy 35; Iraq 30; Guatemala 23; India 22; Mexico 21; Kampuchea 20; Arabia 20; Turkey 20.

One cannot visit places like Baalbek or Thebes without coming away dazed and amazed. Their size diminishes criticism.
No one has explained how the earliest and smallest populations could erect the largest architecture.
I ask you then, what kind of people were they who knew so much more than we do today of engineering, and who constructed giant edifices that still stand?
We see building blocks weighing 200 tons, which would dwarf the largest of our modern earth-moving machinery.
How were these fantastic weights lifted to their resting places on top of great pillars?
If we accept the "block and tackle" explanation in which semi-primitive men raised 70-ton blocks of granite into the air with ropes of vine, then we may as well believe that the moon is really made of green cheese.
The arrangement of the blocks themselves even today would be a difficult task for technicians. It would require, among other things, the use of reinforced concrete platforms able to support the weight of 40-wheeled railroad wagons.
It is hard to avoid the conclusion that some form of machining must have been available, because the work is too precise to have been fashioned by hand. And massive amounts of power were required. These are construction miracles that have not been repeated.

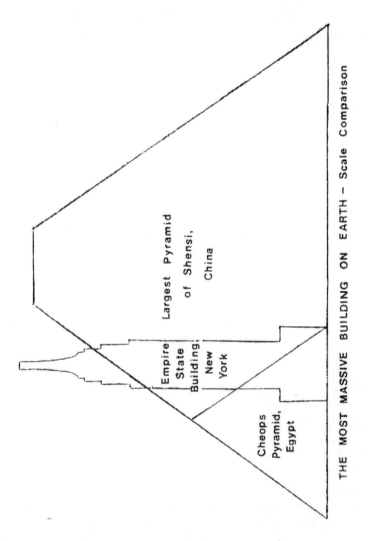

Largest Pyramid
of Shensi,
China

Empire
State
Building,
New
York

Cheops
Pyramid,
Egypt

THE MOST MASSIVE BUILDING ON EARTH — Scale Comparison

Chapter 17

Construction Techniques and House Features—*JOURNEY INTO THE UNEXPECTED*

"It is a human impossibility," gasped Hyatt Verrill.[1]

He's right.

Yet it happened.

The giant mountains of the Peruvian Andes are awesome enough—until one gazes up those extremely perilous slopes and perceives death-defying ruins perched on the summits.

The setting is terrifyingly wild—mountains miles high vanishing into the sky, notched with narrow ledges, slashed with ravines and bottomless gorges.

Waterfalls of an awesome beauty plunge from these immaculate snowy peaks, down into the damp, unknown depths of the canyons.

So rare is the air that even the mules are obliged to stop every ten paces to catch their breath.

Here, "at the frontiers of the impossible," a vanished civilization set gems in stone—astoundingly assembled polygonal walls—suspended over the abyss.

They carved practically vertical stairways up stupendous precipices.

High in the clouds rises one acrobatic stairway of 64 steps, which had to be carved in a place where one could get only a toehold for support.

(Another comprises 600 steps.) Imagine it!

Fig.17-1. This perilous walkway along the face of a sheer cliff has survived repeated earthquakes. (Remember that most skyscrapers would topple during earthquakes. (A removable plank prevented enemy crossings. (Photo: Christiana Dittman)

Fig. 17-2. The ruins of Machu Picchu in the Andes Range, Peru. Note the death-defying terraces perched on the vertical peak behind.

These ingenious "jewelers" in rock ascended a dizzying mountain "no wider than the blade of a sword" and topped it with watchtowers and walls pierced with lookouts. The mountain drops away so abruptly that if a workman slipped his body would not be stopped for 3,000 feet.

Today on all sides, the ruins of temples, fortresses and towers surmount the peaks and cling to the vertical sides of the canyon like ivy. Overlooking a waterfall, a splendid palace rises above the fierce abyss—impossible to reach. How was this palace built?

Terraces were miraculously inlaid into vertical slopes, perched over the canyon fault. How did they hoist up heavy, carved rocks by the thousands?

Site after site is built atop bluffs which are too steep to be accessible. Many seem to have been literally hurled up as though the monstrous stones flew there.

A high, carved niche opens out over the abyss. Under a ridge, shaped like the letter I, the rock was leveled and encrusted with carefully joined stone cubes. Only a daring mountaineer hanging from a rope could possibly reach it. The "builder magicians," I tell you, had no sense of the impossible.

Everywhere loom buildings that defy the laws of equilibrium and gravity—as well as vertigo.

These are a triumph of human daring and of a technology which almost smacks of science fiction.

And would you believe, sometimes the enormous blocks were brought from quarries more than 1,000 miles away!

Many are covered with intricate carvings. No man alive could duplicate such carvings with the stone tools we find. As Hyatt Verrill remarks, "It is not a question of skill, patience, time—it is a human impossibility."[2]

ANCIENT CONSTRUCTION TECHNIQUES

INDIA

1 (S): *The Shaking Towers:* In Ahmedabad, Gujerat, two minarets, 70 feet tall and 25 feet apart, have a peculiarity that is unique in the world. If a small group of people sets one tower in motion by a rhythmical to-and-fro movement, the other tower begins to swing too.

(Secret unknown. The roots of the science behind this are buried deep in time.)

TIBET

2 (W): Ancient texts record that in very ancient times, the people were wise and skillful and built *"great houses of crystal"* (which we may imagine to be like our skyscrapers).

ANTARCTICA
3 (O): There are traditions of a legendary *Rainbow City* where the colors of the rainbow were said to have been used in the construction of the buildings and even in the paving of the streets.

ROME
4 (W): *Glass-storied theater:* Emilio Scauro, one of Sulla's generals, had a three-floored theater built at Rome for 80,000 spectators: the first floor of marble, the second floor of glass, and the third floor of gilded wood.

WORLDWIDE
5 (S): *Use of concrete* (the standard mixture of sand and cement that makes up most building blocks of today) was evidently worldwide:

- Yaxuna to Coba, Mexico
- Cuicuilo, Mexico
- Guatemala
- Quito, Ecuador
- Cuenca, Ecuador
- Marcahuasi, Peru
- Santa Cruz, Bolivia
- Pompeii, Italy
- Tourette-sur-Loup, France
- Couhard, France
- Crete
- Starveco, Yugoslavia
- Egypt
- Northwest China
- Western Australia
- Arkansas, U.S.A.
- Tennessee, U.S.A.
- New Mexico, U.S.A.

At Marcahuasi, in Peru, cement surfacing of slopes was applied over round projecting bosses to hold it in place; and applied in sections with cross lines, to combat the effects of expansion.

Other advanced techniques included the following:

COLOMBIA
6 (S): A fireproof cement.

YUCATAN, MEXICO
CALIFORNIA, U.S.A.
SEABED, BIMINI
ECUADO
MALTA
PERU
EGYPT
7 (S): *Crystalline-white, flint-like building glue, nearly identical, yet superior, to "modern" Portland cement* (superior in its unique combination of two qualities: fast-setting speed and exceeding strength).

Recent examination of many prehistoric buildings has led to detection of this glue.

Traces of iron oxide rust where the glue grips the stonework suggest that iron oxide was added to the cement. Iron oxide grows fingers or hairs at high speed to form a fast-setting, tenacious interlocking network.

PERU
8 (S): Building blocks held together not by mortar but by melted gold and bitumen.

MACHU PICCHU, PERU
9 (S): Future separation of blocks prevented by alternating a polyhedron with a rectangular stone equipped with a hookstone, making a series of keys.

KLAGENFURT, AUSTRIA
10 (S): Huge slabs of marble riveting the stone blocks.

TIAHUANACO, BOLIVIA
PACHACAMAK, PERU
11 (S): Enormous copper clamps; silver bolts 1/2 to 3 tons in weight; gold nails weighing a ton, used to fasten the masonry.

PERU
TAHITI
12 (S): *A softening procedure for hard rock,* enabling it to receive hand or foot imprints by pressure only, as though the granite was putty soft.

EGYPT

13 (S): A large chest hollowed out of a single block of red granite by drilling and chipping; the hardest stone known (diorite) shaped as easily as butter.

The machinery, the cutting tools and the power applied to operate them are still unknown.

Working extremely hard substances was something we could not have done until the development of diamond drills in 1878.

SEABED, BIMINI

(but now raised into jetty material at Fort Lauderdale, Florida)

14 (S): Perfectly drilled five-pointed star holes with sharply defined tips cut right through 12-foot long blocks of granite; other huge 1 / 2 to 6-inch diameter round holes perfectly drilled through 12-foot thick blocks.

(Granite, one of the most abrasive stones, wears expensive diamond drill bits down to nothing very quickly.)

TURKEY

15 (S): Boring of holes finer than the thinnest needle in a block of hard stone.

EGYPT

16 (S): Boring into granite rock with drills that turned 500 times faster than modern power drills.

PERU
TIBET
EGYPT
SUDAN

17 (S): Outer walls sheeted in gold, silver, polished marble, or sparkling white gypsum.

Fig. 17-3. Wall stone with fourteen visible sides, each of which interlocks exactly with adjoining stones. Cuzco, Peru.

184

PERU
ECUADOR
MEXICO
18 (S): Granite building blocks *smoothly polished like glass.*
Practically all buildings of antiquity have been stripped of their outer shiny surfaces, so that today we see only the raw stonework.

SYRIA
BABYLON
MEXICO
SUMERIA
19 (S): Plaster-coated surfaces.

TIBET
BABYLON
20 (S): Decorated enamel or blue porcelain walls.

CHINA
BABYLON
EGYPT
MEXICO
21 (S): Multicolor surfaces on building exteriors.

BRAZIL
22 (S): The use of different-colored stones in the approach steps to buildings.

PERU
23 (S): Steps polished like glass.

TIAHUANACO, BOLIVIA
24 (S): Color-decorated pillars.

GREECE
PERU
25 (W): Hydraulic gates (opened by means of a complicated jet of water).

26 (W): Hydraulic lifts.

Essential to the support of a highly technological society must have been the use of massive water storage dams of "modern" strength. The enigma was, vestiges of these appeared not to exist.

As I sought for evidence, the question kept emerging: Had river rampages obliterated all trace?

Recently, one solution to this mystery fell open in quite a bizarre manner.

ARKANSA, U.S. A

27 (S): Carpet Rock, an area an acre or so in size, which recently split off the Petit Jean mountainside, has a curved grid of ironwork running all through it that gives it the carpet appearance.

Examination, however, shows it to be *reinforced concrete, with the steel gridwork still intact* and little rusted (surprising, until you realize that it was sealed from oxidation until splitting off the cliff only recently).

The whole cliff (Carpet Rock and Petit Jean) is thus seen to be *one vast concrete pour, very, very old.* It was *the spillway of a vast dam* which must have contained the White River and the Arkansas River in one great impounded lake.

Does this sound like the work of semi-primitive men who had to use stone tools, horses and vine ropes? No. The early builders obviously had sophisticated techniques.

In later times, methods became more basic and building less ambitious. The earlier apparatus fell into disuse, gradually disintegrated and was ultimately lost to memory.

FEATURES OF HOUSES

INDUS VALLEY, PAKISTAN
IGURAT, SYRIA
UR, IRAQ
28 (S): Two- and three-story dwellings.

TYRE, LEBANON
KNOSSOS, CRETE
CARTHAGE, TUNISIA
ARIZONA, U.S.A.
29 (S): Houses of five and six stories.

PAKISTAN
BABYLONIA
30 (S): Expert construction in bricks similar to ours heated to about 900 degrees.

ROMAN EMPIRE
31 (W): Sheet-glass windowpanes.

YUGOSLAVIA
32 (S): Cement floors, carefully laid out in large slabs.

CRETE
OKLAHOMA, U.S.A.
33 (S): Inlaid mosaic-tile floors.
ISRAEL
34 (W): Floors covered in gold.

CATAL HUYUK, TURKEY, 3000 B.C.
35 (S): Carpets of so high a quality that they compare favorably with the most modern woven ones.

CRETE
TURKEY
THERA
SUMERIA
36 (S): Wall and cciling frescoes engendering a feeling of a room, not of wood and stone, but of light and color.

PERU
37 (S): Interior walls faced with red stucco varnished.

PERU

ISRAEL
MEXICO
39 (W): Houses "wallpapered" with thin sheets of beaten gold.

ECUADOR
PERU
40 (S): Wallpaper of sheet gold, silver and "aluminum"; every square inch decorated with intricate designs, figures and scenes, in huge rolls artfully riveted together.

(Today, rolls of this are being torn by Indian artifact hunters from the interior walls of long-abandoned, vinechoked buildings in the inaccessible eastern jungle of Ecuador. If only one could glimpse these ancient buildings before they are all stripped!)[3]

ROMAN EMPIRE
41 (W): "Unbreakable" glass walls and floors.

ISRAEL
PERU
42 (W,O): Doors overlaid with copper or gold.

CUZCO, PERU
43 (S): Solid gold guttering.

BAALBEK, LEBANON
44 (S): Rain-gutter water gushing from rows of beautiful carved lion heads in a symbolic roar.

ROMAN EMPIRE
45 (S): Indirect lighting.

CRETE, 1500 B.C.
46 (S): Subtle interior lighting in living rooms and underground vaults.

SAFLIENI, MALTA
KNOSSOS, CRETE
DERINKUYU, TURKEY

47 (S): *Air-conditioning* through filtered air shafts and double isothermic walls.

(In Derinkuyu, there was a city thirteen stories deep in the earth, all served with even temperature!)

CHAVIN DE HUANTAR, PERU

48 (S): An incredible ventilation system, where each floor had its own ventilation, although the building had neither doors nor windows apart from the entrance.

EGYPT

49 (S): Air-conditioning and humidity elimination by ventilation shafts.

KOREA, 2000 B.C.
ROMAN EMPIRE
CRETE
ETRUSCANS, ITALY

50 (S): *Central heating* circulated by means of under-floor vents.

ECUADOR

51 (S): Heavy-walled bronze pipes with a small internal passageway and a thick outer wall—closely resembling modern high-pressure gas pipes (being recovered in the jungle by the thousands).

BYZANTIUM

52 (W): Oil heating.

SOUTHWESTERN U.S.A.

53 (S): Internal steam heat.

SOUTHWESTERN U.S.A.

54 (S): Heated indoor aviaries.

PAKISTAN, 2500 B.C.

Fig. 17-4. Roll of gold wall covering personally dug up by Father Crespi who has a museum in Cuenca, Ecuador. Because gold and silver wall-coverings have intrinsic value they are usually melted into lumps by Indians. (Photo: Richard Wingate)

CRETE
PERU
POMPEII, ITALY
55 (S): A highly efficient *piped water supply.*

ROME
56 (S): Hot water on tap.

SOUTHWESTERN U.S.A.
57 (S): Running water, hot and cold, and indoor plumbing.

MOHENJO-DARO, PAKISTAN
58 (S): En suite running water, bathroom and lavatory with each bedroom (even on the upper floors).

HARAPPA and MOHENJO-DARO, PAKISTAN
IGURAT, SYRIA
CHAN CHAN, PERU
59 (S): Tiled bathrooms with piped hot and cold water.

KNOSSOS, CRETE, 2000 B.C.
60 (S): Apartments (beautifully decorated with frescoes of dolphins and nude girls) containing *flush toilets* with a central system of ceramic pipes and stone drains.

ROMAN EMPIRE
61 (W): Flush toilets

ETRUSCANS
POMPEII, ITALY
PAKISTAN
TEL ASMAR, IRAQ
CRETE
COPAE, GREECE
PERU
62 (S): *A sewage system* from each house, as good as that of the present day.

INDUS VALLEY, PAKISTAN
63 (S): Rubbish disposal chutes from each house.

BRAZILIAN JUNGLE
IGURAT, SYRIA
CUZCO, PERU

64 (S): Garden fountains faced with stone tiles and iridescent displays (The iridescent displays were reported in Cuzco by the Spanish conquisadors when they came upon the Inca empire to ruin it.)

Chapter 18

Town Planning and Social Organization—PERFUME PLEASE, THE GAME STINKS!

During peak hours some street arteries are changed to one-way traffic. Arm-waving policemen stand on duty to cope with congestion. Street signs...No Parking signs...A permanent colored strip set directly into the paved road to divide the two lines of traffic.

A congested twentieth century metropolis? Perhaps. But you could also be standing in old Babylon—Nineveh—Aztec Mexico—or very ancient Italy.

And there are more surprises.

PAKISTAN, 2500 B.C.
GUATEMALA
BABYLON
1 (S): A system of town planning with straight streets and rectangular blocks.

PERU
2 (S): Cities planned with admirable geometric beauty and regularity of patterns.

TOLTECS, MEXICO
3 (W): Building projects covering 400-years-ahead planning. (At present no country in the world has any planning for centuries into the future.)

PAKISTAN
GUATEMALA
BABYLON
4 (S): Wide main streets like modern boulevards.

MEXICO
MARCAHUASI PLATEAU, PERU
CRETE
IGURAT, SYRIA
5 (S): City streets of concrete or flagstones, with parallel drains—and even covered, paved roads.

PERU
6 (O): City roads paved with pure silver.[1]

ANTIOCH, SYRIA
WEST IRIAN
7 (W): Street lighting.

INDUS VALLEY, PAKISTAN
MEXICO
8 (S): An efficient drainage system, with pipes and drains under every street.

POMPEII, ITALY
9 (S): Lead water pipes.

CUZCO, PERU
10 (S): Pipes lined with gold or silver.

TIAHUANACO, BOLIVIA
11 (S): Precision-designed, intricately cut water conduits and overflow pipes (of modern design), with gradient.

PERU
12 (S): A system of canals and stone-lined gutters tunnelled from one terrace to the next, distributing water to all levels, before emptying the excess into a long sink.

(The sink, following an adequate slope, thus prevented seepage and saturation by excess water, which would otherwise have undermined the terraces.) The whole complex indicates *precise calculation of water drainage.*

IGURAT, SYRIA
13 (S): City water supply channelled into town along fine stone canals.

ROME
14 (S): An aqueduct system with a structured plan of anticorrosive, antifriction bronze valves, pumps and fittings constructed to modern standards; *so solidly built that it is still in use;* it could supply water so rapidly that a whole arena could be filled deep enough to float ships for naval battles *during brief intermissions between entertainments.*

TIGRIS VALLEY, IRAQ
CRETE, 2000 B.C.
ETRUSCANS, ITALY
15 (S): Sanitary facilities with twentieth century style coupling pipes; each house connected to the major city sewage system.

MOHENJO-DARO, PAKISTAN
16 (S): A network of canals, pipes and sewers, *with inspection peepholes,* ingeniously devised.

CRETE
17 (S): Mantraps for inspection and repair.

COPAE, GREECE
18 (S): Deep rock-cut air shafts connected to fifty branches of a gigantic sewer-to-the-sea network. (This is an achievement beyond the capabilities of classical or modern Greece.)

PAKISTAN
ISFAHAN, PERSIA
PERU
EGYPT
19 (S,W): Heated public baths.

MAYAN CITIES, GUATEMALA
MINOS PALACE, CRETE
SOME ASIATIC SITES
20 (S): Hot and cold water fountains bordering main streets.

PERU
21(S): Fine, multicolored jets of water spouting from drilled cavities of a public building.

POMPEII, ITALY
22 (W): On hot days, showers of scented water were sprayed over seated sports crowds.

CENTRAL AMERICA
23 (S): Fun-fare contrivances, such as seats suspended from the top of a high mast, which spun around in the air.

SUMERIA
PERU
24 (S): Graves brick-lined, stone-lined. In Peru, grave entrances often covered with a sheet of silver.

SUMERIA
CHALDEA
PERU
25 (W): A formal system of school education, under a specialized faculty.

ALEXANDRIA, EGYPT
26 (W): A library incorporating a university and research institute, with faculties of medicine, mathematics, astronomy, literature and other subjects; also a chemical laboratory, astronomical observatory, anatomical theatre for operations and dissections, and a botanical and zoological garden— instructing 14,000 pupils.

BABYLON
27 (S): Business tycoons dictated letters to secretaries. (Occasionally these have been found, unopened.)

UR, CHALDEA
MOHENJO-DARO, PAKISTAN
INCAS, PERU
28 (S): Business transactions recorded and statistics kept.

CARTHAGE, TUNISIA
29 (W): Floating of joint-stock companies and issuing of public loans.

AZTECS, MEXICO
ISRAEL
ROMAN EMPIRE
INCAS, PERU
30 (W): Census taking.

Chapter 19

Engineering—FORBIDDEN TUNNELS

Have you ever done something you shouldn't, simply because you knew it was forbidden? And for the excitement of not getting caught?

Passing a mental marker that says Danger: Do Not Enter and returning to tell the tale is thrilling.

Not all such excursions are without a price, however.

I'm going to acquaint you, soon, with some mysterious smooth-walled subway systems under Peru. Violate these forbidden passages and stone doors will spring shut behind you. Other ingenious traps will ensure that you never see daylight again.

Theodore Roosevelt, later to become U.S. president, picked up accounts of these sophisticated prehistoric tunnels during his expedition in 1914.

Whatever you call this chapter, it will assuredly prove to be an amazing journey. The ancient roads and canals, though impressive, may elicit a yawn. But I dare you to ponder the incredible tunnel systems and not become spellbound.

Let's get on with our journey.

ROADS

COLOMBIA,
toECUADOR,
toPERU,
to CHILE,
BOLIVIA and
ARGENTINA

1 (S): *The pre-Inca highway system* was the most daring in the world. Linked to a vast network of secondary roads, it reached the Amazon basin, straddled lofty mountain peaks and connected with the coast. Its almost indestructible highways were *paved with granite slabs between two stone retaining walls.*

- *Straight:* Instead of going around impossible barriers, it plunged through them in a direct line, crossing canyons and piercing mountains with tunnels that are still in use today.
- *Signal stations* were perched atop stupendous precipices or mountain summits with sheer 3,000-foot drops.
- *Raised over swamps:* At the standard 24-foot width, one of the causeways rises 8 feet above the marshy countryside for 8 miles.
- *Superior* was this network to the Roman roads, to the Egyptian pyramids and every other construction.
- These roads and bridges were built so well that vehicles use them today.
- Constantly cleaned, they were 'tidy, without a single pebble or weed or wisp of straw."
- *Total length: 19,800 miles.*

Such construction could barely be accomplished by our most modern electro-turbo drills and our most rugged construction machines.

Other features of ancient highway sophistication follow.

MARCAHUASI, PERU
2 (S): Well-protected *covered* roads, at 12,000-foot altitude.

CRETECUICUILO, MEXICOSANTA CRUZ, BOLIVIA
3 (S): Concrete roadways.

MEXICO
4 (S): A 60-mile highway from Coba to Yaxuna, paved with cement and guarded by parapets, running across difficult and marshy country; and city avenues paved with stone or white cement.

GREECE
5 (W): Alexander the Great had plans, cut short by his untimely death, for a highway from Europe to India, *bitumen-sealed all the way.*

MALDEN, in the LINE ISLANDS (PACIFIC)
6 (S): *Basalt-paved highways* connected an inland city to the coastline.

ENGLAND, 2000 B.C.
7 (S): *Wide highways:* The Icknield Way (200 miles long) runs dead-straight on level ground and widens out in some places to the equivalent of a modern four-lane highway.

With a highly developed technology, the ancient races built large cities, gigantic fortresses and *a network of excellent roads,* which (in the case of the Incas) were *used only by pack animals and messengers on foot.* (Doesn't that seem odd? It was as if our modern highways were used only by pedestrians and horses.)

Why, then, were they built? The reason may be that they existed before the Incas and that *their builders intended them for large vehicles.* (If those vehicles moved just above the ground, it would explain the small amount of wear shown.)

CANALS, AQUEDUCTS

ARIZONA, U.S.A.
8 (S): North Canal (9 miles) and South Canal (7 miles), at Hohokam, Pueblo Grande, were comparable to some modern canals.

FLORIDA, U.S.A.
9 (S): One canal 55 feet wide intersects sand ridges to a depth of 40 feet.

NORTH COAST, PERU
10 (S): A 70-mile canal was so efficiently built that it is still in use today.

YUCATAN, MEXICO
11 (S): A network of 30 canals (some up to 160 feet wide) and 25 man-made, large-scale reservoirs, reveal an advanced knowledge of hydraulic engineering.

GUATEMALA, 250 B.C.
12 (S): Recent radar photography of rain forest led to the astonishing discovery of a sophisticated latticework comprising at least 11,185 square miles of irrigation canals, which could have supported millions of people.

CARTHAGE, TUNISIA
13 (S): An aqueduct 87.6 miles long had a capacity of 7,000,000 gallons a day.

FRANCE
14 (S): The Pont du Gard aqueduct, near Nimes, was 160 feet high.

PERSIA, 1000 B.C.
15 (S): *170,000 miles of underground aqueducts* were once constructed to bring mountain water to arid plains. Still extant and functional, this ancient system of irrigation provides 75 percent of the water used in Iran today.

ANDES RANGE, PERU
16 (S): Pre-Incan irrigation works, transforming lofty barren slopes into fertile terraces, could hardly be carried out even with modern turbo drills.

PLATEAU OF MARCAHUASI, PERU
17 (S): An irrigation system incorporated twelve artificial lakes and channels to carry water 4,500 feet lower to a large population.

MOROCCO
18 (S): A network of miles of subterranean passages *up to 250 feet below the surface* was designed to collect water from the subsoil reservoirs under the desert. Ventilated at 100-yard intervals by shafts, this is a titanic work.

Even today, with all our equipment, the creation of such a tunnel system under a desert would present greater problems than building it under one of our big cities.

EGYPT

19 (W): A major surprise is that mighty *Suez Canal.* Contrary to common belief, its first construction was not in 1869! In the days of the early pharaohs, ocean vessels were using the Suez Canal to reach the Indian Ocean, southeastern Asia and Australia. Choked with desert sand, it was rebuilt by the Persians and again dredged by the Arabs. It became blocked once more—and communication between the Mediterranean and the Red Sea ceased until last century.

ANCIENT MINING TUNNELS

UTAH, U.S.A.

20 (S): Remains of coal mining drives are *8,500 feet deep.*

DOMINICA

21 (S): A gold mine *16,000 feet deep* has pits extending about 6 miles. (This region is far less known today than in the fifteenth century, when it was described by Bartholomew Columbus.)

Now here it comes...the shocker.

VAST ARTIFICIAL TUNNELS EXTENDING FOR THOUSANDS OF MILES

You heard it right—a network of intercontinental subways beneath land and sea!

This is the most astonishing and most suppressed archaeological secret: the existence of inexplicable tunnel systems beneath the surface of a great part of the earth. These are part natural and part artificial.

Stories of mysterious subway systems exist in the legends, folklore and myths of almost every country. Reports have persisted for thousands of years.

AFRICA

MOROCCO to SPAIN
22 (S): A huge tunnel (30 miles of which has been explored) runs under the sea between Spain and Morocco.

GENERAL
23 (S): There are descriptions by African travellers of vast tunnels all over the continent; such as one bored under the river Kaoma (south of Lake Tanganyika) so lengthy that it took a caravan from sunrise until noon to pass through.[1]

NORTH AFRICA
24 (S): Livingstone wrote: "Tribes live in underground houses in Rua. Some excavations are said to be 30 miles long."[2]

NIGERIA
25 (0): In the district of Wama, ancient underground tunnels were once used as hiding places by the natives. An old legend mentions a tunnel which stretches hundreds of miles to the Atlantic, near Guinea.

EGYPT
26 (W): A tunnel with a concealed entranceway below one of the Giza pyramids runs "clear to Tibet," according to an old account. Another tunnel at the base of the pyramids is claimed to go southward for 600 miles.

EUROPE

IRELAND
27 (S): Ireland is notoriously riddled with subterranean halls and galleries, whose entrances are to be found within the circular earthworks that surround almost every hilltop.

GREAT BRITAIN
28 (S): A honeycomb of burrowings underlies Chislehurst and Blackheath in Kent. So far 30 miles of tunnel have been located. The system contains geometric-shaped galleries and altar tables.

GREAT BRITAIN
29 (S): There are also extensive tunnels in Yorkshire (though stories of such systems are heard throughout Britain).

FRANCE
30 (S): When a church at Gapennes in Picardy collapsed in 1834, it was found to have been built over a vast network of subterranean passages. This led to an exploration. Enormous tunnels, approximately 100, were found to exist throughout the province.[3]

GERMANY
31(S): There is definite evidence of long subterranean tunnels running beneath Adersbach and Wickelsdorf. During the Thirty Years War, also during the Seven Years War and again in 1866, the local inhabitants took refuge in these labyrinths.

A local tradition calls one of the tunnels "Southern Siberia" because a man "might walk along it until he reached that snowbound region."[4]

SOUTH AMERICA

PERU
32 (S): High in the Andes Mountains, tunnels linking Machu Picchu with other locations burrow for several miles, their *walls lined* with *finely carved stone.* One runs under the bed of the Urubamba River.

ECUADOR
PERU
33 (S): A gigantic system of *interlocking tunnels thousands of miles in length* extends under Ecuador and Peru. It also connects Lima to Cuzco, and goes on to Bolivia, or the sea.

Many hundreds of miles have been explored and measured. Ingeniously constructed entrances are masked beyond discovery; there are *elaborate devices* to trap robbers and hidden doors of carved stones with no sign of a crack or joint. The tunnels are so imposing that some conjecture them to be the work of an unknown race of giants. The Incas, at the time of the Spanish threat, deposited much of their treasure in these caves and sealed some of the entrances.[5]

Fig. 19-1. Insinde and underground system in Spain.

BOLIVIA

34 (S): In the ruins of Tiahuanaco, the nineteenth century naturalist Charles d'Orbigny saw the entrances of galleries leading to a secret underground city.

ECUADOR
COLOMBIA
35 (0): The natives speak of tunnels with *cut-stone walls as smooth as glass* in the mountains. (Some 70,000 artifacts now in a private Ecuador museum were brought by natives from tunnels near Tayos at the confluence of the Santiago and Morona Rivers.)

In August 1976, Scotsman Stanley Hall led a seventy-strong team to investigate another section of the Ecuadorian tunnel system. The expedition was supported by the Universities of Edinburgh and Quito, with assistance from the British and Ecuadorian armies, and accompanied by no less a celebrity than the astronaut Neil Armstrong.

The party fought its way up the raging torrent of the Rio Santiago to arrive at the shaft where, 700 feet below, the entrance to the tunnels lay.

They found the surrounding area dotted with stone pillars, some 20 feet in height and carved with strange hieroglyphics.

The members of the expedition spent two months in the tunnel system, examined over 12 miles of tunnel and took many photographs. They also found evidence of past human presence, but no treasure!

PERU
36 (S): In 1923, scientists from the Lima University, accompanied by experienced speleologists, entered tunnels at Cuzco that advanced toward the coast.

After 12 days, when one solitary member of the expedition staggered out, almost starved, to tell of a confusing underground labyrinth, his colleagues declared him mad. The police dynamited the entrance, to prevent further entry and loss of life.

PERU
37 (S): In 1971, an expedition on Huascaran, the "Mountain of the Incas," removed heavy slabs of rock and descended 200 feet deep until blocked by *six water-tight doors,* which, when pushed, *pivoted on stone balls.*

Beyond was a tunnel lined with incredibly *smooth stone, pitted and grooved.* They followed it for 65 miles, until the sound of surf was heard and 80 feet below the Pacific Ocean, the tunnel was flooded.

PERU

38 (S): After the 1972 Lima earthquake, salvage technicians found large parts of the city to be crossed by unknown tunnels, all leading into the mountains. Their entrances were untraceable due to collapse over the centuries.

AMAZON JUNGLE

39 (W): An explorer reported finding his way into an underground labyrinth *which was illuminated "as though by an emerald sun."* Before retreating (when startled by a large spider), he saw "shadows like men" moving at the end of the passage.

BRAZIL

40 (0): Natives speak of the entrances to a vast network of underground tunnels in the forbidding, unexplored Roncador Mountain Range in the northeastern Matto Grosso. They exist at three different levels and are fanatically guarded by Indians.

BRAZIL

41 (0): Runaway slaves used to enter a tunnel at Ponte Grosse, Parana, and travel all the way to the Matto Grosso underground. When slavery was abolished, they returned by the same route.

BRAZIL

42 (W): The Brazilian radio and press reported the discovery of a subterranean city by a group of scientists. They entered a tunnel which opened on top of a mountain near the Parana and Santa Catarina boundary. Instead of studying it, they fled. (What did they see?)

BRAZIL

43 (0): Two ranchers in the same district told Dr. Raymond Bernard, the American philosopher and archaeologist, that they entered a tunnel and travelled 3 days, finally descending and coming to an illuminated city, in which they saw men, women and children.

BRAZIL

44 (0): Theosophists of Sao Lourence recount that one of their number found a tunnel entrance and travelled all the way from Peru to Brazil in a subterranean passage.

BRAZIL

45 (0): Numerous other supposedly true accounts of journeys through underground tunnels have been related from time to time. The tunnels are described as *smooth-cut, and illuminated,* with radiating side tunnels to ancient subterranean cities. While these are unsubstantiated reports, in the main, they agree in essential details.

In March 1972, independent support to these accounts surfaced quite unexpectedly from the chief of a remote tribe. This "savage" (though to his own people a "prince") emerged from the forest to seek out Brazilian officials and plead against the genocide of his race. It was in Manaus that he met German author Karl Brugger, an authority on South American Indians, a man who ultimately gained his trust and recorded several interviews with him.

BRAZIL

46 (W): Deep in the jungles of northwest Brazil, the mysterious Ugha Mongulala nation are governed by their chief, Tatunca. This man reported to Brugger that in a valley high in the eastern Andes there sits a white stone city, the ancient capital of a once vast jungle empire, from which subterranean passages radiate.

One runs from the Great Temple of the Sun in Akakor, all the way under the enormous Andes range, to finish at the city of Lima, Peru.

Sunk into its light-colored walls at regular intervals are black "hour stones" to mark the distance. About 1920, eighty Ugha Mongulala warriors tramped for 3 months through this tunnel to emerge with bows and arrows in the very heart of Lima, in a futile attempt to rescue fifteen kinsmen. Not one returned.

Another tunnel thrusts 1,000 miles northward under the bed of the "Great River" (the Amazon) to the ruined native city of Akahim on the eastern slopes of the Pico da Neblina, near the Venezuelan border, where, according to Tatunca, a light-skinned tribe is governed by women. (Indeed, white women warriors have been encountered in that very region by explorers and surveyors over the centuries, and as recently as 1973.)

More startling was information on the existence of thirteen ancient underground cities in the Amazon headwaters.

With one exception, these were artificially illuminated. The surface entrances are carefully camouflaged.

Tunnels to these cities radiate from below the temple in Akakor. The cities are many days apart. The sloping walled, flat roofed passages are wide enough for five men. Each city is crossed by canals carrying mountain water, with small tributaries supplying individual buildings and houses.

The secret of the amazing ventilation system is unknown to the natives. Tatunca stated that three of these cities were currently inhabited by his tribe and their allies who had retreated underground to escape extinction.

It is all too real, this extermination of the Amazon tribes. It is deliberate and systematic.

One's heart aches to see their grief, their distress, their tears, Can you imagine mothers, fathers and little children crying out, Why do the white invaders want to wipe us off the face of the earth? That is exactly what is happening.

Initially these uncomplicated but intelligent people greeted Westerners with friendliness, gentleness and smiles. Yet the white invaders were treacherous and cunning. They saw and wanted everything for themselves, for themselves alone. A tree, a piece of fruit, some water, a small heap of earth. Their hearts were cold, unmoved, even when they performed the most terrible acts, to obtain such things.

Like ants, they advanced further up the rivers, insatiable in their hatred, greed and hostility.

In recent decades, cruel men in enormous numbers lusting for wealth and supported by strong, highly superior arms, have advanced ever further: poisoning whole tribes by smallpox carried in pieces of candy; dynamiting jungle natives from the air, then mowing down the survivors with machine guns; and mixing the food of the Indians with arsenic and typhus virus.[6]

After five centuries, from a former forest population of 8 million, only a few thousand are left.

As the European penetrates ever deeper into their territory and they are forced to withdraw from their last fertile lands, many Indians have been reduced to feeding on caterpillars, tree bark and the lichen growing on rocks.

Frightened and confused by this incomprehensible event, tribes have grown increasingly hostile. Thus we hear of savages manned with blowpipes, poison darts and spears, who kill on sight every intruder.

Their hearts are heavy. Angrily they retreat further and further into the jungle; and they know that time will soon run out.

It was in 1968 that the Ugha Mongulala (a proud people with high ethical standards and a unique written history) made an historic decision.

To prevent the discovery of their ancestral white stone city of Akakor by airplanes, the chief's high council gave orders to camouflage all temples, palaces and houses. This once mighty people had lapsed into a state of dismay and despair.

Rather than fight, they now withdrew within shrunken borders. Only small scouting bands were left behind in the abandoned regions to observe the movements of the hostile whites and to forewarn Akakor of an attack.

The situation became still more critical.

By 1971, his surviving subjects dejected and discouraged, the prince advised a slow withdrawal into the underground dwellings. The people gave up their houses and destroyed the buildings of their last remaining settlements, so that white hunters and prospectors would find nothing but abandoned ruins, overgrown by the forests.

They left no sign, no trace that might have pointed the way to Akakor.

Tatunca stated that thirty thousand natives had entered the underground cities. A few remain aboveground to cultivate fields and report on the advance of the enemy. Forbidden to fight when outsiders appear, they must retreat to protect the secret of their former capital city.

One feels outraged that the White Barbarians are above all laws. As the Ugha Mongulala mourn: they "did not come with good intentions, to assume power with kindness and wisdom. Instead...they brought tears, bloodshed..."[7]

Could it be more than coincidence that their inscribed prophecies sound almost biblical?[8] Soon, they predict, a great catastrophe will begin on the other side of the eastern (Atlantic) ocean.

"A war will break out...that will slowly spread over the whole earth. The White Barbarians will destroy each other with weapons that are brighter than a thousand suns. Only a few will survive...The mountains and valleys will tremble. Blood will rain from the sky, and man's flesh will shrink and become soft...Their bodies will disintegrate. In this way the White Barbarians will reap the harvest of their deeds...Then the Gods will return, full of grief for the people who forgot their bequest. And a new world will arise where men, animals, and plants will live together in sacred union. Then the Golden Age will return."[9] So says *The Chronicle of Akakor*.

But for now our journey must resume.

From all evidence, I believe we can substantiate the existence of an underground "road" system stretching as much as 2,500 miles from Mexico to Bolivia, with a branch line running beneath Brazil toward the Atlantic Ocean, as well as a number of subsidiary lines.

We turn now to the Pacific Ocean region.

PACIFIC

EASTER ISLAND
47 (S): Here, too, tunnels lead under the sea.

CAROLINE ISLANDS
48 (S): On Ponape Island are the mouths of impressive underground passages.

CAROLINE ISLANDS
49 (S): On another island, a secret passageway leads down to a terrifying labyrinth.

HAWAIIAN ISLANDS
50 (S): An immense temple lies underground. Also, tunnels are believed to link each of the islands.

SUMATRA
51 (S): A secret passage leads to a vast underground lake on whose shore awesome magic rites are still performed.

OCEANA
52 (0): There are traditions and legends in all Pacific islands of underground cavities reached through secret passages.

ASIA

Artificial labyrinths also stretch under vast areas of Central Asia.

AFGHANISTAN
53 (0): A Mongolian legend claims that a system of tunnels in Afghanistan links up with all other tunnels over the world. The tunnels are lit up by a *green luminescence* which promotes health and life and the growth of plants.

RUSSIA
54 (S): Investigation into a strange bluish light and noises emitted from a "bottomless well" in Azerbaijan, led to the discovery of a whole system of artificial tunnels.

These connected with others in the Georgia and all over the Caucasus. (They are now believed to connect with tunnels in China, Tibet and Mongolia.) One large tunnel led to a spacious hall 65 feet high.

The main entrances to the tunnels are regular in form, *with handsome straight walls and narrow arches—and* almost identical to tunnels in South America.[10]

SIBERIA

55 (S): At Kilyma, near the Cherskiy Mountain Range, a network of tunnels, part artificial, part natural, stretches endlessly toward Mongolia. In the long artificial stretches, *the surface of the wall is almost smooth, as if it had been bored by some kind of machinery.*[11]

SIBERIA

56 (O): There are stories of further subterranean passages in the area of the Altai Mountains. One entrance is at a place called Ergor.

TIBET

57 (O): Tibetans speak of the *green fluorescence* in the tunnels as an underground source of energy, which replaces that of the sun, causing plants to breed and prolonging human life.

They claim *the tunnels go under the Pacific to the Andes* in South America and were "built by giants" when the world was young.

In the summer of 1944, on the Colombia-Ecuador border, journalist John Sheppard came upon a Mongol in meditation with a prayer wheel of the type used in Tibet.

There was suggestion that this was none other than the thirteenth Dalai Lama, who, though supposed to have died in 1933, was in fact never buried in his crypt.

And in Lhasa, the reason given was that he did not die but made the *long underground pilgrimage* to the Andes, the alleged birthplace of Lamaist religion.

And why does Machu Picchu in Peru bear the same name as a mountain and river in Tibet? (The standard appeal to "coincidence" would be too farfetched in this case.)

SINKIANG, CHINESE TURKESTAN

58 (S): Local inhabitants showed the distinguished Russian scientist Nicolas Roerich some long subterranean corridors; they informed him of

people who came out to the towns and spent ancient coins that could not be identified.[12]

KARAKORAM PASS, CHINA
59 (O): Tall white men and women have appeared from secret entrances from inside the mountains, have assisted travellers, and been seen in the dark with torches.

CHINA
60 (S): In July 1961, Professor of Archaeology, Chi Pen Loo, stumbled across a system of tunnels in the Valley of Stones, in the Honan Mountains. They were *smooth and glazed,* with paintings of men on a "flying shield" hunting animals.

61 (S): Ten miles north of Tunhwang (on the southeastern edge of the Gobi Desert on the borders of Tibet) is positive evidence of subterranean passageways.
Behind one of the "Caves of the One Thousand Buddhas" a concealed stairway leads into a more ancient labyrinth of tunnels to disappear in a due south direction.[13]

TIBET
62 (0): A tunnel connected with ancient underground cities is claimed by Buddhist priests to be located beneath the Potala in Lhasa. A massive gold door marks the entrance. [14]

TIBET
63 (0): Other ancient underground galleries extending under the Himalayan foothills, leading far under Mt. Kanchenjunga and in the Altyn Tagh Ridge, are said to contain a collection of several million books. The entrances are thoroughly concealed.

TIBET
64 (W): Tibetan lamas showed the American traveller R.C. Anderson a very old map of underground passages connecting North and South America, Europe and Africa.

INDIA
65 (S): A vast network of underground galleries runs from cave temples, an engineering feat suggesting a high technology in remotest antiquity.[15]

INDIA

66 (W): An ancient tradition of Brahmanic Hindustan speaks of a large island of "unparalleled beauty" which, in ancient times, lay in the middle of a vast sea in Central Asia, north of the Himalayas. Giant men of a Golden Age civilization lived on the island, but there was no communication between them and the mainland, except through tunnels, radiating in all directions, and many hundreds of miles long. These tunnels were said to have had hidden entrances in old ruined cities in India.[16]

NORTH AMERICA

ALASKA

67 (0): Not far from the town of Tanana, in Alaska, Peter Freuchen was shown by local Indians some crevices in the mountains which led to tunnels believed to be inhabited.

The Eskimos have many legends concerning a subterranean world lit by a perpetual light.

ALASKA

68 (O): Eskimos of Alaska and Canada "insist that underground passageways connecting both Asia and the American continent running beneath the Bering Strait were used to accomplish the waves of migration" from Asia.[17]

U.S.A.

69 (0): Apache Indians speak of tunnels that were *"carved out by rays that destroy the living rock"* and go underground from the U.S.A. all the way to Tiahuanaco, in South America.

U.S.A.

70 (0): The Mandan Indians of the Missouri region claimed that they had once been in the subterranean world.

U.S.A.

71(0): The Sioux of North and South Dakota recalled the visit of an Indian brave to an underground city (there is an enduring tradition of subterranean passages in this region).

U.S.A.

72 (W): About 1890, a local newspaper described the discovery of a very ancient cave near Santa Barbara, California.

A large subterranean room had an immense rostrum with steps leading to a throne of marble and a canopy of gold.

An adjoining chamber contained mummies, unknown inscriptions and a ceiling of the sky in detail.

U.S.A.

73 (O): At the turn of the century, an elderly Indian of the Cahroc tribe discovered a tunnel where the Mojave Desert met the Sierra Nevada range.

He trailed it for miles underground. It led to a cavern illuminated by a pale *yellowish-green light* from an invisible source.

U.S.A.

74 (W): In 1904, J.C. Brown came upon an artificial tunnel in the Cascade Mountains. *The walls were lined with tempered copper* and hung with shields and gold wallpieces. Other rooms contained carved drawings and writing. Bones of giant humans lay on the floor.

U.S.A.

75 (W): In 1935, Frank White, prospecting in the mountains and deserts of Southern California, accidentally stumbled upon a small cleft in the rocks. It opened into an underground passage, with *smooth, carefully crafted walls.*

After a half-hour's walk, a progressively brightening *fluorescent green light* glowed over everything. Further on, mummified bodies dressed in leather-looking garments, as well as metal statues. lay about and against the walls.

U.S.A.

76 (O): The Piute Indians speak of people who long ago built a city beneath the stones and the Panamint Mountain Range in Death Valley.

U.S.A.

77 (O): Various reports concern the remains of a splendid city about 75 miles northwest of Portland, Oregon, far down in the earth. It is said to be 8 to 10 miles underground and is reached by a number of tunnels which radiate from it in different directions.[18]

CENTRAL AMERICA

MEXICO
78 (O): A Chiapese tradition recounts that Votan, in a trans-Atlantic visit to Spain and Rome, "went by the road which his brethren, the Culebres, had bored" (i.e., a tunnel which traversed the Atlantic Ocean).[19]

GUATEMALA
79 (O): Adventurer and traveller I. Lloyd Stephens was told by Indians about underground cities beyond Santa Cruz del Quinche, whose people knew *"the formula for the great light."*

He was taken under one of the buildings of the ruined Santa Cruz del Quinche into the entrance of one tunnel by which "one could reach Mexico in an hour."[20]

GUATEMALA
80 (W): Fuentes in 1689 reported amazing tunnels *of the most firm and solid cement,* more than 30 miles long.[21]

WESTERN GUATEMALA
81 (0): A native missionary gave a dying deposition of a journey he had made through a subterranean tunnel leading to a lost city beyond the cordilleras.

MARTINIQUE
82 (0): Similar strange tunnels, very ancient and of unknown origin, were brought to the attention of Christopher Columbus in 1493.

Indications of the reality of these tunnels come also from Sweden, Czechoslovakia, the Balearic Islands and Malta. Most ancient tunnel entrances are now covered by landslides.

The weight of evidence suggests that, whatever the reason, there were once whole cities—linked by an elaborate complex of tunnels—deep beneath the surface of the earth.

Could it be that some of them are still inhabited? Strange noises often resembling the throbbing of machinery have been reported emanating from underground in England, France, Canada, Mexico, Peru, Australia, India, Africa and certain parts of Russia.

As for their origin, I say again, these remarkable achievements, so well attested, needed no astronaut help. They were the constructions of men with an advanced knowledge of engineering.

Most of these fantastic tunnels were constructed in ways beyond our present capabilities—probably by some kind of thermal drill or electron rays, which melted the rock but left no debris.

Interesting, isn't it? The Channel Tunnel, though planned for fifty years by our highly technical engineers, is still not built; for generations they could not agree on the funding or the methods for this comparatively minor tunnel.

Postscript: What we have just discussed does bring to mind an incident which was remembered for centuries in East Anglia—and which, if we did not know better, we might just dismiss as a fable.

In the twelfth or thirteenth century, two "green children" emerged from a cave in Suffolk. They spoke in a strange language. The girl survived and gradually learned English. She described her subterranean homeland as being *illuminated by a constant green glow as if the sun were always just below the horizon* [22]

Enough said.

Chapter 20

Mechanical Devices—MYSTERY OF THE SCREAMING ROBOT

On Malta, there are vestiges of what appear to be a railroad—but it is thousands of years old.

Grooves for the rails and cross ties run beside a narrow strip of rock where no animals pulling a cart could pass. Neither are there any traces of footsteps or hoof marks.

The track, cut into the rock, features sidings and junctions like a modern railway. At one point the track leaves the land and disappears under water for some distance. Mysterious, indeed.

No less intriguing was the robot rooster that screamed.

Is it possible that ancient man possessed machines? It's not only possible. It's true.

GREECE
1 (W): *Steam boilers.*

GREECE
2 (W): *Steam-powered organs.*

EGYPT

3 (W): *A two-cylinder steam engine* which embodied the principles of both the turbine and jet propulsion.

ECUADOR

4 *(S): Numerous woven copper items which bear a resemblance to the modern automobile radiator.* Whatever their use, their design indicates a sophisticated understanding of heat-exchange technology.[1]

GREECE

5 (W): *Petrol vapor machines.*

EGYPT

6 *(W): A speedometer registering the* distance travelled by a vehicle.
If it were not for the repeated burnings of the Alexandrian Library, what stories might we have found concerning motor cars?

YUCATAN, MEXICO

7 (O): The so-called Castillo of Chichen Itza was (according to a very ancient tradition) built over *a "machine"* of similar form *capable of "travelling over great distances and for a very long time."*

ALEXANDRIA, EGYPT

8 (W): Jet engine.

TLALELACO, MEXICO

9 (S): Found 20 feet underground: an object which looks like a miniature jet engine.

ECUADOR

10 (S): Copper gears with a hardness comparable to steel, indicating they were designed for heavy mechanical use.[2]

ECUADOR

11(S): Copper and stone *mechanical devices with circular rollers, bearing an uncanny resemblance to modern metal fabricating machines.*[3]

GREECE

12 (W): *A "machine tool" for cutting screws.*

GREECE
13 (W): *A machine for boring tunnels.*

EGYPT
14 (S): Drills for boring into granite rock, that *turned 500 times faster than modern power drills.*

TURKEY15 (S): Drills that bored holes *finer than the thinnest needle* in hard stone.

MEXICO
16 (S): A 5-ton "steam-roller" for road *maintenance.*

EGYPT
17 *(W): A fire engine* with a double-action pump.

GREECE
18 (W): *Screw pump:* an ingenious interacting system of levers, pulleys and grips for lifting great weights—one use of which was to grab, tilt and sink enemy ships.

FRANCE
19 (W): A sculptured block discovered among Roman remains shows a *multiple harvester used in reaping grain.*

PANAMA
20 (S): *A stylized model of an ancient geared earth-moving machine* contains a system of mechanical gears (including cogwheels on an axle with a rocker arm between them, with two more rocker arms in the rear and a 'jaguar mouth" with teethlike bucket grabs). The spadelike features on side and rear are very obvious.[4] (If this is a prehistoric model of a *real working vehicle,* it would explain some of the construction triumphs of the ancient Americas.)

ECUADOR
21 (S): Found: *mechanical corn mills, wheeled and geared.*[5]

ICA, PERU
22 (W): Stone engravings show people operating *unknown machines.*

CRETE
23 (S): Remains of *puzzling apparatuses* have been found in the palaces and workshops of Knossos.

PERU
24 (W): A clay vessel portrays a man using the index fingers of both hands to operate a kind of *calculating machine, or a switchboard.*[6]

CRETE
25 (S): The Phaistos Disk (discovered in 1908) shows evidence of having been *printed using moveable type* (recurring symbols impressed individually). This shows that the principle of printing by type was known in very early times. (Evidence as to whether it was ever used on paper and other materials is probably lost forever.)

Ancient mounds in Michigan, U.S.A., have likewise yielded objects which appear to have been impressed with dies or type pieces.

GREECE
26 (S): *A bronze astronomical computer* had complex dials, moveable pointers, inscribed plates, as well as twenty interlocking gears, a differential gear and a crown wheel.[7]

SICILY
CHINA
PERSIA
GREECE
27 (W) Machines, often automatic, accurately rotated in imitation of astronomical movements.

MAYA, GUATEMALA
28 (S): *Screw propellers.*

CALIFORNIA, U.S.A.
29 (S): *A mechanized device like a spark plug* has been found inside a rock.[8]

AUSTRIA
30 (S): *A machine-made steel cube (part of a larger mechanism)* has been recovered below ground in a coal mine.

This was accidentally discovered in 1885, when a block of coal was broken open in the Austrian foundry of Isador Braun of Vocklabruck. Braun's son took the mysterious cube to the Salzburg Museum, where it underwent examination by the Austrian physicist Karl Gurls.

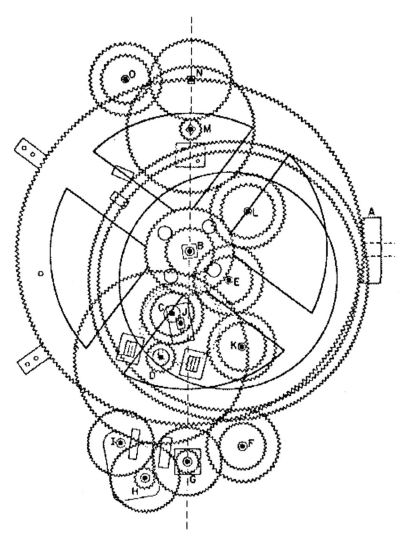

Fig. 20—1. Derek de Solla Price's reconstruction of a calendar computer built by the Greeks in c.65 B.C. and found by sponge-divers off the island of Antikythera.

Fig. 20—2a. Fragments of this ancient mechanical device which were encrusted by the sea.

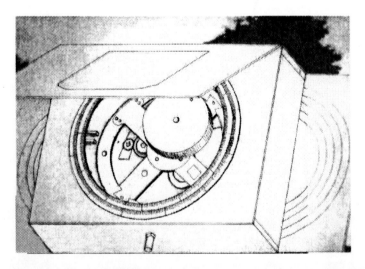

Fig. 20—2b. Originally the Antikythera computer, the size of a typewriter, looked like this (Photo: National Archaeological Museum of Greece; Scientific American)

The object was clearly machine-fabricated, with smooth, sharp surfaces. Four of its sides were flat, and the two remaining sides opposite each other were convex. A deep, even groove ran completely around it.

It remained on exhibit at the museum until 1910. An account of its discovery was published in the scientific journals *Nature* (London, 1886) and *L'Astronomie* (Paris, 1897).

Of antedeluvian origin, it is apparently *a piece of some machine* destroyed and buried during the Flood.

U.S.A.
ENGLAND
GERMANY
RUSSIA
ITALY
FRANCE
31 (S): *Similar objects* with interesting angles have been discovered elsewhere.

CHINA, 1st cent. AD
PERU
32 (W,S): *A seismograph,* providing data to pinpoint the epicenter of an earthquake anywhere in the world.

The application of scientific principles here implied postulates a knowledge of the earth's structure and of the propagation of waves.

EGYPT, 2nd cent. AD.
ATHENS, GREECE
33 (W): *Coin slot-machines* for holy water (the quantity depending on the coin inserted).

EGYPT
34 (W): *An automaton in the form of a cock* was discovered after the Moslem conquest of Egypt, by one of the first caliphs of Cairo, and described in an Arab manuscript known as the *Murtadi.* It was made of red gold and covered with precious stones, with two shiny gems for eyes.

The cock, when approached, uttered a frightening cry and began flapping its wings.

MECHANICAL-ELECTRONIC ROBOTS

CHINA
35 (W): *A walking robot.*

EGYPT over 2,000 years ago
36 (W): *More than 100 different automatons* are recorded.

GREECE
37 (W): *A humanlike robot that walked—and almost ran away!*

PERU
38 (W): *A robot that spoke and gave answers to questions (a computer?).*

CRETE
39 (W): *A bronze Talus metallic creature.*

RHEIMS, FRANCE
40 (W): A bronze automaton which *answered questions.*

REGENSBURG, GERMANY
41 (W): An android that *walked, spoke and performed domestic chores.*

AZTECS, MEXICO
42 (S): Found: *a figurine of a robot.*

Are these residues of automation in a past technological era?

I should qualify that not all scientific achievements of the past were a legacy from before the Flood. There were natural social factors, of course. However, some achievements of early history and prehistory cannot be defined as creations of man's mind at that time, because economic and social conditions were not ripe for them. They would have to be an inheritance from an earlier period.

A mechanical effect of stunning beauty may soon be discovered in the Lin-t-'ung district of China.

Here, where China's earliest emperors lived and died, widespread excavations are presently being undertaken. The most staggering finds are yet to be made. Hidden beneath the picturesque landscape lie hundreds of undisturbed imperial tombs, each filled with art treasures and riches.

In 100 B.C. the Chinese chronicler Suma Chien described unbelievable treasures constructed within the tomb of the first emperor, Chi'n Shi Huang Ti. Constellations, regions of the earth and contemporary buildings were all reproduced. "All the rivers of the country, the Yellow River and the Yangtze, were reproduced in quicksilver and made to flow into a miniature ocean through some *mechanical* means."[9]

The location is known. The tomb, under a mound overgrown with trees and wildflowers, towers 165 feet (16 stories high) against the northern foothills of Mount Li in the Wei River valley of Kansu province.

The archaeologists who finally penetrate this tomb had better take care; the ancient chronicler warned that weaponry was set up "so that any robber breaking in would be killed."[10]

Chapter 21

Everyday Items—THE PHOTO SPIES

Could photographic and listening devices have been known and used in the very distant past? An outrageous suggestion, surely.

Let me introduce to you some Indian records dating to the second millennium B.C. and considered to be copies of still older documents. Whereas the writings of most other nations suffered willful destruction, these have by some miracle survived.

They present epics of gods and men, interspersed with such wealth of a scientific nature that much of it was considered absurd when translated last century.

Modern science is today catching up with many of the concepts expressed in these documents.

Scientists in many countries are now studying a remarkable translation made by Maharshi Bharadwaja called Aeronautics, described as A Manuscript from the Pre-historic Past. It contains fascinating, almost incredible data. This translation has been published by the International Academy of Sanskrit Research in Mysore, India. Its table of contents includes:

The secret of constructing aeroplanes, which will not break, which cannot be cut, will not catch fire, and cannot be destroyed; the secret of making planes motionless; the secret of hearing conversations and other sounds in enemy planes; the secret of receiving photographs of the interior of enemy planes, and more.[1]

Take merely the photographic and audio references in this ancient document. Impossible questions arise, unless we are prepared to understand that there must have been a higher culture or an equally perfect technology before our own.

Many isolated clues from around the world—inconsequential in themselves, but cumulatively meaningful—show that everyday items familiar to us were known and used throughout the "prehistoric" world.

Significantly, these are found in the ruins of inferior civilizations—after the superior technology had vanished. They are suggestive of what must have preceded them.

So here are some of the more modest inventions, but nonetheless surprising to us, that can be found in the "minor" pages of archaeology.

EGYPT, 2750 B.C.
1 (S): Envelopes were used for letters and sealed with the sender's private seal.

EGYPT, 2500 B.C.
2 (S): Eleven rusted razor blades with hieroglyphic writing on them.

BABYLON
3 (S): Sulfur matches.

THERA, 1500 B.C.
4 (W): Boxing gloves.

INDIA
5 (S): Thimbles.

EGYPT, 2700 B.C.
UR, CHALDEA
COSTA RICA TO COLOMBIA
6 (S): Silver and gold foil.

ECUADOR
7 (W): A plaque depicts a clerk writing with a quill pen in a surprisingly modern book.

GENERAL
8 (S): Evidence for paper books has been found on all continents except Australia.

UYCALI and TITICACA, PERU
9 (S): Books of paintings and hieroglyphics.

(Of course, this refutes the conventional assumption that writing was unknown in South America.)

GUATEMALA
EGYPT
10 (O): Books made of gold leaves.

SYRIA, 1400 B.C.
11 (S): Several rooms in one library were devoted entirely to just dictionaries and lexicons!

EGYPT
CHINA
INDIA
12 (S): Technological textbooks.

URARTU, TURKEY
13 (S): Rulers and compasses were used when making elaborate drawings for frescoes.

MEDZAMOR, ARMENIA, 2500 B.C.
14 (S): Metallic paint.

EGYPT, 3000 B.C.
20 (S): A segmented box similar to that used today for cutlery.

EGYPT
21 (S): Camping equipment.

GUATEMALA
22 (S): Diving suits.

EGYPT
23 (W): Plastics: "Glass which could be bent and yet not broken" was reported by the Arab historian Ibn Abd Hokh to have been buried in ancient vaults.[2]

PERU
24 (S): Plastics? Small tubes of a material like glass, but not glass, and of an unknown chemical composition, were found in graves, in the 1940's.

CAPPADOCIA, TURKEY
25 (W): Drinking straws.

EGYPT, 3000 B.C.
SOUTHERN TURKEY
CENTRAL AMERICA
26 (S): Forks and spoons.

UR, CHALDEA
27 (S): Knives of 2.8 percent tin.

INDIA
28 (S): Aluminum cups.

TIAHUANACO, BOLIVIA
CORNWALL, ENGLAND
UR, CHALDEA
MEXICO
PERU
29 (S): Finely executed gold dinnerware.

CRETE
30 (S): Glazed dinnerware and tinted glass goblet.

ROME
31 (S): Thermos containers, keeping liquids and foods either hot or cold, in common use.

URARTU, TURKEY
32 (S): Furniture decorated with gold and silver; bronze legs of tables and beds shaped like goats' feet or horses' hooves.

GERMANY

33 (S): Bed legs made of cast-metal statues balancing on wheels, could be rolled like a sofa on casters! Bronze Age Celts just weren't supposed to have been that sophisticated.

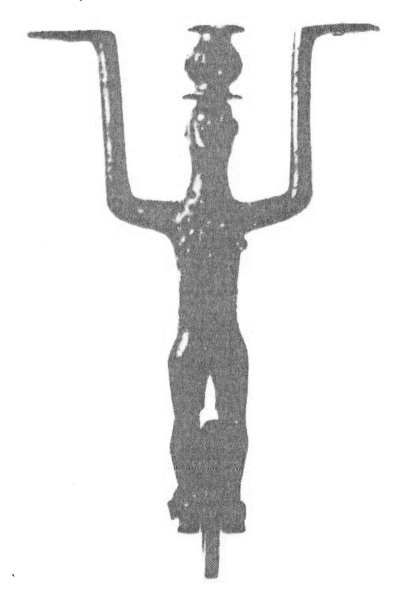

Fig. 21—1. One of eight cast-metal statues that supported the funeral bed of a "Bronze Age" Celtic prince. The bed could be "rolled like a sofa on casters." (Photo: Dr.J. Biel)

ISRAEL, 850 B.C.
EGYPT
34 (W): Beds and ornaments of color-stained ivory.

ECUADOR
35 (S): A magnificent golden bed inscribed with hieroglyphics.

ISRAEL
36 (W): Chairs of ebony, inlaid with ivory and lapis lazuli.

SUMERIA, 3000 B.C.
ECUADOR
37 (W,S): Modern-quality musical instruments in great variety.

SYRIA
38 (S): A musical notation on a 3,400-year-old clay tablet, when translated and played, sounds very pleasing to the modern Western ear. Not unlike guitar music, it was probably written for a harp-accompanied soloist.

ARIZONA, U.S.A. THE MAYA, MEXICO
39 (S): Rubber balls.

Chapter 22

Clothing and Adornment—BIKINI GIRLS OF THE MEDITERRANEAN

S oak up the sun in your bikini, or try on your pantsuit and wig. Then off to a fashion parade.

If twentieth century historians call you primitive because you live thousands of years B.C., then you can smile. Your jewelry is immaculate. You lack nothing in sophistication.

Neither does your "prehistoric" husband live in a cave. He wears well-styled clothes and modern shoes.

Enough to give the traditional prehistorian a seizure.

Here's a short check list…

GOBI DESERT
NEVADA, U.S.A.
ENGLAND
1 (S): Fossilized (prehistoric) shoe prints. with nail heads around the edge, as well as "shoe laces."[1]

MEXICO
PERU
GERMANY
2 (S): Gold and silver footwear with soft-gold soles or rubber soles; gold embellishment.

HELWAN, EGYPT
SUBIS MOUNTAINS, BORNEO
3 (S): Finely woven textiles of extraordinary strength and delicacy, such as could only be produced in highly specialized factories, today.

PERU to MEXICO
4 (S): Cotton grown in various colors (from brown to blue), a technique which modern science has been unable to reproduce.

MOCHICAS of PERU
5 (S): Advanced dyeing techniques: fabrics covered with a mosaic of feathers, in no less than 190 shades of color.

PERU
6 (S): Magnificent textiles, with veils, brocades, and 'gobelins'—far finer than is possible on any modern loom.

RUSSIA, 3000 B.C.
7 (S): Spindle whorls and patterned fabric designs.

PERU
8 (S): Exquisitely patterned lace.

PERU
9 (S): Clothing sewn artistically in multicolored designs, with gold and silver thread.

CHUNG SHAN, CHINA
10 (S): Jade clothes composed of hundreds of pieces of tightly fitted jade particles, sewn with golden thread.

THE MAYA, MEXICO
11 (S): Waterproof clothing.

HONAN MOUNTAINS, CHINA
12 (W): "Modern" jackets and long trousers (depicted in underground tunnel paintings).

SOUTH AFRICA
13 (W): Short-sleeved pullovers, closely fitting breeches, gloves, garters and slippers, and multicolored shirts.

RUSSIA
14 (S): Fur trousers, embroidered shirts, jackets with ivory badges and clasps.[2]

RUSSIA
15 (S): Two-piece suits, styled very much as in the present day).[3]

CRETE
ASIA MINOR
EGYPT, 3000 B.C.
16 (W): Fashions were launched by the elegant women of Crete, and imitated by other countries:

- Very long skirts with flounces
- Later: fuller skirts with flounces
- Bodices decorated with Medici-like collars
- Deeply cut in front, leaving the breasts visible
- Hats of extravagence and variety

FRANCE
17 (W): Pantsuits, short-sleeved jackets, decorated hats, small boots and modern-looking purses.[4]

SICILY
18 (W): Bikinis modelled by skinny young girls, posing in a mode similar to that of today.

SUMERIA, 2900 B.C.
19 (S): An amazingly modern wig.

THERASUMERIA
20 (W,S): Eyelid paint; eye makeup.

EGYPT
21 (S): A woman preserved in a tomb was wearing five shades of lipstick; her hair had been in rollers—and the curls were still in, after 3,000 years.

SUMERIABULGARIA, 3000 B.C.

22 (S): Large earrings, necklaces, cosmetics and expensive jewelry, used with sophistication.

MOHENJO-DARO, PAKISTAN, 3000 B.C.

23 (S): Jewels, rings, bracelets and necklaces of gold, silver and ivory—kept in elegant silver caskets—and "so well finished and so highly polished that it might have come out of a Bond Street jeweller's."

So much for a sampling of ancient fashions. Among the general populace, we see astonishing variety and opulence in clothing; also elegance in which good taste and coordination among clothes, hairdos, headwear and jewelry prevailed.

Beauty sophistication matched our own. Herbal drops were used to enlarge the pupils of the eyes. Green eyeshadow, black eyeliner, face powder and rouge were used in great quantities, as was a bleaching paste for freckles.

From the earliest times, nails held a fascination. Manicuring implements were used, including a cuticle pusher rather like an orange wood stick of today. Women colored their fingernails and toenails bright red.

In taste, people were basically the same as today.

Chapter 23

Art and Sculpture—THE CRYSTAL SKULL

Imagination, you might say. And perhaps I should agree, were it not for the consistent testimony of reputable witnesses.

A crystal skull, during certain phases of the moon, emits capella choir music, melodious tinkling bells and a violet glow.

Scientists have no theory at all to explain the phenomena. The eleven-pound skull was unearthed by Mitchell Hedges at Lubaantun, British Honduras.

It is no secret that prehistoric art and sculpture pose for us some tantalizing mysteries. We are confronted with

- Three-dimensional art
- Four-dimensional art
- Visible then invisible
- Sex-change sculpture
- Eighteen-story-high statues
- Murals in luminous paint
- Carvings designed to produce a fifteen-minute moving picture sequence with the brilliance of a neon sign

Such subtle techniques run counter to the common view of primitives living in caves, using clubs and crude flint tools and looking like ape men!

So far I have not been fortunate enough to hear an explanation of such ultra modern genius that is even tolerably convincing.

Some of this art is so advanced, its techniques are ahead of our time.

ALTAMIRA, SPAIN
LASCAUX, FRANCE
RIBADASELLA, SAHARA
1 (S): Cave paintings of *highly developed and stylized art* which look strangely modern—masterpieces in any period.

- Their dynamic realism and beauty, their flowing lines and contrast, their use of perspective, make them immensely superior to the later animal paintings of Egypt, Babylon, Greece or Crete, and of a level not again reached until the Renaissance in the fifteenth century!
- Sketches and trial pieces found suggest that there were art schools.
- The pictures show shadows and highlights; there is a plan of construction, an idea of composition that makes use of hollows and knobs in the rock. The painters possessed a culture much more advanced than the average inhabitant of the European countryside today.

AJANTA, near BOMBAY, INDIA, 6th cent.
2 *(S): Luminous paints:* Cave murals portraying women carrying gifts lack depth until the light is switched off. In darkness, the figures on the wall appear to be three-dimensional, as if they were made of marble—by the clever employment of luminous paint, the secret of which has been lost forever.

FRANCE
3 (S): *The engraved bones of Glozel are still the finest in the world.*

MOHENJO-DARO, PAKISTAN
MESOPOTAMIA
PERSIAN GULF
4 (S): *Soapstone seals* carved with figures of bulls, elephants, antelope and other animals (one showing a man up a tree with a tiger lurking hungrily below) are *only as big as postage stamps.* So fine is the artwork that it might have been done under a magnifying glass.

HAVEA, BRAZIL
5 (S): *A mountain carved to resemble the head of a bearded man* wearing a spiked helmet: On one side of the mountain (on a small vertical

face 3,000 feet in height) is a carved inscription in *cuneiform characters* some 10 feet tall. It is a mystery how this was done.

PLATEAU OF MARCAHUASI, PERU
6 (S): *Four-dimensional art:*

- Carvings which, according to the angle of vision, have *several faces*—but you have to move into the right spot to distinguish each of them. As you *move,* they *disappear* or *change* into other figures.
- *Many become visible, then invisible* again, seen only at noon, or twilight, or certain other hours, or at one of the solstices—and *at no other time.*
- *A figure of an old man, when photographed, changes into the carved face of a radiant youth.* How can we explain this sculptural mystery, which is revealed only in the photograph? It is hard to see how an artist could achieve this effect even with the benefits of modern science.

The artists needed incomparable skill to make the shapes appear only from certain angles and under certain specific conditions of sunlight.

These examples belong to a vast complex of monuments and sculptures covering a square mile, using whole cliffs; with images of the four main human races and of animals from other parts of the world.

Every type of sculptural technique was used: bas-relief, engraving, and play of light and shade. The sculptors scientifically utilized *the laws of perspective and optics.*

EASTER ISLAND
7 (S): Sculptured heads, although without eyes, have eyebrows carved in such a way as to produce a shadow that simulates the eye in the cavity *at a certain time of the year.*

SOUTH AMERICA
ENGLAND (Stonehenge and Avebury)
FRANCE (Southern Brittany)
8 (S): *Visible, then invisible sculpture* is seen in many places elsewhere.

ONEGA RIVER, RUSSIA
9 (S): *"Neon sign" effect with a moving picture:* An astonishing gallery of 600 sketches has been incised into a cliff of hard granite rising vertically

from lake waters—ingeniously designed to blend the effect of rippling water reflection with setting sunlight.

When the sun nears the horizon, the granite shines dark-red and the various colored lines of the pictures become very clear (the countless tiny crystal prisms of the incisions reflecting much more light than the surrounding smooth areas) and shine intensely.

The luminous pictures then begin to move. The frog seems to turn into an elk, while the hunter makes a movement with the hand; having thrown the axe with his right hand, he puts out his left arm to keep his balance, as the camp fire flickers.

This magnificent spectacle lasts a quarter hour, until the setting sun makes the designs grow weaker.

Like neon lamps going on and off, which seem to move, the same effect is seen here: groups of tiny prisms on the unequal surfaces of the designs act like lamps, so that at moments some become more luminous than others.

Two currents of light—from the setting sun and the moving water—give the impression that the whole design is moving.[1]

The artists must have had a clear idea of what they wanted to show, as well as acute vision and steady hands, since a wrong cut in the sharp silica could have ruined the picture for good; *granite is a canvas which will not allow corrections.*

AUSTRALIA
10 (S): *Are these laser beam carvings?* Punchings of designs and symmetrical forms have been made 4 to 8 inches deep on rock faces 30 to 300 feet up.

Attempts to duplicate the engravings with modern tools failed—the rock would only chip or flake.

"Nothing but a laser beam could leave this impression," claims a scientist.[2]

(Not forgetting that in the United States of America, Apache Indians spoke of tunnels "carved out by rays that destroy the living rock.")

GERMANY
RUSSIA
11 (S): *Faces that change sex:* Giant stones carved to resemble human heads had two faces.

When they were turned 125 degrees, a man's face turned into a woman's face. (Pre-glacial)

THE MAYA, GUATEMALA

12 (S): *Transfer printing:* A pattern drawn on a flat surface was transferred onto a jar *in three dimensions* with an exactitude that few living draftsmen could duplicate. The design was complex.

BRITISH HONDURAS
MEXICO

13 (S): *Two separate crystal skulls,* intricate and beautiful, have no equal anywhere. Each was carved from a solid block of crystal. The larger is in natural size, with a separate, but attached, moveable lower jaw, implying that it was meant to "talk." Use unknown. Each crystal skull has a built-in, nearly perfect set of complicated optical systems that allow almost all the light entering its base to emanate in full spectrum through the hollow eyes. It has been reported that one skull emits strange noises at times.[3]

Today we know that the properties of quartz are very important in semiconductor electronics and radio communications, but with all our experience we could not produce such a work as the crystal skull.

GUIANA
ENGLAND
U.S.A.
CHILE
AFGHANISTAN
PERU

14 (S): *Enormous carvings and drawings* (often too large to be seen from any place on the ground): Human and animal figures from 60 to 330 feet long. Another 825 feet long (part of the Nazca drawings occupying 30 square miles) is the largest work of art in the world.

EGYPT

15 (S): *The titanic portrait statues of the Pharaohs* (up to 89 feet high, with toes, eyes, ears, all of enormous proportions) required an incredible combination of skill and precision. The artist could seldom see all his work at one time.

Fig. 23-1a. A very beautiful skull made of crystal, probably
of Mixtec origin.

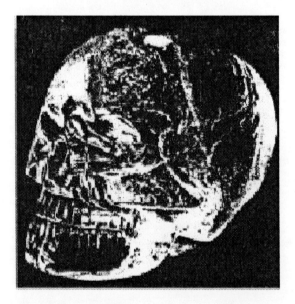

Fig. 23-1b. A skull carved in natural size from a single
block of crystal, believed to be of Aztec origin.

Chapter 24

Health and Medical—WHAT HAPPENED AFTER THE CAR CRASH

Following a serious car accident in 1963, the victim's life was saved in a most unusual manner.

For the delicate operation, Peruvian surgeon Francisco Grano used surgical instruments that had been exhumed from a 3,000-year-old tomb. They were manufactured from an alloy of gold, copper and silver.

Ancient medical practice, it appears, was more than folk herbs.

Rather, medicine and surgery were fantastically advanced millenia ago.

A sophisticated medical science existed worldwide and in some cases is only now being relearned by modern research.

We shall never know everything, but can only wonder at the profusion of medical knowledge and skill that prevailed at the dawn of history.

The following are fragments of that knowledge.

KNOWLEDGE OF INTERNAL BODY FUNCTIONS

INDIA
1 (W): Knowledge of *the nervous system.*

EGYPT

2 (W): A knowledge of *the relationship between the nervous system and the movements of our limbs* enabled an understanding of *the causes of paralysis.* (Forty-eight clinical cases are listed in the Smith Papyrus.)

CHINA, 2650 B.C.
EGYPT
INDIA

3 (W): *The function of the heart in pumping blood through the arteries to circulate throughout the body* was understood and described. (Not until the seventeenth century was this rediscovered. It revolutionized European medicine.)

INDIA

4 (W): *Knowledge of metabolism.*

CHINA

5 (W): *Chemical balance in the body* was understood.

INDIA

6 (W): *Genetics* and the transmission of specific characteristics by heredity was known.

THE BIBLE, 1000 B.C.

7 (W): *Molecular biology:* A knowledge of the sugar/phosphate human cellular DNA-helix tapes and their genetic "blueprints": "Thine eyes did see my substance, yet being unperfect: and in thy book all my members were written, which in continuance were fashioned, when as yet there was none of them."[1]

CHINA, 2650 B.C.
EGYPT, 3000 B.C.
INDIA

8 (W): *Medical and surgical textbooks and diagnostic manuals.*

INDIA

9 (W): *A list diagnosing up to 1120 diseases.*

INDIA

10 (W): *The etiology of a number of diseases not achieved by the Western world until the late nineteenth century.*

HEALTH AND MEDICINE

TIAHUANACO, BOLIVIA
ALEXANDRIA, EGYPT
11 (W): *A college of surgeons; a faculty of medicine.*

CHINA, 3rd cent. B.C.
12 (W): *Pharmacologists.*

CHINA, 3rd cent. B.C.
13 (W): *Specialist doctors.*

CHINA, 3rd cent. B.C.
14 (W): *Veterinarians.*

PERU
EGYPT
15 (W): *A state-sponsored medical aid program,* in which doctors received their remuneration from the government and medical aid was free to all.

THE BIBLE
16 (W): *Dietetic principles* which are only now being recognized by science—including the superiority of fruit, nuts and green vegetables for optimum health; a detailed classification of meats fit and unfit for human consumption; warnings against the consumption of animal fats and blood.[2]

PERU
BRITAIN
17 *(S): Food preservation* (including by vacuum).

THE BIBLE
18 (W): *Quarantine.*[3]
It is significant that the deadly European plagues of the Dark Ages were brought under control by following the quarantine and other rules laid down in the biblical writings in the Book of Leviticus.
With medicine at such a low point during this period, Jewish doctors were highly esteemed.

Has the thought crossed your mind that there might be something more behind this source of information than meets the eye?

EGYPT
THE BIBLE[4]
19 (W): *The practice of hygiene.*

EGYPT
CHINA
THE BIBLE[5]
20 (W): *Antisepsis and sterilization.*

INDIA, 2000 B.C.[6]
CHINA
21 (W): *Immunization and inoculation* (with directions for vaccination and descriptions of its effects).

GREECE
CHINA
EGYPT

EGYPT
INDI
THE BIBLE[7]
23 (W): *Penicillin.*

EGYPT
INDIA
24 (W): Drug prescriptions, such as "take before going to bed," or "take twice a day," in common use.

EGYPT
INDIA
25 (W): *Wonder drugs for "incurable" diseases.* Many of today's "incurable" diseases were, in ancient India, actually cured with medicines that to us are unknown. At present, research is being undertaken in Indian texts, in the hope of recovering some of this lost science.

INDIA, 1st cent. AD.
26 (W): *A pharmaceutical encyclopedia listing over 500 herbal drugs.*

EGYPT,
INDIA,
CHINA,
PERU
ARMENIA, 1500 B.C.
27 (W): *Local and general anaesthesia* (including an unknown mineral drug).

INDIA
28 (W): *Medical methods to counteract the effects of poison gas.*

SUMERIA
29 (W): *Radiation therapy:* A cylinder seal depicts a man lying on a special bed; his face is protected by a mask, while he is being subjected to radiation.

THE BIBLE
30 (W): *Mouth-to-mouth resuscitation.*[8]

CRETE
EGYPT
AUSTRALIA
31 (W,S): *Contraceptives:*
- Contraceptive jelly—Egypt[9]
- Oral contraceptive pills with no harmful side effects—the Australian Aborigines

EGYPT
32 (W): *Urine pregnancy tests and determination of the sex of the unborn child.*

CRETE
33 (W): *Artificial insemination.*

THE BIBLE
34 (W): *Male circumcision practiced not as a puberty rite, but according to the standards of twentieth century medicine—on the eighth day.*[10]

We begin to see the reason for this, at last. Discoveries now show that a newborn baby has a bleeding tendency—until in five to seven days a

249

clotting agent, Vitamin K, is manufactured. *The eighth day* is the day when another clotting element, prothrombin, is at its highest level in a human's entire life—110 percent of normal! Can anyone doubt that here is compelling evidence for a superior source of information back in the beginning?

SURGICAL INSTRUMENTS

POMPEII, ITALY
35 (S): *Gynecology flourishing to* perfection, with instruments almost *identical to those of today.*

CRETE
36 (W): *Adhesives.*

PERU
37 (W): *Tourniquet and forceps.*

PERU
38 (W): *Gauze and absorbent cotton* to bandage surgical incisions.

JERICHO, ISRAEL
39 (S): *Plaster of Paris.*

EGYPT
40 (W): *Broken bones put into splints.*

ITALY, 1st cent. AD.
41 (S): *Surgical instruments* "as fine as anything produced in this line in the twentieth century—screws as threadlike and capable of delicate manipulation as anything today."[11]

INDIA, 5th cent. B.C.
42 (W): As many as *121 surgical instruments described* in an ancient document.

INDIA
43 (W): Curved needles for sutures.

TIAHUANACO, BOLIVIA
44 (S): Bronze surgical knives.

EGYPT
45 (S): Sophisticated medical instruments that are the exact counterparts of the basic tools of modern surgery: forceps, scalpels, clamps, and such.[12]

ARMENIA, 1500 B.C.
GUATEMALA
PERU, 500 B.C.
46 (S): Sharp surgical instruments made of obsidian.

Obsidian (volcanic glass), if you didn't know, is a thousand times sharper than the platinum-plus blades used in other surgical instruments. The cutting surface of obsidian is so sharp that it does not bruise the cells.

In 1975, an American doctor performed successful major surgery with obsidian tools.[13] Obsidian surfaces may eventually revolutionize surgery and could be of special value in cosmetic and plastic surgery.

PERU, 500 B.C.
47 (W): Scalpels, bronze knives, pincers, copper wire and needles for sutures.

EGYPT
48 (W): Artificial nourishment by tubes.

PERU
49 (W): Life-support *systems with tubing:* Heart surgery patients were connected via intricate tubing to life-support systems.

EGYPT
50 (W): *Plasma generator.*

PERU
51(W): *Operating tables.*

FLUOROSCOPES (X-RAY DEVICES) FOR DIAGNOSING INTERNAL INJURIES[14]

INDIA, 500 B.C.
52 (W): When a patient was placed before it, a "gem" "illuminated his body as a lamp lights up all objects in a house, and so revealed the nature of his malady."

CHINA, 206 B.C.
53 (W): "A precious mirror that illuminates the bones of the body" was rectangular (4 by 5-3/4 feet) and gave off a strange light on both sides. The view of the organs of the body that the mirror gave could not be obstructed by any obstacle.

MEXICO
54 (W): From Toro Muerto, a rock drawing shows a man with a rectangle over the chest area; within the rectangle there is a stylized drawing of what appears to be the spinal column and ribs.

AUSTRALIA
55 (W): Aborigines have x-ray paintings portraying animals, reptiles and fish with their internal organs and bones.

Can these be a race memory of an ancient epoch when x-ray equipment was used?

SURGICAL OPERATIONS

PERU
56 (W): Operating rooms were first *cleared and purified.*

PERU
57 (W): *Excisions.*

PERU
58 (W): *Cauterizations.*

PERU
AUSTRALIA
59 (S,W): *Blood transfusions:*

- Many ancient carvings in Peru show pregnant women donating blood to organ transplant recipients. (Could there be an as yet undiscovered retention hormone produced by a woman in pregnancy?)
- In Australia, the Aborigine takes blood either from a vein in the middle of the arm or from one in the inner arm, by means of a hollow reed.

(Blood transference is also done by mouth, but this technique remains unfathomable.) He is aware of the proper vein from which to take blood. Uncannily, he also chooses the fitting donor. Blood transfusion is practiced not only in critical cases of injury and illness, but also to give vitality to the aged. Seemingly the Aboriginal medicine man is *still heir to ancient knowledge.*

PERU
INDIA
60 (W): *Amputations.*

CHINA, 3rd—5th cent. B.C.
INDIA, 6th cent. B.C.
SUMERIA
61 (W): *Eye cataract operations* appear to have been routine.

INDIA
62 (W): *Removal of anal fistulas.*

INDIA
63 (W): *Removal of neck tumors.*

INDIA
64 (W): *Tonsillectomies.*

INDIA
65 (W): *Lithotomies.*

PERU
INDIA
GUATEMALA
66 (W): *Caesarian operations.*

253

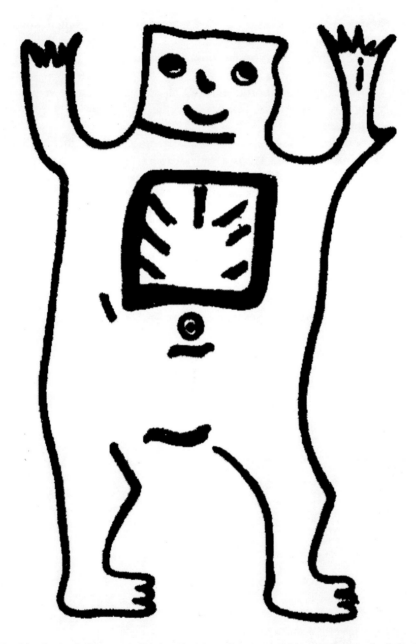

Fig. 24—1. A primitive cave drawing showing what we would identify today as a doctor's fluoroscope and human rib cage.

EGYPT
SUMERIA
PERU
BOLIVIA
67 (W): *Scientific bone surgery,* including scraping the inside of the bone; also bone transplants.

EGYPT
68 (W): *Artificial legs and hands.*
INDIA, 5th cent. B.C.
69 (W): *Plastic surgery.*

PERU
70 (W): *Sinus operations.*

INDIA
71 (W): *Nose transplants.*

SPAIN, 3rd cent. A.D.
PERU
72 (W): *Limb transplants:* In a pictured Spanish operation, the donor was a black man, the recipient a white nobleman. One surgeon is shown still holding the leg he has just amputated.[15] Had these surgeons acquired knowledge of the techniques of gifted surgeons from the dim past?

PERU
73 (W): *Lung, kidney and liver operations and transplants.*

INDIA, 8th cent. B.C.
CHINA, 300 B.C.
74 (W): *Other organ transplants.*

PALESTINE
ASSYRIA (IRAQ)
IRAN
75 (S): *Open-heart surgery:* The ribs were expertly cut, and once an opening had been made, the vacant ribs were further spread apart by retraction. There is evidence that the Russian patient survived 3 to 5 years. (Every feature corresponded to what today is called the "cardiac window," which enables surgeons to perform open-heart surgery.)

PERU[16]
CHINA, 403-221 B.C.
AFRICA, 3rd cent. B.C.
76 (W): *Heart transplants,* using techniques that seem modern by today's standards: The heart is taken out of the patient, who lies on a kind of operating table. Tubes feed him with infusions. A new heart is introduced. Two operators close the arteries. The opening in the chest is closed up.

SKULL OPERATIONS

EGYPT
77 (W): Surgery which required *opening the skull.*

PERU, c. 2000 B.C.
78 (S): Six *extremely fine wires* in the hollow skull of a human who had a bone infection.

SOVIET ARMENIA, c. 2000 B.C.
79 (S): *A bone plug* skillfully inserted into the skull of a woman who had suffered a head injury in her youth, which made a hole 1/4 inch and left bone tissue exposed. Her own cranial bone later grew around the plug and she lived to be about 35.[17] Remains found near Lake Sevan.

LAKE SEVAN, SOVIET ARMENIA
80 (S): *Splinters removed from the brain* of a woman who had received a head blow, in which a blunt object of 1-inch diameter punctured the skull and splintered the inner layers of cranial bone. Surgeons carefully cut a larger hole around the puncture to remove the splinters that had penetrated the brain. Evidence shows that she survived surgery for 15 years.[18]

Even by modern standards, such operations would be considered extremely difficult. Some of these operations are seen to be *technically superior* to modern-day surgery.

RUSSIAN CENTRAL ASIA
81 (S): Even older successful skull operations.

POLYNESIA
PERU

GUANCHES of CANARY ISLANDS
INDIA
TIAHUANACO, BOLIVIA
82 (S): *Trepanning* (setting a gold or silver plate over the brain when the skull has been injured): *Thousands* of skulls have been found in Peru with marks of *successful* trepanning. (One shows five successive trepannings.)
Incan graves show that *85* percent of patients survived!

This is a new technique in modern surgery. The same operation performed at the Hotel Dieu in Paris in 1786 was invariably fatal.
Yet the world is flattering itself today that never before in the history of man has there been such a brainy lot of scientists as are with us now. A simple case of egotism crowned with ignorance.

SUMERIA
83 (W): *Brain operations* were undertaken also in Sumeria.

Brain transplants? A suggestion that such operations once took place will be raised in Chapter 28.

DENTISTRY

MISSOURI, U.S.A. over 3,000 years ago
EGYPT
GUATEMALA
84 (S): *Dental fillings* were made in tooth cavities with a kind of cement. (The *crowns and cement fillings* in Mayan cavities still hold after 1,500 years!)

PERU
85 (S): *Gold inlays and capping.*

EGYPT
BAALBEK, LEBANON
86 (S): *The dental bridge:* Old teeth were placed in the hole between two healthy teeth and fastened with gold wire.

EGYPT
ARIZONA, U.S.A.
ETRUSCANS, ITALY

257

PERU

87 (S): *Artificial teeth,* which looked surprisingly like the product of a modern dentist. (In Arizona, gold artificial teeth; in Peru, teeth of rust-free iron.)

Chapter 25

Electricity—RUINS THAT GLOW IN THE NIGHT

Astonishing—but was it true?

On trek through the forbidding Matto Grosso region of Brazil in 1925, Colonel P.H. Fawcett, D.S.O., was challenged by native reports of mysterious cold lights in some ruined cities of the jungle.

Not only that. There existed, it was claimed, a city still living, inhabited, illuminated at night. Could this really be? Might there be some still surviving remnant of a long lost civilization, which was using "forgotten" knowledge?

Fawcett came out averring he had glimpsed one of these jungle cities. He reentered the region to further pursue his passion, but this time disappeared without trace.

It is noteworthy that few have ever set foot in this "terra prohibida" and returned.

A "lost world" indeed, it is a land infested with enormous swamp creatures, wild beasts and wilder men. This region is generally bounded by the Rio Xingu, the Rio Tapajos and the Amazon.

In regard to the supposed jungle lights, I am somewhat intrigued. The existence of devices which provided lighting at night in ancient times cannot be questioned, because so many classical writers describe them. I was dumbfounded to discover this.

Until 1890, we possessed only candles, torches and oil lamps, and it is easy to think that this was always the case.

However, we must now regard the past use of lighting and electricity as a historical certainty.

PRE-FLOOD

Electricity may have played a vital role in the operation of the Ark of Noah during the Great Flood. Referring to the Ark, two Hebrew words are translated as "window" in the English Bible.

In one reference (Gen. 8:6), the Hebrew word challon ("opening") is used—the window through which Noah released the birds.

The other reference (Gen. 6:16) uses a different word—tsohar, which is translated as "window" but does not mean window or opening at all! Where it is used (twenty-two times in the Old Testament), its meaning is given as "a brightness, a brilliance, the light of the noonday sun," referring to something that "glistens, glitters or shines," or "a light which has its origins in a shining crystal," according to many Jewish scholars of the traditional school.

For centuries Hebrew tradition has described the tsohar as an enormous gem or pearl hung in the Ark, which by some power within itself illuminated the entire vessel.[1]

SUMERIAN LEGEND
1 (W): In the preparation of the "huge boat," Utu (Methuselah) brought "his rays (of the sun) into the boat, in order to give it light."[2]

OLANCHA, CALIFORNIA, U.S. A
2 (S): Again, regarding that device resembling a spark plug found inside sedimentary stone. Examination showed an outer hexagonal layer of an unknown substance enveloping a 3/4-inch wide cylinder made of solid porcelain or ceramic. Circling the ceramic cylinder were rings of copper. In the center of the cylinder was a 2mm shaft of bright metal. The shaft was magnetic. The metallic shaft was corroded at one end, but the other end was affixed to a spring or helix of metal. The finely shaped ceramic and metallic shaft and copper components hint at some form of electrical instrument.[3]

This find, like so many others, is not generally publicized. It is considered too disturbing.

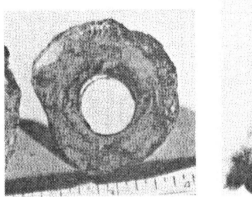
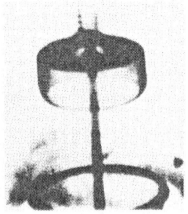

Fig. 25—1a. The Coso artifact, concreted over with fossil shells, after being sawn open.
Fig. 25—1b. X-ray of the left half of the stone reveals an obviously artificial device sealed within.

Fig. 25—1c. Top view of the left half of the object.
Fig. 25—1d and 1e. Side and top x-rays of the right half of the object reveal a similarity to a modern spark plug. (Photos: Ron Calais)

POST-FLOOD

Knowledge of electricity survived the Flood and in one form or another has surfaced throughout the centuries.

INDIA

3 (W): A high tower over a tomb discharged lightning against anyone who approached, striking them dead.

ISRAEL, 1000 B.C.

4 (W): "The house of Solomon the King was illuminated as by day, for in his wisdom he had made shining pearls which were like unto the sun, the moon and the stars in the roof of his house."[4]

FRANCE

5 (W): Electrical knowledge was preserved by the secret Hebrew society, the Kabala.

- A "dazzling lamp that lighted itself" (no oil or wick).
- A door knocker that shocked unwelcome visitors: A Jewish rabbi, named Jechiele, pushed a discharge button in his study, that sent an electric current into the iron knocker on his door.[5]

EGYPT

6 (W): A wall carving depicts a scene where attendants seem to be carrying giant light bulbs, with interior filaments in the shape of snakes, connected to a box or switch with braided cables, and which strongly suggest powerful electric lamps supported by high tension insulators.

(The cables are an exact copy of engineering illustrations as currently used. The cable is shown as very heavy and striated, indicating a bundle of many—multipurpose—conductors rather than a single high-voltage cable.)[6]

EGYPT

7 (W): In an Isis temple a lamp burned, which neither wind nor water could extinguish.

Until the invention of electric lighting in 1890, we possessed only candles, torches and oil lamps—light sources which smoked and left sooty deposits on ceilings.

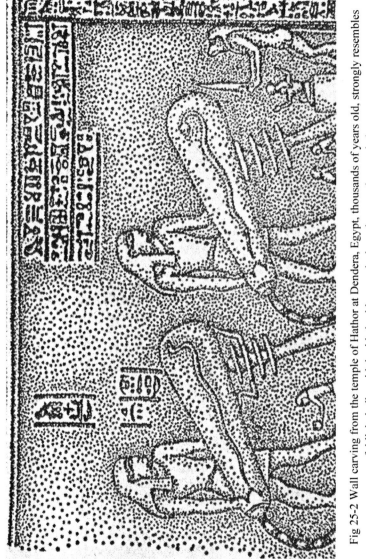

Fig 25-2 Wall carving from the temple of Hathor at Dendera, Egypt, thousands of years old, strongly resembles powerful light bulbs with braided cables attached to what may be a switch or generator.

263

Likewise the Greek and Roman world used torches and oil lamps for illumination—and wherever passageways are still standing between ancient buildings, traces of smoke can be found on the ceilings.

How, then, do we explain the following?

EGYPT

8 (S): No trace of smoke is found in any Egyptian pyramid or in the subterranean tombs of the Pharaohs—which are beautifully carved and painted in several colors. Work of this precision and delicacy requires the equivalent of daylight. (Some tunnels and passageways are too complex for a mirror system to have brought sufficient light into the inner chamber.)

WESTERN EUROPE

9 (S): The walls and c

PERU

10 (S): Low ceilings and passageways of Inca and pre-Inca ruins show no evidence of smoke blackening.

BRAZIL

11 (S): Explorer Fawcett found ancient dwellings in dead cities of the Matto Grosso devoid of lamp smoke.

EGYPT
BABYLON, 2000 B.C.
CENTRAL AUSTRALIA
CHINA
BULGARIA, 3000 B.C.

12 (S): Electroplated objects have been found, indicating the use of electricity.

IRAQ, 250 B.C. TO 650 A.D.

13 (S): Electric dry-cell batteries:[7]

- The first was discovered at Khujut Rabua, near Baghdad (2,000 years old).
- Four more were recovered at Seluecia, near Baghdad.
- Ten more later at Ctesiphon. These batteries are in tested working order, 6 inches high, and utilizing iron, copper, and electrolyte, with asphalt as an insulator.

Those at Ctesiphon were found broken down into their component parts, as though they had been mass-produced and their manufacturer had been interrupted before assembling the pieces into working batteries.

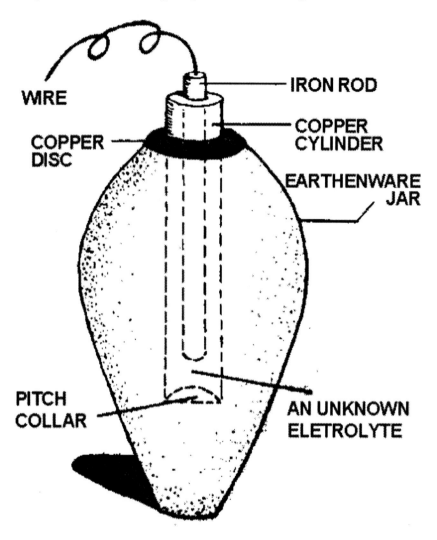

Fig 25-3 An electric battery from ancient Babylon. (Diagram by Andrew Tomas)

Fig 25-4 One of the electric batteries from ancient Babylonia

(A number of electroplated articles have been excavated in the same general area.)

INDIA
14 (W): Agastya, the wise man, is also known in history as "Kumbhayoni," from the word "kumbha" (jar), referring to the jars used by him to make batteries.

INDIA
15 (W): A document from the first millennium B.C. contains a detailed description, not only of how to construct an electric battery, but also how to utilize this battery to "split" water into two gases—the electrolysis of water into hydrogen and oxygen.[8]

ISRAEL
GREECE
EGYPT
ETRUSCANS
16 (W): Legends of lightning conductors and other forms of electricity come from varied sources.

SOUTH AMERICA
17 (S): Electric circuitry has been found.

CHINA-TIBET BORDER
18 (S): Electric disks: In caves, 716 stone disks with drawings and indecipherable hieroglyphics, thousands of years old, have been found. Each had a hole in the center like a gramophone record, from which a double groove traced out a spiral to the circumference. (These were not sound tracks, but a kind of writing.) The disks contained large amounts of cobalt and were rhythmically pulsating as though they had electric charges in them, or were part of an electric circuit.[9]

URAL MOUNTAINS, RUSSIA
19 (S): Gold prospectors are finding up to 40 feet underground ANCIENT, man-made and microscopically TINY artefacts—which resemble control elements used in our latest technology "nano machines". These micro-miniature devices are constructed to the "phi proportion". They have been examined by four scientific institutes in Russia and Finland. (*Report: Central Scientific Research Department of Geology and Exploitation of Precious Metals, Moscow*)

Who, thousands of years ago, was able to manufacture such micro-filigree objects—something our technology is only now just beginning to achieve?

EGYPT
20 (W): Flashes from the eyes of Egyptian idols, such as Isis, may have been produced by electricity, since strange appliances have been found in Egypt by Professor Denis Saurat.

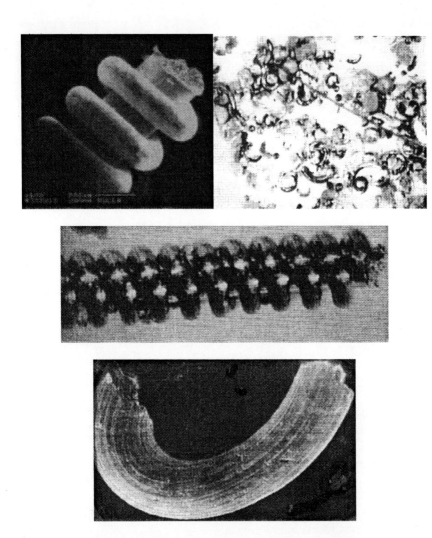

Fig 25-5 Some of the micro-miniature devices dug up in Russia. (Photos: Hausdorf/Moscow University)

EGYPT

21 (W): Ancient tradition speaks of moving walls, secret doors and flashes of light in the depths of pyramid passages. (A generator with an unlimited power supply could account for these phenomena.)

More recently, within the Great Pyramid a phenomenon has been detected which "defies all known laws of science and electronics." When an attempt was made with modern electronic equipment to chart the unseen interior, the readings were thrown into utter confusion.[10] Our Space Age scientists were baffled.

Somewhere inside the pyramid there appears to be a force field. The question arises, What is generating it?

EVER-BURNING LAMPS

ROME

22 (W): Numa Pompilius, the second king of Rome, had a perpetual light shining in the dome of his temple.

23 (W): A lamp which burned at the entrance to a temple to Jupiter-Ammon had remained alight for centuries. It could not be extinguished by wind or rain.

HIERAPOLIS, SYRIA, 2nd cent. AD.

24 (W): A shining jewel in the forehead of the goddess Hera brilliantly illuminated the whole temple at night.

LEBANON, 2nd cent.

25 (W): The temple of Jupiter in Baalbek was provided with a type of lighting generated by glowing "stones."26 (W): A beautiful lamp in the temple of Minerva could burn for a year. (AD. 70)

ANTIOCH, SYRIA, 6th cent.

27 (W): An ever-burning lamp was found with an inscription indicating it had been burning more than 500 years.

ENGLAND

28 (W): During the early Middle Ages, a third century perpetual lamp was found that had burned for several centuries.

ROME

29 (W): When the sepulchre of Pallis was opened in 1401, the tomb was found to be illuminated by a perpetual lamp which had been alight for more than 2,000 years.

(Nothing could put it out, until it was broken to pieces by desecrators.)

EDESSA, SYRIA, 11 cent.

30 (W): Kedrenus, the Byzantium historian, records having seen a perpetual lamp, which had been burning for 500 years.

AFRICA, 4th cent.

31 (W): St. Augustine described an everburning lamp he saw at the temple of Venus.

VIA APPIA, ROME

32 (W): A sealed mausoleum (with a sarcophagus containing the body of a shapely and beautiful patrician girl), opened in April 1485, contained at her feet a lighted lamp which had been burning for 1,500 years!

The body was that of Cicero's daughter, Tullia. She lay in an unknown, transparent, all-preserving fluid.

When the preserver was removed, her lifelike form with red lips and dark hair was seen by 20,000 people. The lamp continued to burn for some time.

EGYPT

33 (W): Many of these lighted lamps have been found in the subterranean vaults of Memphis, but after exposure to air, the lights went out.

INDIA

34 (W): A number of these lamps are known to have existed in Brahmin temples.

INDIA

35 (S): In a deep well inside the temple of Trevandrum, Travancore, was seen a great golden lamp which had been lit over 120 years before.

TIBET

36 (S): The Abbe Evariste-Regis Hue (1813—1860) claimed that he examined an ever-burning lamp.

INDIA
37 (O): There is an age-old tradition of the magic lamps of the Nagas, living in underground abodes in the Himalayas.

TIBET
38 (S): In the 1920s, in a dungeon beneath the Dalai Lama's monastery in Lhasa, two American travellers, Anderson and Shearer, saw a light that has supposedly burned for thousands of years.

FRANCE
39 (S): Some very strange and very beautiful lamps have been found at Lascaux, but we do not know how they worked.[11]

BRAZIL
40 (O): Again, in the 1920s, Colonel Fawcett was told by natives of the Matto Grosso forest that mysterious cold lights had been seen by them in lost cities. He reported, "The interior of the lofty buildings is lit up by a great square crystal on a pillar. So brightly does it shine that it makes the eyes blink and dazzle. It never goes out."[12]

BRAZIL
41 (S): In 1601, Barco Centenera, a memoirist of the Spanish conquistadores, described their discovery in the ruins of El Gran Moxo (an island city near the sources of the Rio Paraguay) of a large "electric" lamp in good working order: "On the summit of a 7-3/4 meter pillar was a great moon which illuminated all the lake, dispelling darkness."[13] Location: in the Matto Grosso, latitude 14 degrees 35 minutes south, longitude 57 degrees 30 minutes west, near the modern town of Diamantino.

BRAZIL
42 (O): According to the reports of several researchers during the early 1970s, an underground city, known by natives of the Ugha Mongulala tribe as Akakor, lies deep within the thick northwestern Brazilian jungle. Unknown machines lie therein, as do lights which never go out. Four human bodies have been seen, lying in a preserving liquid. The spot is considered sacred by the tribe.

ECUADOR
43 (O): Natives, who for years have been bringing ancient artifacts to the Maria Auxiliadora Museum in Cuenca, describe immense deserted cities which still shine with a mysterious, cool bluish light when the sun goes

down. Location: near Tayos, at the confluence of the Santiago and Morona Rivers—dense and dangerous jungle country.

Unfortunately, aerial exploration in this part of the world is virtually impossible.

COLOMBIA
44 (O): The Guarari Indians have a tradition that the ancient population of Colombia "made fire and light by strange means."

MEXICO
45 (O): A legend existed among the Maya and the Aztecs about cities where the lights never went out by day or night.

U.S.A.
46 (O): The Mandans (white Indians of North America) remember an age when their ancestors lived in "cities with inextinguishable lights beyond the sea."

U.S.A.
47 (O): The ethnographer Baker was told by a Canadian Indian, who was a wise man of a secret totemic society, about an ancient time when further south there were *"great shining cities"*.

PERU
48 (S): The 'Tombo del Yuca" bears an inscription which is phosphorescent and the top of the rock itself gives off a light like that of the ever-burning lamps. Location: At Ylo, on the Pacific coast south of Arequipa.

AUSTRALIA
49 (S): Only a few decades ago, three "'booyas" (round stones set in a large bamboo socket) existed in the Torres Strait Islands. When a chief pointed the round stone toward the sky, a thunderbolt of greenish blue flashed. This "cold light" was so brilliant that the spectators seemed to be enveloped in it.

INDONESIA
50 (S): A village in Irian Jaya, near Mt. Wilhelmina, has a layout of artificial illumination that in brightness is said to equal any system we have in the Western world.[14]

Travellers who penetrated this hamlet lost amid high mountains, said they 'were terrified to see many moons suspended in the air and shining with great brightness.'[15]

Other visitors have described these "moons" as 10-foot diameter spheres of stone that began to glow with a mysterious bright light as soon as the sun disappeared behind the tangled overgrowth of the jungle. Mounted on tall pillars, they glow with a strange neon-like light, illuminating all the streets.[16]

Perpetual lamps are found also in Islamic tradition. The secret was apparently universal.

The lamps functioned indefinitely without oil or any product that was burned or consumed. Touching them was prohibited under pain of provoking an explosion capable of destroying an entire town.

There is no doubt that the ancients knew of energies other than electric power, if they could construct perpetual lamps that burned for hundreds of years. Probably they had more sources of light than we can imagine. Did they utilize chemical power or some form of radiology?

It seems that they knew more about matter and light, about the ether and its properties, than the scientists of the twentieth century can ever know or imagine.

We know how to generate electricity from coal, from water power and from nuclear reactors. These scientists went much further. They were very likely able to extract free energy from the atmosphere for lighting, heating, moving great weights and for instruments used in household chores—not to mention defense, as we shall later observe.

VIEWING DEVICES

UXMAL, MEXICO
(S): John Stephens, nineteenth century explorer who relocated lost Maya cities, discovered an artifact he described as a smooth, black, glasslike surface, which priests consulted when making vital decisions. This magical black screen, used for communication—might we today have called it a television receiver?

INDIA 3000 B.C.
52 (W): An expert on the ancient document, the Rig-Veda (Padrhasi Sivirammamurti, a curator at the National Museum in New Delhi) claims that the Veda covers an entire range of technical knowledge, including television, in great detail.

EGYPT
53 (W): Wall engravings in the Temple of Dendera (of the Ptolemaic period) depict men handling what could be Crookes electron tubes, the forerunner of the modern television tube. (see Item 6)

BOOK OF ENOCH
54 (W): Azaziel taught men to make 'magic mirrors"; distant scenes and people could clearly be seen in them.

ROME
55 (W): Description of a "magic mirror": "It was a looking glass of enormous dimensions, lying over a well not very deep. Whoever goes down into this well, hears everything that is said upon earth. And whoever looks in the mirror, sees in it all the cities and nations of the world."[17]

Was this science fiction written for idle patricians or was it a chronicle of some past in which magic mirrors were as commonplace as they are today?

CHINA
56 (W): All descriptions of scientific development in China in the first millennium B.C. refer to "magic mirrors."

They are mirrors which have extremely complicated high reliefs on the back of the looking-glass.

When direct sunlight falls on the mirror, the high reliefs which are separated from the surface by a reflecting glass, become visible. This does not happen in artificial light.

If they are set up in pairs, they transmit images, like television.

The phenomenon is scientifically inexplicable, by present knowledge.

Some of these mirrors are still supposed to exist in private collections. We do not understand how they were made or what they were used for.

ARABIA
FRANCE
GREECE
ENGLAND
ISRAE
THE MAORI

57 (W, O): Old legends refer to "magic mirrors" or "glass globes" whereby the viewer could inspect and record events occurring at a great distance.

BRAZIL

58 (W): The remote western Amazon Ugha Mongulala tribe, who now live in a comparatively primitive state, have inherited an ancient written history which they still treasure. This chronicle states quite plainly that their former masters "had magic stones to look into the distance so that they could see cities, rivers, hills and lakes. Whatever happened on earth or in the sky was reflected in the stones."[18]

INDIA

59 (S): Early this century, Maxim Gorky, the celebrated Russian writer, met a Hindu yogi in the Caucasus, who asked Gorky if he wanted to see something in his album. Gorky said he wished to see pictures of India. The Hindu put the album on the writer's knees and asked him to turn the pages. These polished copper sheets depicted beautiful cities, temples and landscapes of India, which Gorky thoroughly enjoyed. When he finished looking at the pictures, Gorky returned the album to the Hindu. The yogi blew on it and smilingly said: "Now will you have another look?" Gorky recalls: "I opened the album and found nothing but blank copper plates without a trace of any pictures! Remarkable people, these Hindus!"[19]

CHINA

60 (W): Objects could be seen and heard many hundreds of miles away.

SPEAKING DEVICES

THE BIBLE

61 (W): The question was asked of Job (c. 2500 B.C.): "Canst thou send lightnings [electrical impulses] that they may go, and say unto thee, Here we are?"[20]

TIBET

62 (W): Speech at a distance was cultivated by the ancient Hsing Nu civilization.

PHOENICIA

63 (W): References to "speaking stones" and "animated stones" come from the twelfth century B.C. and the second century A.D.

64 (W): The Christian historian Eusebius carried a "speaking stone" on his chest, which answered his questions in a small voice resembling a "low whistling." (AD. 300)

65 (W): Arnabius confessed that whenever he got hold of a "speaking stone" he was always tempted to put in a question. The answer came in a "clear and sharp small voice." (AD. 300) Are we using these stones today, calling them transistors?

BABYLON
EGYPT
PERU
CLUSIUM, ITALY

66 (W): Singing buildings, singing and speaking statues (teraphim) and talking vases appear frequently in ancient records.

Chapter 26

Flight—THE MERCURY SECRET

S o you thought that manned flight began with the Wright Brothers in 1903?

Surprise!   Would you believe that flying machines could cross the oceans and cover the vast distances between continents in the earliest times?

Listen to this.   People all over the world have retained separate memories of a period when aviation was a well-known concept, and flight was a frequent occurrence.

What is more, their writings demonstrate a knowledge of aerodynamics and an awareness of the factors of take-off propulsion, braking and landing.

But first I should draw your attention to some giant drawings found all over the globe.   The question is, Why are so many of these designed to be seen only from above?

PETROGLYPHS MADE TO BE SEEN FROM THE AIR

ENGLAND

1 (S): The Long Man of Wilmington, Sussex, is *a human outline 226 feet long,* formed by an immense ditch.   The figure can be seen solely from above and even then one has to be high up.

ENGLAND

2 (S): The *Gog and Magog giants* on hills near Cambridge are of such dimensions as to suggest that their construction was controlled from the air.

ENGLAND

3 (S): There's a *360-foot-long white horse* at Uffington in the Berkshire Downs.

ENGLAND

4 (S): The famous *Cerne Abbas giant,* a 180-foot-human figure, is outlined by chalk trenches on a Dorset hillside.

ENGLAND

5 (S): The Great Zodiac of Glastenbury was *a huge stone calendar, laid out in a circle 30 miles in circumference,* and apparently meant to be seen from above.

WISCONSIN, U.S.A.

6 (S): Then there are the *Elephant and Serpent mounds* in Wisconsin.

CALIFORNIA, U.S.A.

7 (S): The *Mojave Maze.*

OHIO, U.S.A.

8 *(S): The Great Serpent mound* of Bush Creek over 1300 feet long. Its open jaws are 60 feet.

CALIFORNIA, U.S.A.

9 (S): *The horse,* 40 feet long; *the giantess* 87 feet high; and *the giant* 96 feet tall—all three at Bligh.

ARIZONA, U.S.A.

10 (S): The 150-foot-tall *giant* at Sacaton.

LOUISIANA, U.S.A.

11 (S): Six enormous *octagons with a total length of 11.2 miles,* near Poverty Point.

MADISON, WISCONSIN, U.S.A.
12 (S): *Colossal gravel carvings of birds* that measure 202 feet wing to wing.

KURINGAI CHASE, NEW SOUTH WALES, AUSTRALIA
13 (S): *A 58-foot whale and men up to 34 feet in length.*

PERU
14 (S): On the Nazca plain, pictures traced on the ground are *so large that they can be seen only from the air.* One is 825 feet long! An amazing series of geometric patterns, interspersed with artistically sophisticated pictures of flowers, birds, animals, insects and people, covers 30 square miles.

Why were they designed so big? Why were they made in such a way that they are perfectly visible from above, but impossible to spot from the ground?

(Thus they were not recognized for what they were until 1939, when a plane flew over them.)

Even the original artists could only have recognized the perfection of their creations from the air. What is more, a deviation of just a few inches would spoil the proportions, which, as we see them on aerial photographs, are perfect.

This is not on a human scale. It suggests, rather, a civilization of titans. And they evidently possessed highly developed instruments for reckoning. There are lines which go for miles, remaining absolutely straight while jumping over (or through) a mountain. They are laid out straighter than by the best of modern survey techniques.

TARAPACAR DESERT, CHILE
15 (S): *A stylized figure of a man is 330 feet long.*

PERU
CHILE
16 (S): There are said to be *many* other sites of the Nazca kind in Peru and Chile.

PERU
17 (S): The Candlestick of the Andes, *an 820-foot-high* three-armed stone trident on the cliffside of the Bay of Pisco, can be seen 12 miles out at sea; but *it is oriented skyward.* Lying in a bay, it cannot be seen from all

sides by passing ships and would have been excessively large for coastal shipping.

MACHU PICCHU, PERU
ZIMBABWE, RHODESIA
18 (S): In two ancient countries there survive high oval towers like silos which have no aperture in their walls, *as though they were designed to be entered only by flying beings.*

So much for vague speculation; let's advance to actual reports of manned flight—and better still, tangible evidence.

HANG GLIDING

CRETE
19 (W): A Greek legend relates that Daedalus *constructed wings* for himself and his son Icarus, whom he advised neither to fly high, lest the glue should melt in the sun and the wings should drop off, nor to fly too near the sea, lest the pinions be detached by the damp. Just a tale?

PERU
20 (S): Four pieces of Nazcan *fabric* from tombs were examined under a microscope. They proved to have *a finer weave than present-day parachute material and a tighter weave than that used by modern hot-air balloonists*— 205 X 110 threads per square inch, compared with 160 x 90.

PERU
21 (W): Many of the textiles from Nazca depict *flying men.*

PERU
22 (O): An Incan legend tells of a boy named Antarqui who *flew behind the enemy lines* and reported their positions—thus helping the Incas in battle.

FLIGHT

SUMERIA
23 (W): Sumerian cylinder seals show *great numbers of machines flying in the sky*, as matter-of-factly as if it were a daily occurrence.

BRITISH ISLES
24 (O): Druid legends speak of *"magical machines capable of travelling on land, sea and air"*. (One of them was the famous Roth Fail.)

CELTS, BRITAIN
25 (O): Bran's chariot *did not touch the water.*

CELTS
26 (O): Manannan's flying machine took him *from Ireland to England* by night.

DRUID TRADITION, BRITAIN
27 (O): Abiris, of Britain, travelled through the air to Greece, with the aid of a "golden arrow."

IRELAND
28 (O): Mog Ruith possessed a flying machine and engaged in an aerial battle over Ireland with a Druid rival.

His craft was not of metal but of stone. A portion of it was erected as a standing stone by his daughter, Tlachtga, at Cnamchoill near Tipperary.

DRUIDIC TRADITION
29 (O): Like Mog Ruith, Bladad (the father of King Lear) possessed a flying machine activated by the ley line energies. Both airborne vessels ended in disaster. Bladad's crashed at Ludgate Hill on the site of St. Paul's Cathedral.

(Often flights would end in disaster with an eclipse terminating the power source along the lines. This is scientifically valid—see Chapter 4, explaining ley lines.)

BRITISH ISLES
30 (O): Celtic traditions frequently describe "flying animals covered with iron armor, which have neither bones nor skeletons and which do not require food."[1]

CLOERA, IRELAND
31 (W): When the large metal anchor of *an aerial vessel* caught in the door of a church, the crew, unable to free it, cut the rope and the dirigible (?), liberated, sailed out of sight. (But the anchor remained fixed in the door for centuries, bearing witness to the event.)

BABYLON
32 (W): The "Halkatha" set of laws: *To operate a flying machine* is a great privilege. Knowledge of flying is most ancient, a gift of the gods for saving lives."[2]

CHALDEA, 3000 B.C.
33 (W): A detailed account (occupying almost 100 pages of English translation) instructs *how to build and operate an aircraft,* with the various parts such as vibrating spheres, graphite rods and copper coils. On the subject of flight, the writer comments on wind resistance, gliding and stability.[3]

ASIA MINOR
34 (W): A Hittite tale describes a search for the missing Telepinu, in which 'Shamash sent out *"a swift eagle"* to find him.

ASSYRIA, 1500 B.C.
35 (W): A seal engraving shows two *"eagle men"* saluting a tower. Numerous depictions of such "eagles" (or bird men) have been found—men wearing costumes or uniforms that gave them an eagle appearance.

BABYLON, 2700 B.C.
36 (W): The *Epic of Etana* describes *a flight miles in altitude by means of an eagle.*

In July 1969, Neil Armstrong, from the Apollo II spacecraft, beamed back the message: "The *eagle* has landed."

"Eagle" was the name of the separation lunar module that landed on the moon. When it first separated from the orbiting spacecraft, the astronauts told mission control, "The *eagle* has wings."

"Eagle" was the symbol of the astronauts also, worn as an emblem on their suits. As in the Babylonian story, they were "eagles" who could fly and speak.

MESOPOTAMIA

37 (W): Other texts speak of kings *"flying on the wings of birds";* of "rising from the lower horizons to the lofty ones"; and of a flying god "who stretched over unknown distances, for countless hours."

(Even in recent times, African Bantu natives described a geologist's light aircraft as *a giant bird* with the roar of a thousand lions!)

IRAN

38 (W): Taimuraz, the third king of Iran, visited a statue cave gallery in the mountains of Khaf (Caucasus) *on a winged steed* (aircraft).

CHINA, 2258—2208 B.C.

39 (W): Emperor Shun not only *constructed a flying craft,* but also *tested a parachute.*

CHINA, 1766 B.C.

40 (W): Emperor Cheng Tang ordered *a flying apparatus* built and run on a test flight to Honan province.

CHINA, 340—278 B.C.

41(W): In a poem entitled "Li Sao", Chu Yuan tells of an aerial voyage he made at a great height in the direction of the Kun Lun Mountains. This *aerial survey in a jade-colored craft* described how it was unaffected by the wind and dust far below.[4]

CHINA, 4th cent. A.D.

42 (W): *A helicopter:* A "flying car" of wood possessed "rotating blades" that caused the car to travel skyward.

CHINA

43 (W): Paintings in an underground passage system (discovered 1961) show *men on a "flying shield"* dressed in modern jackets and long trousers blowing darts at fleeing animals.

CHINA

44 (W): A stone carving on a grave depicts a dragon chariot flying high *above the clouds.*

CHINA
45 (W): *There exist numerous other legends* about "aerial carriages", "wooden birds" and "flying dragons."

CHINA
46 (W): Unlike ourselves, the Chinese did not have to invent a new term when the airplane appeared this century: they already had one in their vocabulary—"fei chi" *(flying chariot).*

CEYLON, 4th cent. A.D.
47 (W): Gunarvarman travelled *in a flying craft to Java—a distance of 2,000 miles.*

TIBET
48 (W): Records describe *two warring nations who used flying vehicles* and fiery weapons.

TIBET
49 (W): According to an ancient document, *the knowledge of the flying machines ("pearls of the sky") "is secret and not for the masses."*[5]

CHINA-TIBET BORDER
50 (W): Inscriptions relate that "the Dropa descended from the clouds on their machines"; they *lost their aircraft during a dangerous landing in high mountains* and suffered great grief in their failure to build a new one.

TIBET
51 (W): According to the Indian epic, *Ramayana,* Rama *flew in a controlled aerial vehicle from Ceylon* to Mount Kailas (in Tibet).

TIBET
52 (W): A Tibetan text contains a description of *an "enormous flying wagon made of a black metal with an iron base, not drawn by horses or elephants but by machines as large as those animals.*[6]

TIBET
53 (W): An old book bound in animal hide and tied with leather thongs, shows a drawing of *an egg-shaped device flying over a high mountain.*

RUSSIA
54 (W): There survives *an ancient relief of an airship.*

NEPAL

55 (W): At the command of his king, Rumanvit requested the court designers to construct a flying vehicle, but they informed him that they were unable. They knew the workings of many machines, but *the secret of flying machines was known only to the "Yavanas"*. A Yavana eventually came from the west and fulfilled the king's wish to see the world from the air, but without revealing to him the mechanics of flying.[7]

"Yavana" is derived from Javan, a grandson of Noah, whose descendants inhabited *Greece and Mediterranean islands* several centuries after the Flood. Noorbergen ventures the opinion that there was "a conscious effort on the part of the high civilization centers not to proliferate advanced technology among those post-Babel peoples who had lost knowledge, but rather to keep that technology for their own use and power."[8]

And speaking of the Yavanas (the Greeks)...

GREECE, 400-365 B.C.

56 (W): Archytas of Tarentum set in motion *a flying machine* in the form of a wooden dove by means of compressed air.

GREECE

57 (W): Grecian legends of *"winged beasts" and "winged sandals"* may all be poetically distorted remembrances of ancient aircraft.

It would appear that winged representations throughout the world are nothing more than the memory of facts far in the past. It is the core of the myth, saga or legend that has to be grasped.

ETHIOPIA

58 (W): Familiar to us all is the Bible story of the visit to King Solomon by a queen from the south.

Now comes the discovery of the Ethiopian epic *Kebra Nagast* (c. 850 B.C.), which tells the story from the other side. It records that King Solomon of Israel lavished on a visiting Ethiopian queen enormous riches and gifts...and a vessel wherein one could traverse the air." Carrying a cargo of animals as well as men, via Egypt, it "travelled in one day a distance which (usually) took three months to traverse."[9]

INDIA

59 (O): In Srinagar, India, is a mountain called Tahkti Suleiman ("Solomon's Mountain").

Very strange that a mountain in India's highlands should be named after a Hebrew king—except that Mohammedan tradition declares King Solomon flew there in a flying machine and arranged for the construction of the temple on the summit.

INDIA

60 (W): One type of aircraft used in India was *as big as a temple and five stories high.*[10]

INDIA

61(W): *The Mahabharata* (written 500 B.C., but referring to a period 1,000 to 2,000 years earlier) makes repeated references to great god-kings riding about in *vimanas* or "celestial cars," described as *"aerial chariots with sides of iron clad with wings".* They were used both for peaceful transportation and in war.

There is mention of some flying cars which have crashed and are out of action, others standing on the ground, others already in the air.

The vimana was *shaped like a sphere* and borne along at great speed on a mighty wind generated by mercury. It *moved in any way the pilot might desire, up or down, forward or backward.*

INDIA

62 (W): *The Ramayana* (likewise very ancient) describes one vimana as *"furnished with window compartments and excellent seats."*

"Bhima flew along in his car, resplendent as the sun and loud as thunder...The flying chariot shone like a flame in the night sky of summer."

The vimana was *a double-deck circular aircraft with portholes and a dome.* It flew with the "speed of the wind" and gave forth a "melodious sound." A pilot had to be well trained; otherwise no vimana was placed in his hands. The craft *performed maneuvers which only helicopters can do partially today, i.e., stop and remain motionless* in the sky.

Detailed descriptions of the ocean and landscape from a great aerial height are given.

The vimanas were *kept in hangars,* and employed for *warfare, travel* or *sport.* "A vimana *rose vertically into the air* with a whole family on board, and with a tremendous noise."

INDIA

63 (W): The ancient *Samarangana Sutradhara* relates that *"the chariot was automatic; big and well-painted, it had two floors and many rooms and windows."*

This document deals with take-off, *cruising for thousands of miles,* normal and forced landings, and even with possible collisions of aircraft with birds.

The advantages and disadvantages of *different types of aircraft* are discussed at length, as to their relative capabilities of ascent, cruising speed and descent, and recommendations given regarding suitable metals for construction.

Also dealt with are informative details on how to take pictures of *enemy planes,* methods of determining their approach pattern, means of rendering their pilots unconscious, and how to destroy enemy planes. The secret of making planes invisible, and the secret of hearing conversations and other sounds in enemy planes is documented.

A description of *the fuel power source:*

"Within it must be placed the mercury engine, with its heating apparatus made of iron underneath.

"In the larger craft, because it is built heavier, four strong containers of mercury must be built into the interior. When these are heated by controlled fire from the iron containers, the vimana possesses thunder power through the mercury. The iron engine must have properly welded joints to be filled with mercury, and when fire is conducted to the upper part, it develops power with the roar of a lion. By means of *the energy latent in mercury,* the driving whirlwind is set in motion, and the traveller sitting inside the vimana may travel in the air, to such a distance as to look like a pearl in the sky."

The intricate knowledge of aircraft and flying was deliberately controlled by a select few.

Precautions were taken against industrial espionage and unlicensed manufacture.

The mercury was heated by "a special flame capable of being directed." (A laser?)

Sir Isaac Newton wrote: "Because the way by which mercury may be impregnated, it has been thought fit to be concealed by others that have known it, and therefore may possibly be an inlet to something more noble, not to be communicated without immense danger to the world."[11]

What it is about mercury that could be of "immense danger" to the world we do not know. Yet it seems apparent that the ancients were well aware of the practical application of mercury.

The secret is still beyond our present technology. However, at an international space congress in Paris, in 1959, there was talk of producing an "iono-mercurial engine"; and in 1966 the French were planning to launch a satellite powered by a "mercury solar furnace".

TURKESTAN
GOBI DESERT

64 (S): Russian excavators recently discovered in caves what may be *age-old instruments used in aircraft flight.* These are hemispherical objects of glass or porcelain, ending in a cone, each carefully sealed and each containing *a single drop of mercury*[12]

INDIA

65 (W): *The Mahavira* records that "an aerial chariot, the Pushpaka, conveys many people to the ancient capital of Ayodhya. *The sky is full of stupendous flying-machines,* dark as night, but picked out by lights with a yellowish glare."[13]

INDIA

66 (W): *The Vedas* tell us of vimanas *of various types and sizes:* the "agnihotravimana" with two engines, the "elephant vimana" with more, and other types named after the kingfisher, ibis, etc.—very much as we now christen aircraft types. Doesn't that flying "elephant" remind one of our "jumbo" jets?

INDIA

67 (W): *The Valmiki* says: "The sky chariot...is gilded and lustrous throughout...it leaps above the hill and the wooded valley, winged like lightning...covered in smoke and flowing lamps, speedy and round of prow."[14]

INDIA

68 (W): The Sanskrit term "vimana vidya" means *the science of building and piloting airships.*

INDIA

69 (W): *G.R.* Josyer, director of the International Academy of Sanskrit Research in Mysore, has translated into English the 3,000-year-old *Vymanika Shastra,* meaning "the Science of Aeronautics".[15] It has eight chapters *(6,000 lines), with diagrams, on the construction of three types of aircraft.*

Information covers:

- The design of a helicopter-type cargo plane and drawings for double- and triple-decked passenger planes for as many as 500 people.
- Plans for an aircraft that flew in the air, travelled under water, or floated pontoonlike on the water.
- The qualifications and training of pilots.
- The planes were equipped with cameras, radio and a kind of radar, as well as apparatuses that could not catch fire or break.
- Instructions on how to make the aircraft invisible to enemies, how to paralyze other aircraft, how to create the illusion of a star-spangled sky, how to zig-zag in the sky like a serpent, how to see inside an enemy's airplane, how to spy on "all activities going on down below on the ground".
- Also the correct proportions of certain chemicals which will envelop the aircraft and give it the appearance of a cloud.

This document contains formulas which would make our aircraft manufacturers gape in astonishment, and if mastered would herald a new era in aviation.

INDIA

70 (W): The wise sage Agastya is credited, among other things, with having *built an airship.*

INDIA

71(W): *The Pantachantra* records that six young men constructed a *dirigible airship* which could take off, fly or land. The zeppelin was operated by a complex control system, providing a safe, fast flight and perfect maneuverability.

EGYPT

72 (W): A legend tells of a king within the belly of *a "white bird"* which came down in a *"trail of fire."*

EGYPT
73 (S): *Fourteen model airplanes* found in various tombs may be replicas of full size airplanes of over 2,000 years ago.

One model recently flew perfectly, demonstrating a knowledge of aerodynamics on the part of its makers.[16]

As most Egyptian tomb models are linked to larger originals, it is possible that under the desert sands there may be remains of life-size gliders.

Clearly the models were not accidental or merely toys. Rather, they were the end product of an enormous body of computation and experimentation, embodying principles of aircraft design that have taken European and American designers a century of experimental work to discover and perfect.

EASTER ISLAND
74 (W): Easter Island fragments speak of—*"flying men in hats"*.

AUSTRALIA
75 (O): An Arnhem Land Aboriginal legend speaks of *a great silver bird which landed* upon a plateau to lay a big silver egg *out of which the first tribesmen hatched.* They were white-skinned.

AUSTRALIA
76 (O): A legend from the Ayers Rock region recalls *a great red-colored egg which tried to land safely but broke (crash-landed). Out of it emerged white people and their children.*

In time the great egg rusted away until its remains had merged with the ground.

AUSTRALIA
77 (O): The Dharuk tribe of New South Wales spoke of *Biramea the Bird Man, who laid a great egg* near the present town of Linden, *from which their ancestors hatched.*

PONAPE ISLAND
78 (O): Light-skinned men came from the west in *"shining boats"* that *"flew above the sea".*

Their stay was brief, but the natives still speak of the "magical works" the ancient Westerners performed.

MANGAREVA, GAMBIER ISLAND
79 (O): A *"flying canoe"* with great wings *"clasped tightly to the side"* appeared and its pilots were *able to fly great distances—as* far as the Hawaiian Islands, nearly *2,500 miles away.*

ISLAND OF TARA-VAI
80 (W): A detailed description and an actual artist's model of the ancient flying canoe.

(The wings in particular remind one of the winged solar disk of Horus, pictured in Egyptian art.)

NEW ZEALAND
81 (O): Maori legends speak of Pourangahua, who flew from Hawaiki to New Zealand on a magic bird. "I come and a new heaven turns above me" (refering to the Southern Hemisphere sky, with different constellations above.)

NEW ZEALAND
82 (O): Maui "fished up" (or discovered) *the North Island of New Zealand,* which is called "the fish of Maui" and *is shaped like a ray-fish* with its open mouth in the south and the long tail in the north with one fin on the hook—but this shape can only be seen on the map, or from high above the earth!

GREENLAND
83 (O): Certain Eskimo tribes *were flown* from Central Asia to t

BRITISH COLUMBIA, CANADA
84 (O): The Haida Indians in the Queen Charlotte Islands retain the tradition of great sages who *descended from the sky on "disks of fire".*

CANADA
85 (O): Canadian Indians tell of the ancient times when "demons came and made slaves of our people and sent the young to die among the rocks and below the ground (mining?). But then arrived *the thunderbird,* and our people were freed. We learned about the marvellous cities of the thunderbird, which were beyond the big lakes and rivers to the south.

"Many of our people left us and saw these shining cities and witnessed the grand homes and the mystery of *men who flew upon the skies.* But then the demons returned, and there was terrible destruction. Those of our people who had gone southward returned to declare that all life in the cities was gone—nothing but silence remained."[17]

The name "thunderbird" (or "firebird") is used by the Indians of the U.S.A., Canada and Alaska. This is the animal we see at the top of the totem pole.

U.S.A.
86 (O): The Hopi Indians of the southwest United States have a similar tradition of *people who made a "patuwvota" which soared through the sky. On this, many of them flew to attack a great city.*
Soon others from many nations were making "patuwvotas" and flew to attack one another.[18]

U.S.A.
87 (O): Piute Indians tell of the "Hav-Musuvs" who travelled from the Gulf of California to Death Valley (when it was still green and fertile) and built subterranean cities in caves.
They *flew in huge silent craft, which had weapons.*

MEXICO
88 (W): Paintings in Mexico City show *Quetzalcoatl flying in a winged ship.* He is said to have descended at Vera Cruz.

TABASCO, MEXICO
89 (W): A carved monolith portrays *a man sitting inside a dragon, his feet working pedals,* his left hand on a "gear lever," his right hand carrying a small box, his head enveloped in a helmet; directly in front of his lips is an apparatus that might be identified as a microphone.

MEXICO
90 (W): King Netzahualcoyotl of the Aztecs *designed aircraft.*

MEXICO
91 (W): *Pictorial representations of what appear to be aircraft or rockets* have been increasingly identified or recognized in the art of the ancient cultures of Central and South America.

MEXICO
92 (W): Maya documents from Yucatan speak of *"creatures arriving on flying ships."*

SALVADOR, BRAZIL

93 (W): An unearthed vase shows *men flying above a group of palms in curious machines which leave a trail of smoke behind them.*[19]

COSTA RICA
VENEZUELA
COLOMBIA

94 (S): *Models resembling modern jet airplanes* have been discovered in various tombs.

They possess delta wings, engine housing, a cockpit, windshield, flanged tail and elevators.

These models have passed aerodynamic tests; fourteen models are known to exist, some with two sets of wings.[20]

BRAZILIAN JUNGLE

95 (0): Fables tell of *"wizards in flying boats"* who stayed briefly, then *"flew away on their colored ships."*

PERU

96 (0): There are many Peruvian legends telling of *men who flew.*

BOLIVIA

97 (W): There are three rows of *"flying kings"* on the gateway of the Sun at Tiahuanaco.

BOLIVIA

98 (0): Indians of the La Paz region say that thousands of years ago their ancestors travelled in *great golden disks which were kept airborne by means of sound vibrations at a certain pitch, produced by continual hammer blows.*

Kept airborne by the vibrations of continual hammer blows? *(Point 98)* Really???

You know, this is not so absurd. Vibrations of a set frequency may have had the effect of increasing the atomic energy of gold, thus reducing the weight of the disk and enabling it to overcome the force of gravity.

In what is now a dead city of the Deccan (in India) monks today are said to free metals from terrestrial gravity and endow them with energy. The method? Striking them incessantly with tiny hammers; it is the sound thus produced which effects the change.

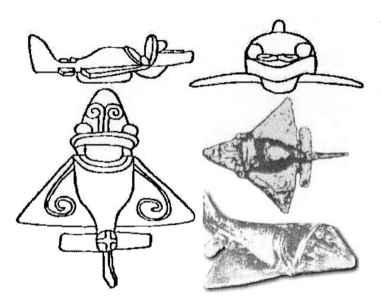

Fig. 26—1a. A gold jet from Colombia, South America. Its features are more mechanical than biological. Experts at the Aeronautical Institute of New York concur that it does not represent any known type of winged creature. It appears to be a model of an ancient jet aircraft.

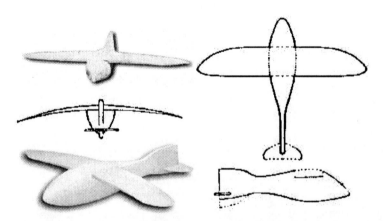

Fig. 26—1b. This object, once thought to be a bird, was found in a tomb at Saqqara, Egypt, in 1898. Stuffed in a box of bird models in one of Cairo Museum's store-rooms, it was rediscovered in 1969 and found to fly perfectly as a glider, though there are indications that it may originally have possessed a propulsion mechanism at the tail. The design is highly sophisticated.

Certain crystals can make a connection between mechanical and electrical energy—the so-called piezoelectric effect. A sharp blow to a quartz crystal under pressure can cause thousands of volts of electricity to be discharged from it.

In photography, the modern Flipflash-10, a rectangular flash that lasts for ten pictures, receives its electricity from a piezoelectric crystal inside the camera. When struck by a tiny hammer triggered by the shutter, this crystal converts the mechanical impact into electrical energy.

(Why not experiment for yourself? If you strike a block of quartz with a hammer, a burst of power will cause a hundred-watt globe wired to it to blaze up momentarily.)

...Even as I write, fresh developments emerge. Researcher William Deiches has discovered something most surprising.

EGYPT

99 (S): A breastplate found in the tomb of Tutankhamen bore a diagram which upon analysis was found to depict parts of a plane. (Like other unexplained tomb drawings, it had long been considered just a pretty picture.) In 1982, Deiches built from the diagram a working model—and yes, it flew!

Deiches' theory that aircraft were in regular use 4,000 years ago so impressed the British Royal Aeronautical Society that in August 1984 they endorsed his plan to obtain a financial sponsor so that he can build a replica of this ancient plane.

MIGHT ANCIENT AIRCRAFT BE FOUND?

One is led to contemplate the intriguing possibility, however remote, of such a discovery. Craft could be of any size and of surprising shapes.

Did you notice how frequently ancient flying machines were described as shaped like an "egg", a "hat", a "sphere" or a "disk"? (See items 53, 61, 62, 74, 75, 76, 77, 84 and 98.)

While it is the purpose of this work to present positive knowledge rather than vague speculation, I submit the following reports as a matter of interest.

Consider them in the context of what has preceded. After all, Professor W.B. Emery, who had spent most of his life digging in Egypt, did say, "There is more lying under the sands than has ever been found."

EGYPT

100 (S): During the early period of Egypt's overtures with Israel, permission was accorded to Israeli archaeologists (if we are to accept one magazine report) to dig near the Snofru Pyramid at Dahshur.

Late in February 1979, at a depth of 50 feet, they broke into a cave, which to their astonishment contained a 40-foot disk-shaped craft. Photographs of the craft, which was equipped with ultrasophisticated devices, were delivered to Israel's Defense Ministry.

On March 2, in a lightning raid, Golani Brigade commandos took charge of the object. It was brought to Tel Aviv.

Initial tests with weaponry as well as with rejuvenating chemicals found on board allegedly left officials half-stunned.

Egyptian archaeologists shortly after unearthed a second craft under the Bent Pyramid and were under pressure to release it to the United States.[1]

I suspect that this report may not be verifiable due to policies of secrecy on the part of the three governments. Nevertheless, some credibility is suggested in light of the following fact.

EGYPT

101 (W): While visiting Lhasa, Tibet, in the 1920s the American travellers Anderson and Shearer were shown statements from ancient manuscripts to the effect that an airship was buried inside the Great Pyramid at Giza, Egypt.[2]

It should be noted that this information is independent from the first both in place and time.

BRAZIL

102 (0): Deep in the jungles of northwestern Brazil the Ugha Mongulala tribe have severed contact with the outside world. In 1972, their chief Tatunca supplied to Karl Brugger details concerning underground chambers littered with metal objects and equipment. One relic is asserted to be a rocketlike flying machine with a brilliant golden sheen. It can hold only two men and is described as having neither sails nor rudder. Nearby sits a strange bowl-shaped vehicle with seven long legs which "resemble curved bamboo sticks and are moveable."[3]

It must be said that certain additional features in the chief's account are consistent with discoveries on other continents. He referred to:

1. Ever-burning lights (see Chapter 25, items 21 to 49).
2. Bodies immersed in a preserving fluid (compare Chapter 25, item 31).
3. Corpses with six fingers and toes. Similarly endowed humans appear in biblical records[4] and in recent tomb discoveries.

In my opinion, such unlikely elements in the tale of a remote tribesman do tend to endow the report, as a whole, with a certain credibility.

Investigation of Tatunca Nara on other matters has disclosed the fact that on each point where his credibility can be checked, he has told the truth.

On September 25, 1972, at the chief's invitation, Brugger and a cameraman set out on a six-week journey from Manaus to Tatunca's distant jungle homeland. Ultimately the "green hell", with its savage surprises, took its mental and physical toll. The two Europeans were forced to turn back when only ten days from their destination. The chief, garbed in loincloth and paint, continued on alone.

ENERGY SOURCES

In this chapter, we have detected traces of an ancient power technology more advanced than our own:

1. *Energy from sound waves generated by magnetized rods or hammering* (see item 98).

    Sanskrit books state plainly that aircraft could be driven solely by the power of sound, tunes and rhythms.

    Interestingly, in modern automobile tests, an ultrasonic reactor attached to a carburetor almost doubled petrol mileage with very little exhaust gas. This simple gadget was based on a system of harmonic resonance within the atomic structure of liquids.
2. *The power latent in mercury* (see items 61, 63 and 64).
3. *Electromagnetic energy obtained directly from the atmosphere* (see item 29; also Chapter 27, item 1; and Chapter 28, item 25).

A number of scientists believe that electromagnetic energy supersedes the orthodox laws of gravity. The fundamental characteristics of gravity still elude analysis by modern physics.

Were you aware that magnetic currents can be used not only to neutralize gravity but as motive power?

Spinning objects made of selected materials have been shown to generate an electromagnetic energy field when placed in rapid relative motion. If this force field is made to undulate, a secondary gravitational field is produced, which can "neutralize" earth's gravity.

Disk airfoils three feet in diameter and incorporating an electrical condenser charged with 150 kilovolts have been made to fly under their own power. The disks moved under the influence of interaction between electrical and gravitational fields, in a fifty-foot-diameter course.

An electromagnetic force field would cause the vibratory frequency of an object to be altered in such a way that it opposes the frequency of the gravitational field. It would act upon all parts of the craft simultaneously. A vehicle thus propelled would be able to change direction, accelerate to thousands of miles an hour, or stop.

Do you see, man now uses the sledge-hammer approach to high-altitude, high-speed flight. He has to increase power in the form of brute thrust many times over in order to achieve just twice the speed.

By his present methods, man actually fights against the forces that resist his efforts.

But in using a gravitic field to provide the basic propulsive force, he would make his adversary work for him. If the coupling effect between gravity and electricity can actually be harnessed and used for propulsion purposes, then we would have a free and inexhaustible power supply.

If we could thus conquer gravity, the headaches of transmission of power from the engine to wheels or propellers would cease to exist. The oil-consuming car engine and hydroelectric generators would become obsolete. The work of the world could be done with tiny amounts of energy. Construction of large buildings and bridges would be revolutionized by temporary induced weightlessness.

I think you'll agree, we seem to have lost something.

Chapter 27

To the moon and beyond—WERE WE ON THE MOON IN 2309 B.C.?

In 1926, Professor A.W. Bickerton declared the concept of shooting at the moon to be foolish and impossible. In 1935, the noted astronomer F.R. Moulton wrote that man could never travel in outer space. In 1957, Dr. Richard van der Riet Wooley (former Astronomer Royal) called the idea of space travel "utter bilge". Eight months later *Sputnik I* was orbiting the earth.

In a remote northern area of Tibet lie the ruins of the Hsing Nu capital, discovered by Duparc in 1725.

Within the city, Duparc came upon a mass of monoliths (once coated with silver), a pyramid, part of a tower of blue porcelain, and a royal palace, containing thrones with sun and moon images. There was also a large milky white stone surrounded by exquisite drawings.

Now for the stunning sequel. In 1952, a Soviet expedition arrived. The group was shown by Tibetan monks some ancient documents, whose descriptions agreed with those of Duparc.

But here is the breathtaking part: the milky white stone, so said the documents, was "brought from the moon."

Moon rock? Is it possible? Could man actually have left this earth and gone to the moon in ages past? Was space travel a natural adjunct to his civilization? Are there clues?

Indeed there are. Indications of the reality of ancient space travel do come from widely separated parts of the world. Written and oral tradition is widespread—and, it seems, reliable.

Chinese historians in particular never tried to please their rulers at the expense of truth. Death was preferred to untruthful reports of history. As an example we have the fate of historians in the reign of Chi in 547 B.C. We should therefore take seriously the historical reports of China, even if they seem at first to he far-fetched.

There is a tendency in scientific circles nowadays to regard ancient documents and even mythology and folklore - as sources of history. Anthony Roberts expresses it this way: "Legends are like time-capsules that preserve their contents through ages of ignorance."[1]

In regard to some of the chronicles cited hereafter, internal evidence will carry its own proofs of authenticity.

My first source is an old manuscript described by James Churchward, the English scholar who wrote decades before people spoke of artificial satellites and spaceships.[2]

INDIA

1 (W): *Vehicles that could revolve around the earth (i.e., satellites):* "Their fuel is drawn from the air in a very simple and cheap way. The motor is something like a modern turbine: it works from one chamber to another and does not stop or stall unless switched off. If nothing happens it continues to function. The ship in which it is built *could revolve as long as it liked around Earth, only falling when the parts of which it is made were burnt up.*

INDIA

2 (W): Philosophers and scientists who *orbited the earth* "below the moon and above the clouds" are spoken of in the ancient *Surya Siddhanta.*[3]

Giant satellites made of shiny metal and turning about an axis are described in detail in ancient Sanskrit texts, right down to their dimensions and interiors, as well as smaller craft that fly between them and the earth.

CHALDEA

3 (W): *Two "modern" rockets emitting rays at the rear,* a box like a loudspeaker and a "copy" of a Gemini capsule—are engraved on a copper chisel unearthed at Ur.

SUMERIA

4 (W): Pictographic texts describe three related objects on display in Sippar: the golden sphere (command module?), the "GIR" (a long arrow-shaped object, divided into several compartments) and the "alikmahrati," meaning "advancer that makes vessel go" (i.e., a motor, or an engine). *Together they look very much like a three-part rocket ship.*

Another explicit sign is the combination of two words "DIN" and 'GIR." When joined together to form the word "gods," *the tail of the finlike "gir" fits perfectly into the opening of the rocketlike "din,"* which exhausts fire from its tail.

PERU

5 (W): A clay vessel 8½ inches high portrays *a kind of "space capsule" on which motor and exhaust are clearly recognizable.*

ITALY

6 (W): A painting discovered in the niche of a room under Rome's Palatine Hill, in 1961, portrays *what appears to be a rocket. It stands on a launching pad. From it run guys or cables; behind is a tall wall, resembling a counterblast wall.*

JAPAN

7 (S): Excavations have uncovered clay figurines of *people clad in peculiar "space suits", with helmets entirely covering their heads.* On the helmets are representations of something like *slit-type glasses, breath - filters, antennae, hearing aids and even night-sight devices.*

INDIA

8 (W): *The Mahabharata* describes "two storey sky chariots with many windows, ejecting red flame, that race up into the sky until they look like comets...*to the regions of both the sun and the stars.* "[4]

GUATEMALA

9 (W): Another ancient description mentions "a circular chariot of gold, measuring 12,000 cubits in circumference and *able to reach the stars*"[5]

INDIA

10 (W): Other references speak of:

- Pushan sailing in golden ships across the ocean of the sky
- Garuda (a celestial bird) carrying Lord Vishnu in cosmic journeys

- Aerial flights "through the region of the sky firmament which is above the region of the winds"[6]
- The *Ancients of Space Dimensions.*[7]

NEW ZEALAND
11(O): Maori legends tell of flying *machines and journeys to the moon.*

CHINA, 3rd cent. B.C.
12 (W): Chuang Tzu, in a work entitled *Travel to the Infinite,* relates *a trip he made into space to 32,500 miles from the earth.*

TIBET
MONGOLIA
13 (W): Ancient Buddhist books speak of *"iron serpents which devour space with fire and smoke, reaching as far as the distant stars."*

TIBET
14 (W): The three levels of a pyramid in the Hsing Nu capital commemorated three historical periods in the remote past: the pre-space travel era, the time *when men were able to visit one of the heavenly bodies,* and then afterward when they came back to earth and lost the power of space travel. It was here that there reposed on the altar *a "stone brought from the moon".*

BABYLON
15 (W): The *Epic of Etana* (4,700 years old) supplies us with *very accurate descriptions of the earth's surface from progressive* altitudes— descriptions which were not verified in our own era until the high-altitude aerial flights of the 1950s and the first space shots of the 1960s.

The description of this ancient space flight depicts exactly what happens when man leaves the earth (the concept of the round earth which becomes small, due to perspective as distance increases, and changes into particular colors).[8]

BOOK OF ENOCH
16 (W): The *Book of Enoch* says that *in space* "it was hot as fire and cold as ice" (where *objects get hot on the side illuminated by the sun and icy cold on the shaded side)* and "a dark abyss."[9]

YUNNAN PROVINCE, CHINA

17 (W): Engravings of *cylindrical rocketlike machines,* which are shown *climbing skyward,* were discovered on a pyramid which suddenly emerged from the floor of Lake Kun-Ming during an earthquake.

GREECE

18 (W): Lucian pictured *the moon* as *a body like the earth* which *could be reached in 8 days* and wrote a "fiction" (?) of a moon trip.

CHINA

19 (W): *"Desolate, cold and glassy":* In the year 2309 B.c. the engineer of Emperor Yao decided to go to the moon. The "celestial bird" provided him with information on his trip. He explored space by "mounting the current of luminous air" (the exhaust of a fiery rocket?).

Hou Yih flew into space where "he did not perceive the rotary movement of the sun."[10] (This statement is of paramount importance in corroborating the story because it is only in space that man cannot see the sun rise or set.)

On the moon he saw the 'frozenlooking horizon" and *erected a building, "the Palace of Cold".*

His wife Chang Ngo likewise flew to the moon, which she found a "luminous sphere, *shining like glass, of enormous size and very cold;* the light of the moon has its birth in the sun," she declared. (Chang Ngo's moon exploration report was correct. *Apollo II* astronauts found the moon desolate with a glasslike soil—and parts of it even paved with pieces of glass. Most of the moon, at any given time, is in the throes of extreme cold. It plunges to minus 250 degrees Fahrenheit at midnight.)

The ancient Greek scientist Empedocles had also declared that the moon was made of glass. Such precise knowledge implies on-site inspection of the moon in the remote past.

CHINA

20 (W): A story from this same period states that an enormous ship appeared on the sea at night with brilliant lights which were extinguished during the day. *It could also sail to the moon and the stars,* hence its name, "a ship hanging among the stars" or "the boat to the moon".

This giant ship which could travel in the sky or sail the seas was seen for 12 years.[11]

303

CHINA

21 (W): "The Shi Ching" book says that when the Emperor saw crime and vice rising in the world, "he commanded Chong and Li to cut off communication between the earth and the sky—and since then there has been no more going up or down."[12]

Is this not a clear indication of *the cessation of space travel* in the past?

TIBET

22 (W): Sanskrit documents discovered by the Chinese at Lhasa are claimed to contain *directions for building interplanetary spaceships. Flight to the moon* is mentioned (though it is not stated whether this was undertaken or just planned). The Chinese have stated that certain of the data were being studied for inclusion in their space program.

23 (S): *Relics on the moon?* Reports have been made concerning strange messages on the surface of the moon.

- An object shaped like a sword near the crater Birt
- Strange cross formations in the crater Eratosthenes and at Fra Mauro
- Angular lines in the crater Gassendi and seven spots in the shape of the Greek capital Gamma on the floor of the crater Littrow
- Two giant sets of letters under Mare Serenitalis, to the left of Mare Tranquilitatis, which read: "PYAX" and "JAW"—black letters, easily discernible
- Strange tracks running right up the wall of a crater.

If such geometric constructions were found on earth, speculation would rage as to the men who left them.

Not every discovery has been announced by NASA—and exploration has scarcely begun. Already NASA has run out of budget for further moon visits. It is by no means impossible that future astronauts will discover objects or installations showing that other human beings came to the moon in the distant past.

24 (S): It was July 20, 1969, the occasion of the first moon landing. During the last reconnaissance flight around the moon, preceding the landing, one of the astronauts made an unexpected announcement: he had just seen the contours of what seemed to be *some sort of seven-story structure.*

What was it that he saw? Might it have been the "Palace of Cold"? Why did they subsequently delete this from rebroadcasts? (But it was too late. We had already heard it.)

If there is a single, ancient, long-abandoned edifice on the moon, if there is a single object indicating earlier intelligence, if there is still one recognizable rock drawing to be found, then just think what such a find would do to our conventional history.

But wait! News is now filtering through—not from the moon, hut from 40 million miles away on the small planet Mars.

25 (S): A Soviet scientist who defected to the West claims that photographs taken by an orbiting satellite clearly show the ruined temples of a civilization—on the planet Mars!

The 58-year-old scientist was a high-echelon member of an elite team that has worked together since 1961 when *Vostok I* carried Yuri A. Gagarin as the first man in space.

But Russia's growing emphasis on the development of a nuclearized "Star Wars" satellite system in space prompted him to flee Russia. He now lives under an assumed identity in Switzerland.

He reports that several years ago, a Soviet satellite was launched for Mars. It reached that destination in 1982 and has been orbiting the Red Planet ever since.

Its sole purpose was to beam photographs and other data back to a manned satellite orbiting Earth. The task was accomplished with incredible success.

The photographs are computer-enhanced and in full color. The detail they show is far beyond anything produced in America. And there is no mistaking what they reveal.

The city scanned by the satellite's camera is three times the size of Moscow and it is ringed by wide boulevards, one inside the other and linked together by smaller avenues, like the spokes of a cartwheel.

The temples must have been huge. Most are in ruins, as though crumbled by a tremendous Marsquake. But some still support slate-grey domes that measure two to four miles in diameter.

The Soviet Union will never admit to this incredible discovery because it would reveal too much of their technological progress.

End of the story? No, not quite. On February 4, 1985, the Melbourne, Australia, *Age* reported the belief of thirty U.S. scientists that two photographs sent back from Mars in 1976 by the *Viking* spacecraft indicate the existence of an ancient civilization.

Richard Hoagland, science writer and member of the group of scientists known as the Mars Investigation Group, said the photos show what appear to be four huge pyramids lined up symmetrically with a face.

Dr.C. West Churchman, a professor at the University of California at Berkeley, said there are too many details pointing to the possibility of an extinct habitation on Mars.

What then, I ask, is the real truth about our past? Have we been to Mars before?

Chapter 28

Some intriguing secrets—COULD SCIENCE MAKE YOU INVISIBLE?

S ome of the data now to be presented may seem preposterous to the mind educated to a blind faith in modern science.

Yet I have reservations about scientific dogmatism, because what is science today will be fallacy tomorrow and what was science ten or twenty years ago is fallacy today.

Certainly, as evidence piles up of a forgotten prehistoric science, it is difficult to shake off the feeling that our ancestors knew a lot more than we do.

They possessed superior intelligence and technological skill—often to a degree that the modern mind finds staggering.

Their attainments stare us in the face; their secrets defy us. Consider these as food for thought.

EGYPT
1 (W): A mysterious vase of red crystal, when it was filled with water, *weighed the same as when it was empty.*

LEBANON
2 (W): *Fire that burned in water* was used by the Greeks to defeat the Arabs in 674 and in 716, and then the Russians in 941 and in 1043. This was a devastating weapon: in the battle of 716, 800 Arab warships were totally destroyed.

The secret formula was brought to Greece by a fleeing architect who had excavated it in ancient Baalbek.

This viscous product has never been reproduced, even by modern napalm specialists.

EGYPT

3 (W): *Singing statues:*

- The statue of Memnon, and its twin, emitted a thin, high-pitched sound like a chord on a harp. It was a phenomenon heard at dawn, for about 200 years; the sound at first was said to be sweetly melodious. (One theory suggests a complex mechanism hidden in the depths of the statue, activated by the rising sun working on a lens hidden in the figure's lips.)
- Similar sounds were heard at sunrise in the granite cave at Syene.
- Also in the Karnak temple.

After certain repairs on the statue, the musical sounds ceased. This indicates that the "music" was due to some complicated mechanism triggered by the sun's rays—a mechanism which was inadvertently damaged during the restoration work.

"ELECTRIC EYE" SOUNDS TO OPEN DOORS

GREECE

4 (W): *"Singing houses" are believed to have been devices for the automatic opening and closing of doors;* a kind of concealed "carillon" activated by weights or by the footsteps of the passers-by.

NORTHERN AUSTRALIA

5 (O): Entrances in cliffs were opened by mysterious means (for example, "by blowing on the cliff face").

KARNAK, THEBES and ABYDON, EGYPT

6 (W): Heavy portals of temples were opened wide by a certain word pronounced (by chosen priests) in a prescribed tone.

THE ORIENT

7 (W): "Magic" doors giving access to temples, crypts and caves are frequently mentioned in tales.

ALEXANDRIA, EGYPT

8 (W): *Harmonious sounds issued from beaks of birds made of metal.*

The principle was apparently that of sounds emitted at a certain pitch and touching off a spring mechanism, or else of sounds or ultrasounds acting upon an electric cell, as light would do. The "open sesame" principle which operates in nature, by a low-pitched note, was evidently understood.

MEDITERRANEAN REGION
HARZ MOUNTAINS
ASIA
ICELAND

9 (W): Doors which open and close *themselves, and shutters which close automatically, have been described* countless times.

ALEXANDRIA, EGYPT, 1st cent. A.D.

10 (W): *Artificial rain of perfumed water* was activated by a hidden device.

11 (W): *"Magical" lighting and sound effects* caused a temple to be wrapped in clouds or bathed in unearthly light; darkness appeared in daytime; night suddenly lit up; lamps burned of their own accord; images of gods would blaze; and claps of thunder ring out.

ISFAHAN, PERSIA

12 (W): *Large public baths were heated* by a crucible which was in turn heated *by the flame of a single candle!* (What was this ingenious mechanism that could amplify the energy of the fire of the candle thousands of times?)

SYRIA, 2nd cent. A.D.

13 (W): The *eyes* of the goddess Hera (a statue in a temple at Hierapolis) *followed a person no matter where he moved.*

STATUES RISING FROM BELOW GROUND OR SUSPENDED IN MID-AIR

GREECE, 4th cent. B.C.

14 (W): A vault constructed with "magnetic stones" so that idols could be suspended in mid-air.

ALEXANDRIA, EGYPT, 400 A.D.
15 (W): A sun disk ascending into the air "by magnetism" in the temple of Serapis.

SYRIA, 2nd cent. A.D.
16 (W): An image of a deity raised into the air.

ASIA MINOR, 5th cent. A.D.
17 (W): An iron Cupid suspended between the ceiling and floor of a Diana temple.

TIBET
18 (W): An embalmed body poised a span from the ground.

MEDINA, ARABIA
19 (W): Mahomet's coffin suspended for a long period high up in a mosque.

BIZAN, ABYSSINIA
20 (W): A "flying rod" motionless for centuries, mid-air, in a church.

HELIOPOLIS, EGYPT
21 (W): The statue of Apollo was maneuvered into position while floating in the air.

On the basis of the foregoing, I think we should reconsider the method by which those enormous stone blocks strewn throughout the world were set in place.

The explanation offered by the ancients—who lived closer to the events than we—cannot lightly be brushed aside. Even the legends of their local descendants should at least be given a hearing.

Outrageous though individual accounts may sound, a comparison does reveal an interesting thread of agreement running through them all—the concept that the stones were made to levitate.

SOUTH AMERICA
22 (0): The local explanation for the enormous building blocks in ancient cities of the Andes is that godlike heroes *made the stones fly* from distant quarries.

PONAPE, CAROLINE ISLANDS
23 (0): Local natives relate that the cyclopean ruins of Nan Madol were originally built by the casting of a spell which caused the basaltic prisms *to fly through the air* and settle down in the right positions.[1]

EASTER ISLAND
24 (0): Local native tradition relates that the statue builders had techniques which utilized the mysterious *vibratory energy* of "mana".

INDIA
25 (W): Ancient texts refer to the secrets of *anti-gravity* (weightlessness), of *telekinesis* and the *exploitation of cosmic energy*.

ENGLAND
26 (W): Historical legend asserted that *some form of machinery* gave a lift to the large blocks of Stonehenge.[2]

BABYLON
27 (W): Tablets indicate that *by means of sounds* the priests were able to raise into the air heavy rocks which a thousand men could not have lifted.[3]

EGYPT
28 (W): Certain Arab sources contain curious tales about the manner in which the earlier pyramids were erected. One says that the stones were wrapped in papyrus, then *struck with a rod. They became weightless and moved through the air* for some 150 feet. The procedure was repeated until the pyramid was reached and the stone placed.

EGYPT
29 (W): Coptic writings indicate how the blocks were *levitated by the sound of chanting.*

The relationship between sound and weightlessness is still a mystery to us. We are reminded, again, of the Bolivian legend that flying vehicles were kept airborne by vibrations at a certain pitch generated by continual hammer blows.

Here, perhaps, is the explanation for those technologically impossible prehistoric constructions, many of which seem literally to have been thrown up to the tops of mountains and perched on the edges of precipices, as if the giant stones had flown there!

It is possible that in a particular village in present-day India we see demonstrated the principle behind this ancient secret. Stones are levitated when the right number of people place their index finger on a rock and do the correct chanting. Success in this instance appears to hinge on sound waves and biocurrents from the fingers.

30 (S): *A process for softening hard rock, by utilizing a radioactive plant extract,* may have been used by the Incas and others in shaping stones.

- An earthenware jug in a Peruvian grave contained a black fluid that, when spilled on rocks, turned them into a soft, malleable putty.
- American archaeologist A. Hyatt Verrill saw remnants of this substance in the possession of an Indian witch doctor.
- Fawcett, the British explorer, reported that on a walk along the River Perene, in Peru, large spurs were corroded to stumps in one day by the juice of plants about a foot high with dark-reddish fleshy leaves.
- A small bird in the Bolivian Andes bores holes in solid rock by rubbing a leaf on the rock until it is soft and can be pecked away.

EGYPT
THE ARABS
CHINA
INDIA
FRANCE
ENGLAN
SWITZERLAND
SUMERIA

31(W): *Reports of alchemy (the transmutation of metals, including lead into gold)* come to us from widespread sources.

The fact of an advanced culture and technology in protohistory can clarify why ancient alchemists believed in transmutation of the elements.

A remote age during which nuclear science was practiced implies the use of atomic energy for many purposes. Some ideas, such as transmutation, which the alchemists kept alive in their endless search to turn lead into gold, most likely stemmed from ancient knowledge that manipulation of atomic structures could convert one element into another.

Today, with instruments such as the strong-focusing synchrotron, the transmutation of metals has begun to look quite good.

It has now been reported that Soviet scientists have found a cheap way of converting lead into gold. They were conducting an experiment in nuclear bombardment when they found the lead shielding inside an advanced nuclear reactor had changed into gold. They were able to repeat the process under laboratory conditions.

Russian scientists have also grown real diamonds in a carbon dioxide bath under low pressure.

But such breakthroughs are *possible only in the most sophisticated contemporary physics.* The idea that such processes were known thousands of years ago, and then forgotten, jolts the mind.

INVISIBILITY APPARATUS

GREECE
32 (W): A "magical" helmet, when placed on the head, rendered the wearer invisible. (Was this "helmet" an electronic device to diffract or deflect light rays, thereby acting as a protective agent?)

DRUIDS, ENGLAND
33 (W): A "magic mist" was created, to render the producers invisible. (This might have been linked with light diffraction devices.)

LHASA, TIBET
34 (W): Manuscripts are said to reveal the secret of "antima" (the "cap of invisibility").

GERMANY
35 (W): The heroic Siegfried won from the dwarf king Alberich a cloak that when worn rendered him invisible. He used it afterward in successful duels. The ancient Germans firmly believed in a cloak of invisibility.

INDIA
36 (W): Ancient texts reveal "the secret of making planes invisible".

INDIA
37 (W): Weapons and flying objects were able to render themselves "invisible to the enemy".[4]

INDIA

38 (W): The ancient destroyer Shiva sometimes disappeared into thin air before enemy eyes.

PERU

39 (W): *Visible-invisible bridge:* A city in the Andes was protected by a rocky defile which could only be crossed by a bridge. Constructed of ionized matter, this pre-Incan bridge was made to appear and disappear at will.[5]

Of course, all solid objects have a vibration frequency within the range perceptible to the human eye. Some scientists consider that it might be possible to alter the vibration frequency into vibrations outside the visible range.

In October 1943, secret experiments allegedly took place from the Philadelphia Naval Yard in which an electromagnetic force field was created and a ship of the U.S. Navy, fully crewed, was made to disappear. In other words, ship and crew became totally invisible. Pulsating energy fields produced an electronic camouflage. The explanation can probably be found in Einstein's unified field theory.

Despite detailed evidence as to names, places and times, the event is still officially denied.

Yet, significantly, since then the Great Powers have developed infrared cannons sensitive not only to the visible shape of objects, but also to their thermal radiation. Indicating that they seriously consider the possibility of war between invisible combatants.

In particular, the United States has been investigating means of providing an electronic "cloak of invisibility" for its aircraft carriers at sea. The enemy would then attack an electronically depicted but nonexistent target.

A product of similar research is the Stealth aircraft.

40 (W): *Time viewing devices:* The construction of the "Al Muchefi Mirror" was outlined according to the laws of perspective and under proper astronomical configurations—a mirror in which one could see a panorama of Time.

If this be true, then the former cultures were one step ahead of us—they had Time Television.

In his book *Readable Relativity.* the British scientist Clement V. Durell writes: "But all events, past, present and future as we call them, are present

314

in our four-dimensional space-time continuum, a universe without past or present, as static as a pile of films which can be formed into a reel for the cinematograph."[6]

Some years ago, an unprogrammed broadcast appeared on American television sets. Investigation showed that the program seen had been transmitted four years earlier by a station that had since closed down.

Did our predecessors have the technology to tune into past events at will? To retrieve vibration waves from those events, which were still rippling somewhere through space?

PERU
INDIA
SUMERIA

41(W): *Brain transplants,* the ultimate in neurosurgery, appear to have been carried out in several ancient cultures, according to written and pictorial evidence.

IMPOSSIBLE, of course! That's one's instant response to such a suggestion. Good material for a science fiction horror, that's all.

Could it be that we are too hasty to dismiss that which we do not understand? Some recent astonishing developments make skepticism look almost naive.

Dr. Robert White of Cleveland Western Reserve Medical School has transplanted an isolated brain into the body of another monkey in an apparently successful operation.

Russian experimenters have temporarily succeeded with total head transplants on dogs.

The major problem in a transplant of this nature is to make the neuroconnections that will enable the brain to be supported by and to control its new body. Clearly, success in the West is still years away; the difficulties are so immense.

And in a human transplant, powerful moral and sociological questions arise. May I boldly suggest that a brain transplant recipient is himself probably no longer alive? It is the memory, the character, the personality— yes, the very life of the donor that survives. Well?

Now for some startling news. The ultimate breakthrough may have already occurred. In northeast China, during April 1984, a team of micro-surgeons successfully transplanted the head of a corpse onto the body of a living man. The 31-year-old recipient had a massive brain tumor and was being kept alive on life support apparatus. The head was taken from a man who had died after he was almost decapitated in a factory accident in Shensi

315

Province. The surgical team used newly developed, computer-controlled, microlaser techniques.

The fourteen-hour operation was described by one of the team, CAT-scan specialist Chen Lee, who later fled to Europe. From his thirteen notebooks, he plans to write a book about the mind-boggling successes of China's recent transplant experiments.

Then on July 7, 1986, Soviet medical journals reported an experiment at a research facility near Moscow, in which surgeons had switched the heads of two "prime specimens". Although both young men emerged from the surgery with their senses intact, attempts to reattach the spinal cords of their new bodies were unsuccessful and the men were paralyzed from the neck down.

German cancer specialist Dr. Hans Frankl, in Russia to treat victims of the Chernobyl nuclear disaster, was horrified to learn from Soviet doctors that the experiment had been preceded by at least 14 failed attempts.

In Europe, researchers and theologians were quick to condemn the experiments on apparently healthy subjects as "an outrage" and a "godless disregard for human life."

Ancient neurological skills now become more believable, don't they?

Chapter 29

Weaponry—TOO LATE FOR ESCAPE

In the forest areas between the Indian mountains of Rajmahal and the Ganges, the explorer De Camp came upon unknown charred ruins.

A number of huge masses appeared fused together and hollowed at various points "like lumps of tin struck by a stream of molten steel." The result could not be due to ordinary fire, however violent.

Further south, the British official J. Campbell stumbled upon similar ruins, with a half-vitrified courtyard, produced by an unknown agent.

Similar reports have come from other travellers in the jungle areas, reports of ruined buildings with walls "like thick slabs of crystal," likewise holed, split and corroded by some mysterious force.

The explorer-hunter H.J. Hamilton received a substantial shock when he entered a low-domed building. He recalls that:

suddenly the ground gave way under my feet with a curious noise. I got into a safe place and then widened the hole, which had appeared, with my rifle-butt and lowered myself into it. I was in a long and narrow corridor which got its light from the space where the dome had split. At the bottom I saw a kind of table and chair, made of the same 'crystal' as the walls.

An odd shape was crouching on the seat, with vaguely human features.

Looking at it from close by, I thought it might be a statue damaged in the course of time but then I glanced at something which filled me with horror: under the 'glass' which covered that 'statue' a skeleton could clearly be seen!

Walls, furniture, people—melted, then crystallized.

No natural burning flame or volcanic eruption could have produced a heat intense enough to cause this phenomenon. Only the heat released through atomic energy could have done this damage.

Advanced weaponry in ancient times? It's more startling than fiction!

FIREARMS

BRITAIN
1 (O): Myths from Druidic times speak of rods which spit fire and could kill.

BROKEN HILL, RHODESIA
2 (S): The Museum of Natural History, London, possesses a human skull from a very early period of history, found 60 feet underground.

On the left side of the skull is a hole, perfectly round, with no radial cracks as would have resulted from an arrow or a spear.

Only a high-speed projectile such as a bullet could have made such a hole. The left side of the skull directly opposite the hole is shattered, having been blown out from the inside.

The same feature is seen in modern victims of high-powered rifles.

A forensic authority from Berlin has positively stated that the neat hole and the shattering effect could not have been caused by anything but a bullet.

LENA RIVER, RUSSIA
3 (S): The Paleontological Museum of the U.S.S.R., Moscow, has a skull of a "prehistoric" aurochs bison pierced by a small round hole, of an almost polished appearance, without radial cracks—indicating a projectile entered at high velocity.

This was not of recent times, because the animal (now extinct) was alive—as shown by the edges of the wound which calcified over (indicating it survived the shot).

This is evidence of the destructive ability of a developed people, who did not use primitive clubs.

318

INDIA

4 (W): Bullets of iron, lead shot, explosives of saltpeter, sulfur and charcoal—as well as cylindrical cannons which made a noise like thunder—were used in 3000 B.C.

Much later, guns were fired and rockets dispatched against Alexander the Great.

OTHER WEAPONS

THE ARABS
5 (W): Rocket torpedoes were developed.

CARTHAGE
6 (W): Land mines were used by Hannibal to destroy the Roman army.

BYZANTIUM, GREECE
7 (W): Marines often carried bronze-lined portable flame-throwers, so small that they could be carried like a pistol.

CHINAGREECE
8 (W): Solar mirrors were utilized to incinerate the enemy.

ARABIA
9 (W): Electromagnets withdrew the nails of ships as a means of destroying the enemy.

GREECE
10 (W): Fire that burned in water: A chemical warfare weapon, manufactured by a formula which included petroleum and saltpeter or naphtha and sulfur, was self-igniting.

It was delivered by rockets, catapults or through flame-throwers, and, on striking other ships, would continue to burn despite water thrown on it—even burning on water.

INDIA
11 (W): Nerve gas used in warfare: "Poison was produced, covering the earth with deadly fumes" which "stupified...—the poison that would have destroyed the world."

CHINA, 1000 B.C.
12 (W): Poison gas bombs were exploded on the enemy.

U.S.A.
13 (O): A tiny metal tube released a "rain of cactus thorns" (an electric discharge?) which paralyzed the victim for almost the entire period from sunrise to sunset.

A second tube could kill through unknown rays or discharge (perhaps, for example, by UHF ultrasonic sound waves?

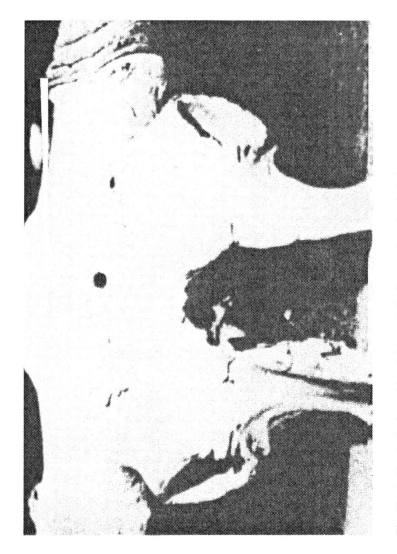

Fig. 29—1. The skull of a prehistoric bison. Ballistic tests show that the hole was made by a firearm and that the wound healed, indicating that the animal survived the shot.

INDIA
14 (W): Chemical and biological warfare: "Samhara" was a missile that crippled and "Mohanastra" was a weapon that produced a state of complete paralysis.

INDIA
15 (W): Killer beams: Kapilla's lance could burn 50,000 men to ashes in seconds.
(Sounds like either nuclear energy used as a beam, or some kind of laser weapon.)

INDIA
16 (W): Super bombs:
- "Saura" (a giant of giant H-bombs)
- "Agniratha" (a remote-control jet bomber)
- "Sikharastra" (a bomb with napalmlike effects)
- "Avidiastra" (attacking the nerve system)
- "Prasvapana" (a weapon inducing sleep)

SIBERIA

INDIA
18 (W): Flying spears that could ruin whole cities. (Missiles with nuclear warheads?)

ATOMIC THEORY

The ancients somehow knew about the infinitely small.

EGYPT
19 (W): The atomic theory was known in Egypt.

GREECE
20 (W): "In reality there is nothing but atoms and space."[1]

PHOENICIA
21(W): The atom's divisibility (now being corroborated as new atomic particles are being discovered all the time).

ROME
22 (W): Atoms "rushing everlastingly through all space" "undergo myriad changes under the disturbing impact of collisions." "It is impossible to see the atoms because they are too small."[2]

ISRAEL
23 (W): The atomic structure of matter and its polarity.

SUMERIA
24 (W): One Akkadian picture tablet instantly brings to mind a model of an atom: a circle of balls arranged next to each other that radiate alternately.

INDIA
25 (W): India understood:

- The molecular composition of matter: "There are vast worlds within the hollows of each atom, multifarious as the specks in a sunbeam"[3]; that is, the atoms which themselves contain particles are, however, mostly empty space.
  (We can totally agree. Each atom is indeed built like a solar system, consisting of a nucleus with electrons buzzing around it, in the same manner as the planets move around the sun.)
- The interrelation of molecules, heat being the cause of molecular change.

INDIA
26 (W): The size of the atom: The "Varahamira Table" (c. 550 AD.) gives a mathematical figure that compares closely with the actual size of a hydrogen atom.[4]
(Were these figures handed down from a much more distant time?)
It appears fantastic that this ancient science recognized the atomic structure of matter and realized how small is its ultimate particle.
Here was a knowledge of nuclear physics rivalling that of today.

INDIA
27 (W): Atomic divisions of time: In the ancient Hindu book, the *Bihath Sathaka*, we find reference to the "kashta," equivalent to three one-hundred-millionths (0.00000003) of a second—and at the other extreme the "kalpa," a period of 4.32 billion years.[5]

Modern Sanskrit scholars have no idea why such a small fraction of a second was necessary in antiquity. All they know is that it was used in the past, and they are obliged to preserve the tradition.

Time divisions of any kind, however, imply that the duration of something has been measured. And here is the crunch: How could it have been measured without precision instruments? Without sensitive instruments, three one-hundred-millionths of a second would be absolutely meaningless.

The only phenomena in nature that can be measured in billions of years or in millionths of a second are the disintegration rates of radioisotopes—ranging from those of elements like uranium 238 (with a half-life of 4.51 billion years) to subatomic particles with mean half-lives measured in miniscule fractions of seconds.

It is significant that the "kashta" is very close to the life spans of certain mesons and hyperons.

If the ancients had a technology that could study and measure nuclear and subnuclear matter, then means for using atomic energy was also accessible to them.

USE OF RADIOACTIVITY

28 (S): Scientists have found a number of uranium deposits that appear to have been mined or depleted anciently.

EGYPT
29 (S): In the tombs of the Pharaohs, the pitch used to preserve corpses contains highly radioactive substances.

The cloth used for swathing is radioactive. The burial chambers were probably full of radioactive dust. (Perhaps the priests made use of this to protect the tombs from desecrators.)

But more importantly—and the significance of this is absolutely world-shaking—researchers have recently unlocked a time capsule, a number of documents "buried" in incomprehensible terms until our day.

When translated last century, they were not understood. Nor could they be until modern knowledge "caught up" with former knowledge and was able to recognize it.[6]

These very ancient documents contain what is now startlingly familiar language. Their contents are quite alarming.

Here are eyewitness reports that raise the compelling question:

Did nuclear war wipe out large sections of the civilized world in the third millennium B.C.?

USE OF ATOMIC WEAPONS

A. *In Ancient Documents*
INDIA 2449 B.C.

30 (W): An Indian text recounts in detail how aircraft were used to launch a weapon that devastated three cities. The record is unnervingly similar to an eyewitness report of an atomic bomb explosion. It describes:

> —the brightness of the blast
> —the column of rising smoke and fire
> —the fallout
> —intense shockwaves and heatwaves
> —the appearance of the victims
> —the effects of radiation poisoning

The historical text states:

- An iron thunderbolt contained "the power of the universe."
- "An incandescent column of smoke and flame, as bright as ten thousand suns, rose in all its splendour."
- "Clouds roared upward."
- "Blood-coloured clouds swept down onto the earth."
- "Fierce winds began to blow." Elephants miles away were knocked off their feet.
- "The earth shook, scorched by the terrible violent heat of this weapon."
- "Corpses were so burnt that they were no longer recognizable."
- "Hair and nails fell out. Pottery broke without cause. Birds were turned white. After a few hours, all foodstuffs were infected."
- "Thousands of war vehicles fell down on all sides...thousands of corpses burnt to ashes."
- "Never before have we seen such an awful weapon, and never before have we heard of such a weapon."[7]

—The war zone: the upper regions of the Ganges.

Passages from this ancient Sanskrit text, the *Mahabharata* are a nerve chiller. The cold terror of the survivors still lives in its pages.

Until we started to experiment with radioactive substances, no person on earth could have described radiation sickness, for the simple reason that such a disease did not exist.

Yet radiation sickness, in clinical detail, is described: the hair loss, vomiting, weakness and eventual death—classic symptoms of radiation poisoning.

More significantly, it states that one could save himself by removing all metal from his person and immersing himself in the water of rivers. The reason can only be in order to wash away contaminated particles—the exact procedure followed today.

BABYLONIA

31 (W): The "Gilgamish Epic" recounts a day when "the heavens cried out, the earth bellowed an answer, lightning flashed forth, fire flamed upwards, it rained down death. The brightness vanished, the fire was extinguished. Everyone who was struck by the lightning was turned to ashes."[8]

TIBET, re GOBI, MONGOLIA

32 (W): The Tibetan "Stanzas of Dzyan" depict a holocaust engulfing two warring nations who engaged in aerial warfare, utilizing blinding rays, spheres of flame, shining darts and lightning The nations were:[9]

- The "Dark-faced" and the "Yellow-faced" (i.e., the Mongolians of the Gobi civilization). A few of the Yellow-faced escaped the flooding and nuclear destruction, but the Dark-faced appear to have been annihilated.
- The "straight-eye" (peoples of Europe and the Middle East) were among the survivors, apparently having been also involved in this nuclear conflict.

MEXICO, re U.S. A

33 (W): Ancient Mayan texts describe the destructive effects (unfortunately quite recognizable to us after Hiroshima) of a fire from the sky that put out eyes and decomposed flesh and entrails. Great cities to the north (i.e., in the U.S.A.) were destroyed.[10]

CANADA, re U.S.A.

34 (0): Canadian Indians speak of "men who flew upon the skies" and had shining cities and grand homes "to the south" (i.e., in the U.S.A.). Then an enemy nation came "and there was terrible destruction. All life in the cities was gone—nothing but silence remained."[11]

U.S.A.

35 (0): Hopi Indians recount that "some of these of the Third World" flew to a great city, attacked it and returned so quickly that the inhabitants did not know where their attackers came from. Soon many nations flew to attack one another. "So corruption and destruction came."[12]

B. Physical Evidence

GABON, WEST AFRICA

36 (S): In Africa, there are remains of a prehistoric nuclear chain reaction that cannot be explained by natural means. Discovered down a mine, the remains appear to be residue from an artificially produced pre-Flood nuclear reaction.

INDIA

37 (S): There are Indian remains which strongly suggest that an atomic war was waged in the distant past:[13]

- Precisely in the region specified in the old records, that is, between the Ganges and the Rajamahal Mountains, there are numerous charred ruins which have yet to be explored. Indications are that these ruins were not burned by ordinary fire. In many instances, they appear as huge masses fused together, with deeply pitted surfaces "like tin struck by a stream of molten steel."
- Further south, in jungle-claimed areas of the Deccan, are more such ruins. The walls have been glazed, corroded and split by tremendous heat. In some buildings, even the surfaces of the stone furniture have been vitrified (i.e., melted, then crystallized).
- In the same region a human skeleton was found with radioactivity fifty times above the normal level.

No natural-burning flame or volcanic eruption could have produced a heat intense enough for this. The heat of millions of degrees, that of thermonuclear reactions, is necessary.

PAKISTAN

38 (S): Skeletons in Mohenjo-Daro and Harappa are extremely radioactive.

The ruins of these ancient Indus Valley cities are immense. They are thought to have contained well over a million people each. Practically nothing is known of their histories, except that both were destroyed suddenly. In Mohenjo-Daro, in an epicenter 150 feet wide, everything was crystallized, fused or melted; 180 feet from the center, the bricks are melted on one side, indicating a blast.

Ancient Indian texts speak of a city's people being given 7 days to get out—a clear warning of total destruction.

Excavations down to the street level revealed forty-four scattered skeletons, as if doom had come so suddenly they could not get into their houses.

All the skeletons were flattened to the ground. A father, mother and child were found flattened in the street, face down and still holding hands.

The skeletons, after thousands of years, are still among the most radioactive that have ever been found, on a par with those of Hiroshima and Nagasaki.[14]

IRAQ

39 (S): Melted ruins of a ziggurat structure not far from ancient Babylon appear as though "fire had struck the tower and split it down to the very foundation."

Brickwork was changed to a vitrified state, completely molten. The whole ruin is like a burnt mountain. Even large boulders found in the vicinity of the ruins have been vitrified.[15]

What power could have melted the bricks? Nothing but a monster thunderbolt or an atom bomb!

Here is something else. Did you know that when the first atomic bomb exploded in New Mexico, the desert sand turned to fused green glass?

Listen...

BABYLONIA

40 (S): In 1947, archaeologists on one site uncovered, in succession:

- A layer of agrarian culture
- An older layer of herdsman culture
- A still older layer of "cave man" culture
- Then they reached another layer—of fused green glass!

Lightning may occasionally fuse sand, but when it does, the fusing occurs in a distinctive, rootlike pattern. Only a nuclear explosion could produce an entire layer, a whole stratum of fused green glass.

GOBI DESERT, MONGOLIA
41 (S): The desert surface of the Gobi near Lob Nor Lake is covered with vitreous sand from Red China's atomic tests.

But the desert has certain areas of similar glassy sand which have been present for thousands of years.

There are ruins, almost formless, which bear the marks of blistering by enormous heat. It is indeed difficult to believe that once men lived, loved, ruled, and died here.

ISRAEL
42 (S): In 1952 archaeologists unearthed, at the 16-foot level, a layer of fused green glass 1/4-inch thick and covering an area of several hundred square feet. It was made of fused quartz sand similar in appearance to sand at the atomic test sites of Nevada and the Gobi.

SOUTH-CENTRAL TURKEY
43 (S): At Catal Huyuk, archaeologists came upon thick layers of burned brick at the VIa level. The blocks had been fused together by heat so intense that it had penetrated more than 3 feet below floor level, where it had carbonized earth, skeletons and burial gifts that had been interred with them. The enormous heat had halted all bacterial decay.

NORTH SYRIA
44 (S): So completely were the royal buildings burned at Alalakh that the wall plaster was vitrified and in some areas basalt wall slabs had actually melted.

SOUTHERN SAHARA DESERT
45 (S): Albion W. Hart, an engineer graduate from Massachusetts Institute of Technology, while traversing a desert in the interior of Africa, was puzzled by "a large expanse of greenish glass which covered the sands as far as he could see."

Not until 50 years later, when he passed the White Sands area after the first atomic test there, did he recognize the same type of silica fusion.

EGYPT

46 (S): Fused green glass has been found also in sites of the Old and Middle Kingdoms of Egypt.

LOFOTEN ISLANDS (off Norway)
SCOTLAND
IRELAND
CANARY ISLANDS

47 (S): Prehistoric forts and towers in Europe have had their walls vitrified and stones fused by an unknown energy, usually along their western wall, but sometimes on the inner sides of the eastern wall as well—so intense was the heat!

Many sites show melting to a depth of one foot, "turned to glasslike frozen treacle."[16]

ISLE OF MAN

48 (S): The stones of the innermost cell of a long barrow near Maughold were in like manner fused together.

WESTERN PACIFIC

49 (S): Similar vitrifications have been observed in the Western Pacific.

PERU

50 (S): At Cuzco, an area of 18,000 square yards of mountain rock has been fused and crystallized. Likewise, a number of the dressed granite blocks of the nearby Sacsahuaman fortress have been vitrified through intense radiated heat.[17]

BRAZIL

51 (S): The ruins of Sete Cidades (Seven Cities) in the Province of Piaui are "a monstrous chaos," having been melted through extremely high energies. Squashed between the stone layers protrude pieces of rusting metal that leave streaks like "red tears" down the crystallized wall surface.

U.S.A.

52 (S): In the western United States, ruins exist in southern California, Colorado, Arizona and Nevada, in which the radiated heat was so intense as to liquify the rock surface.

- Between the Gila and San Juan Rivers, a huge region is covered with remains. "Ruins of cities…burnt out and vitrified in part, full

330

of fused stones and craters caused by fires which were hot enough to liquify rock or metal. There are paving stones and houses torn with monstrous cracks."[18]

- In the center of a ruined city in Death Valley (with lines of streets a mile long and positions of buildings still visible), stands an enormous structure on a tall rock. The southern side of rock and building has been melted and vitrified.
- And in the Mohave Desert exist several circular patches of fused glass.

EASTER ISLAND

53 (W): Unique wood carvings with Semitic features show the effects of nuclear radiation on a human body-invariably representing an emaciated body with goitered glands, swollen groin, clenched mouth, wasted sunken cheeks, collapsed cervical vertebrae, with a distinct break between the lumbar and the dorsal vertebrae, popped eyes, and distended stomach—all in remarkable detail. These are the unmistakable nightmare symptoms of exposure to a severe dosage of nuclear radiation.

Does this perhaps tie in with the remains of fiery destruction discovered on the island?

Pioneer nuclear scientist Professor Frederick Soddy (Nobel Prize winner and the discoverer of isotopes), envisaging a past civilization which had mastered atomic energy, said, in 1909:

Can we not read into them (the prehistoric traditions) some justification for the belief that some former forgotten race of men attained not only to the knowledge we have so recently won, but also to the power that is not yet ours?

The specter of past atomic warfare is increasingly more tenable as new information comes to light.

Whatever we choose to imagine, there is always the hard fact: there is already too much evidence from too many parts of the world to call it nonsense. It is a fact, or it couldn't turn up so often.

The secret was known; inevitably justification was found to use it. Civilian populations disappeared.

Do we see the warning? This is the jest to end all jesting. Once more a universal time fuse is alight.

EPILOGUE

The wisdom and technical splendor of the antedeluvian civilization was so astounding that it has never been equalled.

Even after the Deluge, the reconstituted world system was conceived by races with an intelligence far superior to our own; there is evidence, literally, by the ton that says so.

In many ways their civilization was comparable to ours. They had air travel and underwater devices. They were very "modern."

I don't think you can construct that supercivilization and find exactly another United States. They travelled on a different orientation. Whether in lighting or transport, they reached the same results by a different method.

Because of the fragmentary and incomplete nature of our knowledge concerning them, any attempt at exposition is necessarily imperfect.

However, the evidence points to scientific knowledge that was worldwide at the same time.

And it appears that work stopped on a global scale, more or less overnight. Genius perverted by a materialistic philosophy culminated in corruption and violence. You know the sequel.

Striking parallels exist between that period and our own.

More to the point, there are some ancient biblical prophecies that foretell the appearance in the sky of blood, fire and mushroom pillars of smoke, to occur in that final age when men acquire the ability to destroy the earth. It is stated plainly that the world's cities will be devastated, that "the elements shall melt with fervent heat."[1]

According to this, we are heading toward the day when everything stops—toward the moment when Earth's pendulum will shudder and stop in midswing!

333

There is something unique about Bible prophecy. Indeed, this Book makes audacious claims for itself, actually challenging the world to prove whether it is a divine message to us, by testing its prophecies.[2] Were you aware that one-third of the Bible comprises prophecy? And something else. It informs us that an unseen Overlord has been quietly shaping human history; that He will reveal His intentions before causing certain events to occur.[3]

Come to think of it, the prophecies to date have been uncannily accurate.

Events leading to the twentieth century have been outlined step by step in correct sequence. Then there is the current scenario—our explosion of knowledge, the awakening to strength of weak Asian nations, a militarily aggressive Russia, the 1967 return of Israel to Jerusalem,[4] a coming economic-political union of ten nations, or groups of nations, in Europe. The list goes on. All these are to occur against a background of increasing earthquakes, famines, war and unprecedented social breakdown.

Then come predictions more startling than fiction! Soon uncontrollable panic grips the nations; they see no way out.[5] A charismatic leader (already clearly identified) arises with "the solution". For the first time since ancient Babylon, all nations are drawn into one world government. (An electronic network already in place makes this easy.) The world leader cancels the existing currencies and establishes a worldwide number system. Every person on earth is required to receive an imprint.[6] Dissidents are not tolerated. For a short season, the planet is "at peace". The world dictator is popular.

The utter wickedness of this man is not exposed to the world until too late. Suddenly all hell breaks loose. World trade collapses,[7] religious extremism mounts,[8] and we are plunged into "a time of trouble, such as never was since there was a nation even to that same time."[9] The Bible predicts that so great will be the devastation that unless the conflict is halted, no life will be left on earth.[10] It will be stopped—just in time, but only because of the supernatural intervention of the Creator.

Undoubtedly, human history is racing toward some appalling catastrophe. The good news is that the Bible has clearly foreseen the events. It does offer evidence that the Creator is still in control—and will do what man cannot do—act decisively to save the human race from total destruction.

So, who is to blame? Human perversity is the main reason for the mess the world is in. But, you ask. Is it likely that an all-powerful, caring Creator would allow any of His creatures to go wrong? The answer is, Of course!— if He decided to give man free will. Tell me, would it be a better world if

He had not given us free will, but instead controlled our every move, where we were just robots? Think about that.

As it is, we have freedom of choice. We can demonstrate hatred or love, as we wish. Let's face it, if we did not have free will, then love, generosity and other qualities would be unsatisfying, even meaningless, and life would not be worth living.

As stated earlier, man was created noble. He has perverted his own character by misusing the free will that God gave him. No, you are not in a process of evolution which will enable you to create your own paradise here on earth. Such a philosophy is dangerous; it will lull millions into being unprepared for the climactic events ahead.

As the prophecies lead us unerringly along the trail toward Armageddon, the Flood of Noah sounds a warning.[11] The information we have dug up concerning our past suddenly becomes relevant, like a time bomb ready to explode.

But after D-Day—what then? For those who choose it and qualify, there is a new world...a world in which eternal youth, loving concern and security are the norm; where transformed individuals are able to live in harmony.

If all this be true, then I suppose people aplenty are going to miss out. And wouldn't some of them just love to be there! Think of it—a whole new world to mess up!

APPENDIX

Notes on the Crespi Collection

(A) The Genuine

Richard Wingate, in *Lost Outpost of Atlantis,* offers evidence for the authenticity of the bulk of the Crespi Collection. He writes:

- "Similar epigraphy in Father Crespi's collection was also labelled a clumsy Indian fraud until better trained scholars discovered some inscriptions were written in classically pure Egyptian hieroglyphics, Egyptian hieratic, Libyan and Celt-Iberian, and Punic." (p. 108)
- Concerning the large numbers of brass and bronze high-pressure air pipes: Such pipes simply can't be purchased in Ecuador today...We were told by importers that we would have to special order pipes of these specifications from Germany, and the cost would be substantial. These technological artifacts, of course, don't fetch high prices on the market." (p. 139)
- Concerning artifacts that are made of pure or alloyed gold: The native gold panners "hardly have the leisure or the inclination to fake heavy artifacts of gold and then sell them for less than the bullion value of the precious metal." (p. 139)The "heavy mineral crust enamel coating" of many artifacts indicates that they were "buried under searing volcanic heat." (p. 139)
- Concerning sophisticated artifacts, like the Phoenician calendars, the golden Middle Eastern helmets, the golden armor, and the

golden plaques: these "would bring hundreds of thousands of dollars and perhaps millions on the private market; to suggest that a sophisticated forger unloaded them on the priest for a low price is to deny the greed that motivates forgery!" (p. 140)

- Concerning a cast steel shield: "Steel casting is beyond the metallurgical capacity of present day Tayos Indians." (p. 143)

(B) Fakes

Regarding fakes (which Crespi knowingly purchases in his casual, humanitarian style, at the same time chiding the seller): "The modern solder and hacksaw marks give them away." (p. 136)

(C) Hybrid real-fakes

- Far from creating fakes in order to reap high profits, some of the Indian diggers in Ecuador have cut up and reshaped genuinely ancient and priceless materials in order to get any kind of price at all for it. We have mentioned earlier the ebony column…carved with the Ecuadorian national seal and decorated with gold cut from a sheet of mysterious ancient wallpaper." (p. 139)
- Picture (p. 36)—"Obviously genuine copper 'radiators' were redecorated by Indian discoverers."
- Picture (p. 39)—"Heavy brass 'bass viol' a real-fake soldered together from original thick wall sheeting." The brass sheet metal is genuine and very old, but the instrument was crafted by modern forgers. One can see where existing designs on the brass sheets were cut through in the manufacture of the article.
- Picture (p. 142)—"Genuine silver wrapped gold trimmed elephant. Yet decorated with modern brass thumb tacks."
- Picture (p. 146)—"Bottom of tin can. Clumsily fire blackened to simulate real volcanic mineral patina on genuine objects. The carbon on this olive oil can be rubbed off on a sheet of paper. The black patina on most of Crespi's material is enameled to the metal."

In summary: "The genuine green porphyry patina on many of the articles,…the enormous quantities of cheaply bought gold articles, the metallurgical uniqueness of some of the artifacts (such as the platinum nose cone and the radiators), the Mideastern artistic motifs, and the abundance of artides for which little or no market exists (such as the air pipes and the 'wallpaper') pose difficult questions for those who carelessly write the collection off as a hoax." (p. 140)

BIBLIOGRAPHY

The Advertiser (Adelaide, Australia).

Aelian, Claudus, Varia Historia. A.D. 200. Tr. by Thomas Stanley. London: Thomas Dring, 1665.

Aeronautics, A Manuscript from the Prehistoric Past. Tr. by G.R. Josyer. Mysore: Coronation Press, Mysore, 1973.

The Age (Melbourne, Australia).

Albright, W.F. *Recent Discoveries in Bible Lands.* New York: Funk and Wagnalls Co., *1955*.

American Antiquity.

Ancient Astronauts (New York).

Anthropology Review.

Antiquity.

Archaeological Journal.

Archaeology.

Arnett, Kevin. *Mysteries, Myths or Marvels?* London: Sphere Books Ltd., 1977.

Art and Archaeology.

Asimov, Isaac, "Can Decreasing Entropy Exist in the Universe?" *Science Digest* (May 1973).

Australian Post.

Aztec Codices: "Chimal Popoca," "Telleriana Remensis," "Dresden," "Mexicanus Vatican."

Ballinger, Bill. *Lost City of Stone.* New York: Simon and Schuster, 1978.

Baring-Gould, Sabine. *Cliff Castles and Cave Dwellings of Europe.* London: Seeley, 1911.

Bayley, Harold. *Archaic England*. London: Chapman and Hall, 1919.

Beckley, Timothy Green, *The Subterranean World*. Clarksbury, West Va.: Saucerian Books, 1971.

Bergier, Jacques. *Mysteries of the Earth*. London: Future Publications, Ltd., 1974.

Berlitz, Charles, *The Bermuda Triangle*. St. Albans, U.K.: Panther Books, Ltd., 1977.

-*Doomsday: 1999*, St. Albans, U.K., Granada: 1982

-*Mysteries from Forgotten Worlds*. London: Transworld Publishers, Ltd., 1978.

-*Mystery of Atlantis*. St. Albans, U.K.: Panther Books, Ltd., 1977.

Berlitz, Charles, and Moore, William. *The Philadelphia Experiment*. St. Albans, U.K.: Panther Books, Ltd., 1979.

Bernard, Dr. Raymond. *The Hollow Earth*. New York: Bell Publishing Co., 1979.

The Bible. King James Version.

The Book of Enoch. Tr. by Richard Lawrence. San Diego: Wizards Bookshelf, 1977.

Brewster, David. *Statements Concerning a Nail Found Imbedded in Sandstone from Kin goodie Quarry, North Britain*. Report of the British Association, 1844.

Bridgman, P.W. "Reflections on Thermodynamics," *American Scientist* 41 (Oct. 1953).

Brugger, Karl. *The Chronicle of Akakor*. New York: Delacorte Press, 1977.

Burgess, E. *Surya Siddhanta*. New York, 1860.

Cantelon, Willard, *The Day the Dollar Dies*. Plainfield, N.J.: Logos International, 1973.

Castle, E.W. and Thiering, B.B. *Some Trust in Chariots*. Sydney, Australia: Westbrooks Pty. Ltd., 1972.

Caston, Margaret. *Rocks and Minerals*. (No. 396) Washington, D.C.: Heldref Publications, 1972.

Cathie, Bruce. *Harmonic 33*. London: Sphere Books, Ltd., 1980. - *Harmonic 288*, London: Sphere Books, Ltd., 1981.

Cathie, B.L. and Temm, P.N. *Harmonic 695*. Wellington, N.Z.: A.H. and A.W. Reed, 1977.

Charroux, Robert. *Legacy of the Gods*. London: Sphere Books, Ltd., 1974.

-*Lost Worlds*, Fontana, 1974.

-The Mysterious Unknown. London: Transworld Publishers, Ltd., 1975.

China Pictorial, Peking, Nov. 8, 1958.

China Reconstructs. Peking, August, 1961.

Churchward, James. *The Children of Mu.* New York: Ives Washburn, 1956.

Cohane, John Philip. *The Key.* New York: Crown Publishers, Inc., 1970.

Collyns, Robin. *Laser Beams From Star Cities.* London: Sphere Books, Ltd., 1977.

Corliss, William R. *The Unexplained.* New York: Bantam, 1976.

Creation Research Society Quarterly (Ann Arbor, Mich.: Creation Research Society).

Dawson, Sir John William. *The Historical Deluge in Relation to Scientific Discovery.* Chicago: Fleming H. Revell Co., 1895.

De Camp, Sprague L., and De Camp, Catherine. *Citadels of Mystery.* London: Fontana Books, 1972.

De la Vega, Garcilaso. *Royal Commentaries of the Incas. Tr.* by Harold V. Livermore. Austin: University of Texas Press, 1966.

Deyo, Stan. *The Cosmic Conspiracy.* Perth: West Australian Texas Trading, 1979.

Dickhoff, Robert Ernest. *Agharta.* Boston: Humphries, 1951.

Duplantier, Gene. *Subterranean Worlds of Planet Earth.* Canada: SS and S Publications, 1980.

Durant, Will. *Story of Civilization.* New York: Simon and Schuster, 1951.

Durell, Clement V. *Readable Relativity.*

Ebon, Martin, *The World's Great Unsolved Mysteries.* New York: New American Library, 1981.

Economist (London).

Edwards, Frank. *Strange World.* New York: Bantam Books, 1973. - *Stranger Than Science.* New York: Bantam Books, 1973.

Eitel, E.J. *Feng-shui: The Rudiments of Natural Science in China.* Cokaygne, 1973.

The Epic of Gilgamesh. Tr. by N.K. Sanders. Middlesex, England: Penguin Books, 1960.

Exposure, Vol.6, No. 1, 1999

Fate.

Fawcett, Colonel P.H. *Exploration Fawcett.* London: Hutchinson, 1953.

343

Fell, Barry. *America B.C.: Ancient Settlers in the New World*. London: Wildwood House Ltd., 1978.

Fix, William R. *Star Maps*. Toronto, Canada: Jonathan-James Books, 1979.

Fowler, Raymond *E.U.F.O.'s: Interplanetary Visitors*. New York: Prentice-Hall, 1979.

Geoffrey of Monmouth. *Historia Regum Brittanniae,* twelfth century. Middlesex, England: Penguin Books, 1966.

Goetz, Delia, and Morley, Sylvanus G., *Popul Vuh*. From the Spanish translation by Adrian Recinos. Norman, Okla.: University of Oklahoma Press, 1950.

Goodman, Jeffrey. *Psychic Archaeology*. New York: Berkeley Publishing Corp., 1978.

Gorbovsky, A. *Riddles of Ancient History*. Moscow, 1968.

-Riddles of the Ancient Past.

-Vie Nueve, June 29, 1962.

Hapgood, Charles. *Maps of the Ancient Sea Kings*. Radnor, Pa.: Chilton Books, 1966.

Hawkins, Gerald. *Beyond Stonehenge*. Hutchinson, 1973.

-Stonehenge Decoded. Souvenir Press, 1966.

Hayward, Alan. *God Is*. Nashville, Te.: Thomas Nelson Publishers, 1980.

Hitching, Francis. *Earth Magic*. London: Pan Books, Ltd., 1977.

-The World Atlas of Mysteries. London: Pan Books, Ltd., 1978.

Hornet, Marcel. *Sons of the Sun*. London: Neville Spearman, 1963.

Howard-Vyse, R.W. *Operations Carried On At The Pyramids of Gizeh in 1837*. 3 vols. London: J. Fraser, 1840—1842.

Howarth, Sir Henry. *The Mammoth and the Flood*. London: Sampson Low, Marston Searle, and Risington, 1887.

Howells, William. *Mankind So Far*. New York: Doubleday and Co., Inc., 1947.

Hue, Abbe Evariste-Regis. *De la Tartarie et du Tibet.*

Humboldt, Baron Friedrich Alexander. *Views of Nature. Tr.* by E.C. Otto. London: HG. Bohn, 1850.

Idriess, I. *Drums of Mer*. Sydney, Australia: Angus and Robertson, 1962.

Johnson, George, and Tanner, Don. *The Bible and the Bermuda Triangle*. Plainfield, N.J.: Logos International, 1977.

Johnson, Ken. *The Ancient Magic of the Pyramids*. London: Transworld Publishers, Ltd., 1978.

Josyer, G.R. *Vymanika Shastra.* Translation of *Maharishi Bharadwaja.* Mysore, India: Coronation Press, 1973.

Kazantsev, Aleksandr. *Steps of the Future.* Moscow: State Publishing House, 1963.

Keller, Werner. *The Bible as History. Tr.* by William Neil. New York: Bantam Books. 1974.

Kolosimo, Peter. *Not of This World.* New York: Bantam Books, 1973.

-*Spaceships in Prehistory.* Secaucus, N.J.: University Books, Inc., 1976.

-*Timeless Earth.* New York: Bantam Books., 1975.

Kramer S.N. *History Begins at Sumer.* New York: Doubleday. 1959.

Landsburg, Alan. *In Search of Lost Civilizations.* London: Transworld Publishers, Ltd., 1977.

Landsburg, Alan and Landsburg, Sally. *The Outer Space Connection.* London: Transworld Publishers, Ltd., 1975.

Laufer, B. *The Prehistory of Aviation.* Chicago: Field Museum of Natural History, 1928.

Le Poer Trench, Brinsley. *Secret of the Ages. St.* Albans, U.K.: Panther Books, Ltd., 1976.

Leonard, George H. *Someone Else Is On Our Moon.* London: Sphere Books, Ltd., 1978.

Levi, Eliphas. *Histoire de Ia Magie. Tr.* by Arthur Edward White. London: Rider and Co., 1948.

Lockyer, J. Norman. *Stonehenge and Other British Monuments Astronomically Considered.* London: Macmillan, 1906.

Lucian. *Vera Historia. Ed.* by C.S. Jerram. Oxford: Clarendon Press, 1936.

Maclellan, Alec. *The Lost World ofAgharti.* London: Souvenir Press, 1982.

The Mahabharata. Tr. by E.R. Rice. New York: Oxford, 1934.

The Mahavira. Ahmedabad: Sri Jaina Siddhanta Society, 1948—1951.

Man (London).

Medical History Bulletin.

Mebta, C.N. *The Flight of Hanuman to Lanka.* Bombay: Narayan Niketan, 1940.

Michell, John. *Astro-Archaeology.* Thames and Hudson, 1977.

-*The View Over Atlantis.* London: Abacus (Sphere), 1973.

Mooney, Richard E. *Gods of Air and Darkness.* London: Souvenir Press, 1975.

Morris, Henry M. *The Scientific Case for Creation.* San Diego: Creation-Life Publishers, 1977.

-*The Bible and Modern Science.* Chicago: Moody Press, 1968.

Muller, Fredrich Max. *The Sacred Books of the East.* Oxford: Clarendon Press, 1879—1924.

National Enquirer.

National Geographic.

Nature (London).

Neuberger, A. *Technical Arts and Sciences of the Ancients. Tr.* by Henry L. Brose. Dublin: Brome and Nolan, Ltd., 1969.

New York Times.

Noorbergen, Rene. *Secrets of the Lost Races.*U.K.: New English Library, 1980.

-*Treasures of the Lost Races.* London, England: W. H Allen, 1983.

Norville, Roy. *Giants.* Wellingborough, England: Aquarian Press, 1979.

Paranormal and Psychic Australian (Sydney).

Pauwels, Louis. *The Eternal Man.* New York: Avon, 1972.

-*The Morning of the Magicians.* New York: Avon, 1968.

Payne, F.C. *The Seal of God.* Adelaide, Australia: Hunkin, Ellis and King, Ltd., 1961.

Price, Derek J. de Solla. "An Ancient Greek Computer," *Scientific American,* June 1969.

The Queen of Sheba and Her Only Son Menyelek. Tr. by Sir E.A. Wallis Budge. London: Philip Lee Warner, 1932.

Readers' Digest.

Rehwinkel, Alfred M. *The Flood. St.* Louis, Mo.: Concordia Publishing House, 1951.

Reiche, Maria. *Mystery on the Desert.* Nazca, Peru: Maria Reiche, 1976.

Roberts, Anthony. *Sowers of Thunder.* London: Rider and Company, 1978.

Roerich, Nicolas. *Altai Himalaya: A Travel Diary.* London: Jarrolds, 1930.

-*The Indestructible.* Riga: Uguns, 1936.

-*Shambala.* New York: Frederick A. Stokes, 1930.

-*Gateway to the Future.* (Vrata v. Budushschie). Riga: Uguns, 1936.

Rome, J., and Rome, L. *Life of the Incas of Ancient Peru.* Geneva: Liber, 1978.

Saga.

Schaeffer, Claude F.A. *The Cuneiform Texts of Ras Shamra Ugarit.* *Tr.* by G.C. Dunning and K.M. Richardson. London: Oxford University Press, 1939.

Schul, Bill, and Pettit, Ed. *The Psychic Power of Pyramids.* New York: Fawcett Publications, 1979.

Science Digest.

Science Journal.

Science News.

Scientific American.

Scientific Australian.

Search.

Signs of the Times (Warburton, Australia).

Sitchin, Zecharia. *The Twelfth Planet.* New York: Avon, 1978.

Smith, Warren. *This Hollow Earth.* London: Sphere Books, Ltd., 1977.

Soddy, Frederick. *Interpretation of Radium.* London: John Murray, 1909.

Steiger, Brad. *Mysteries of Time and Space.* Englewood Cliffs, N.J.: Prentice-Hall. Inc. 1974.

-*Worlds Before Our Own.* New York: Berkeley Publishing Corp., 1979.

Stephens, John Lloyd. *Incidents of Travel in Central America, Chiapas and Yucatan.* 1838—1839, Vols. I and II. New York: Dover Publications, 1969.

Story, Ronald. *The Space Gods Revealed.* New York: Harper and Row, 1976.

Strabo. *Geography of the World.* (63 B.C. to after AD. 20).

The *Sun* (Melbourne, Australia).

Thom, Alexander. *Megalithic Sites in Britain.* Oxford University Press, 1967.

Time.

Tomas, Andrew. *Atlantis: From Legend to Discovery.* London: Sphere, 1978.

- *We Are Not the First.* London: Sphere, 1971.

Tompkins, Peter. *Secrets of the Great Pyramid.* New York: Harper and Row, 1971.

U.F.O. Report (New York).

Vandenberg, Philipp. *The Curse of the Pharaohs.* New York: Pocket Books, Inc., 1976.

von Danicken, Erich. *According to the Evidence.* London: Souvenir Press, 1977.

-*Chariots of the Gods.* New York: Bantam Books, 1971.

-*The Gold of the Gods.* London: Souvenir Press, 1973.

-*Return to the Stars.* London: Souvenir Press, 1970.

-*Signs of the Gods.* London: Corgi, 1981.

von Hassler, Gerd. *Lost Survivors of the Deluge.* New York: American Library, 1978.

Velikovsky, Immanuel. *Ages in Chaos.* London: Sphere Books, Ltd., 1976.

-*Earth in Upheaval.* London: Sphere Books, Ltd., 1978.

-*Worlds in Collision.* London: Sphere Books, Ltd., 1978.

Verrill, Alphius Hyatt. *America's Ancient Civilizations.* New York: G.P. Putnam's Sons, 1953.

Waisbard, Simone. *The Mysteries of Machu Picchu.* New York: Hearst Corp., 1979.

Waters, Frank. *Book of the Hopi.* New York: Ballantine, 1974.

Watkins, Alfred. *The Old Straight Track.* London: Garnstone Press, 1971.

Watson, Lyall. *Supernature.* London: Coronet, 1976.

Whitcomb, John C., Jr., and Morris, Henry M. *The Genesis Flood.* Philadelphia, U.S.A.: The Presbyterian and Reformed Publishing Co., 1976.

White, A.J. "Radio Carbon Dating." *Creation Research Society Quarterly.* (Dec. 1972): 156—158.

Wilkins, Harold T. *Mysteries of Ancient South America.* Secaucus, N.J.: Citadel Press, 1974.

Wilson, Clifford. *The Chariots Still Crash.* Old Tappan, N.J.: Fleming H. Revell and Co., 1976.

-*Crash Go the Chariots.* New York: Lancer Books, 1972.

-*Gods in Chariots.* San Diego, Calif.: Creation-Life Publishers Inc., 1975.

-*The War of the Chariots.* Melbourne, Australia: S. John Bacon Pty. Ltd., 1978.

Wilson, Don. *Secrets of Our Spaceship Moon.* London: Sphere Books, Ltd., 1980.

-*Our Mysterious Spaceship Moon.* New York, N.Y.: Dell, 1975.

Wingate, Richard. *Lost Outpost of Atlantis.* New York: Dodd, Mead & Company, Inc., 1980.

Woolley, Sir Leonard. *The Sumerians.* New York: Norton, 1965.

Zink, David D. *The Ancient Stones Speak.* New York: E.P. Dutton, 1979.

OTHER BOOKS
By Jonathan Gray

Further information and orders: http://beforeus.com

ARK OF THE COVENANT
THE DISCOVERY THEY TRIED TO HIDE. When Jonathan Gray set out to disprove an amateur archaeologist's claims, he never counted on being targeted for murder—or facing political pressure to keep a major discovery underground.   Fast moving, spell-binding, well documented. Revealing…forgotten voyages, secret tunnels, acts of intrigue.

STING OF THE SCORPION
ASTROLOGY EXPOSED—THE TRUTH BEHIND STAR NAMES AND SIGNS.

Ancient civilisations believed that a serpent - which represented the devil - took control of the world. They believed a virgin's baby would fight the serpent, defeat him and bring peace, life and happiness back to mankind. The pictures on the sky map were used to describe the story and NOT to tell people's fortunes through the stars. The NAMES of the stars, as well as the star sign PICTURES told that story.

CURSE OF THE HATANA GODS

A STUNNING REAL-LIFE ADVENTURE. One of the most isolated islands on earth is Rotuma, ancient home to a race of GIANTS. But Rotuma shielded a sinister secret, for which there was no scientific explanation. They called it THE CURSE OF HATANA. The evidence for the ANCIENT GIANTS and the incredible story of a face-to-face encounter with the CURSE.

64 SECRETS STILL AHEAD OF US

64 ways in which an earlier, forgotten science and technology was superior to our own. Learn of secret formulas that could revolutionise modern aviation, construction and medicine—advanced secrets we once knew and have forgotten.

THE ARK CONSPIRACY

COVER-UPS, BETRAYALS AND MIRACLES. The cloak-and-dagger story behind the alleged discovery of Noah's Ark; attempts to suppress the news. Why some people reject the discovery. And why others say this could be the real thing. A true-life thriller: archaeology at its most exciting.

THE BIZARRE ORIGIN OF EGYPT'S ANCIENT GODS

A 4,000-year-old scandal that affects our society today. Would you like to know why the most popular man in the world was executed? How a beautiful woman impersonated someone else, so as to be queen? Discover the advanced technology used by ancient Egyptians to make a "dead" man come "alive".

THE LOST WORLD OF GIANTS

Were there really humans 12-15 feet tall? Discovered!—tools, artifacts and houses of ancient giants. Up to 97 giant discoveries all over the earth, and now ACTUAL PHOTOGRAPHS! Also, amazing reports of long-lived humans. "Killer" facts that shake the evolution theory!

THE KILLING OF PARADISE PLANET

Imagine it! What if everything in your life changed suddenly in 24 hours? This picks up where Dead Men's secrets left off. **THE WORLD BEFORE THE GREAT DISASTER**. Was there a time when people could lived for 600 years? Did humans sunbake under Antarctica's palm trees?...sheltered under a giant, protective canopy?...atmosphere and temperature controlled?...a paradise planet? But then something happened...SUDDENLY.

SURPRISE WITNESS

A whole planet SUDDENLY left dead, from New Zealand to Norway. Waves thousands of feet high. Robust tropical animals frozen in a flash. Mountain lions and deep sea creatures swept together onto hilltops. **THE TRUTH ABOUT THE GLOBAL FLOOD**. Mirror-smooth buildings from a high civilization entombed 3 kilometers deep. Were dinosaurs really seen by men? Are there dinosaurs still alive?

THE CORPSE CAME BACK

This story unfolds like a mystery thriller...the action-packed, true, fascinating story of the settling down of our earth **AFTER THE GREAT DISASTER** of Noah, and its effect upon human history. Cities swallowed by the sea. The rapid birth of the Grand Canyon. The seaport that climbed a mountain range. The mummy that came up with a volcano. Bandits of a strange lost city. Bells that ring under the sea. Long-vanished civilizations, jungle-choked ruins and startling secrets of the Great Pyramid and Stonehenge. Who were the mystery persons in Australia before the Aborigines? What Hiroshima-sized calamity occurs on earth every two days?

DISCOVERIES: QUESTIONS ANSWERED * Paperback, 340 pages

All the questions asked are answered, concerning the Ron Wyatt discoveries. Did Wyatt lie about the blood? Did Gray "seriously edit" an Admiralty letter to prove a Red sea land bridge? What's behind the "Answers in Genesis"-Standish attack in the discoveries? Did scientists prove "Noah's Ark" to be a fake? Over 280 questions. Certificates, private letters and facts never before revealed. Input by numerous people. Our most explosive publication ever! Spiralbound.

SINAI'S EXCITING SECRETS * *Spiral bound 76 pages*
Things are happening at Mount Sinai in Arabia - a new top secret radar base; bedouins digging up graves. New information and photos can now be revealed to the world. A compilation of data.

OTHER BOOKS by Jonathan Gray
- *CURSE OF THE PHARAOHS*
- *MYSTERIOUS LOST CITIES*
- *THE MAN WHO NEEDED 2 GRAVES*
- *INTO THE UNKNOWN*
- *IN A COFFIN IN EGYPT*
- *HOW TO LIVE 20 YEARS LONGER...AND LOVE IT!*
- *HOW LONG WAS JESUS CHRIST IN HIS TOMB?*

NEWSLETTER BOOK (back issues, Vol. 1)
SPIRAL-BOUND BOOK OF THE FIRST TEN ISSUES OF *UPDATE INTERNATIONAL*. Covers all discoveries in which Jonathan Gray and his associates are involved, with extra information, as well as ancient giants, dinosaurs, mysteries of ancient South America, surprises in the Grand Canyon, and more. Scores of photos, maps, diagrams.

NEWSLETTER BOOK (back issues, Vol. 2)
SPIRAL-BOUND BOOK OF *UPDATE INTERNATIONAL* ISSUES 11 TO 20. Updated information on the discoveries in which Jonathan Gray and his associates are involved, as well as giants, pyramids in China, ancient Egyptians in Australia, lost technology. and much more. Scores of photos, maps, diagrams. Also INDEX to all QUESTIONS and topics found in Volumes 1 & 2.

NEWSLETTER BOOK (back issues, Vol. 3)
SPIRAL-BOUND BOOK OF *UPDATE INTERNATIONAL* ISSUES 21 TO 30. Further updates on the discoveries in which Jonathan Gray and his associates are involved. Includes mystery of the mammoths, the Ice Age, tunnels under Egypt, ancient giants, discoveries in astronomy, lost

technology and much more. Scores of photos, maps, diagrams, letters from readers, etc. Also INDEX to all topics in Volume 3.

NEWSLETTER BOOK (back issues, Vol. 4)
SPIRAL-BOUND BOOK OF *UPDATE INTERNATIONAL* ISSUES 31 TO 40. More updates on the discoveries in which Jonathan Gray and his associates are involved. Includes Egyptian Pacific discovery voyages, sinister events in Israel, the search for the infamous Tower of Babel, lost technology and much more. Scores of photos, maps, diagrams, letters from readers, etc. Also INDEX to all topics in Volumes 1 to 4.

NEWSLETTER

REGULAR NEWSLETTER
QUARTERLY *UPDATE INTERNATIONAL* NEWSLETTER SUBSCRIPTION. All recent developments and new materials are announced in here. Plus other significant archaeological finds around the world, and news of other important world developments relating to the coming New World Order.

VIDEOS

SURPRISING DISCOVERIES 1—
Secrets of the Lost Races
Fantastic secrets of ancient cities. Mysterious underground tunnel systems. World survey accurately mapped 4,000 years ago. Who really were the first to fly? Evidence of incredible nuclear battles. Ancient technology

---

SURPRISING DISCOVERIES 2—
(a) Has Noah's Ark Been Found? Search for the lost Ark. Something big in the mountains…what is it? Scientific probes and discoveries.

(b) Into the Forbidden Valley. The dark secret of a sinister village chief puts the lives of archaeologists in danger. Is Noah's grave here?

SURPRISING DISCOVERIES 3—
The Lost Cities of Sodom and Gomorrah
Dead Sea cities deep in ash and sulphur balls that rained from the sky. Shock from the past. A furnace by day, scary by night.

SURPRISING DISCOVERIES 4—
(a) And the Sea Will Tell Runaway slaves trapped by a super-power's well-equipped army—and the army vanishes! **In search of Pharaoh's lost army**...a grim discovery on the sea floor.

(b) Smuggled Out of the Desert Amazing, forbidden movie footage of the true Mount Sinai.   See biblical remains mentioned in the book of Exodus!

SURPRISING DISCOVERIES 5—Ark of the Covenant
4-part story.   How the ARK OF THE COVENANT mysteriously vanished; the strange "coincidences" that overshadowed the search; and the surprise inside Skull Hill for which no one was prepared. Will the Ark play a role in the events under the New World Order?

SURPRISING DISCOVERIES 6—Strange Signs in the Sky
From the glories of distant galaxies...to the CODED MESSAGE of the ancient sky maps. What were the ancients trying to tell us? Why does a MAN tread on SCORPIO'S head and fight with the SERPENT for the CROWN? Why does VIRGO hold a CHILD in her arms called IESU? Why did some ancient sages follow a star to a precise spot on earth? What did they know? How were they so sure what they would find? An amazing SIGN seen over the North Polar star NOW...and linked to a prophecy.

SURPRISING DISCOVERIES 7 - Secrets of Ancient South America
Into the unmapped jungle of the Amazon headwaters…where savages shrink human heads. Up into the dizzy heights of the Andes mountains…to the lost city of women, ancient Inca fortress in the clouds. And the strange floating islands of Lake Titicaca…a vertical 2 miles above sea level.

SURPRISING DISCOVERIES 8 - In a Coffin in Egypt
Mysteries and wonders of ancient Egypt. Into the secret tunnels of Sakkara. Deep under the desert sands, a mysterious tomb. Joseph's Canal and grain pits. The incredible story of a vanishing mummy…and prophecies to make Nostradamus look pale.

CD-ROM: ARK OF THE COVENANT - for Macintosh and Windows
Reports on the Ark of the Covenant, Noah's Ark, Sodom and Gomorrah, Red Sea Crossing, and Mount Sinai discoveries. Up to 8 hours of interactive viewing, including one hour of exclusive new video footage. Provides on the Internet an international on-line conference for discussion and debate.

TO ORDER contact us at info@archaeologyanswers.com

NOTES

Chapter 1: The Day The Earth Tipped Over

1. Discoveries in both polar regions of ancient warm water coral beds, vast coal deposits from former forests, and thousands of square miles of tropical to subtropical animal and vegetal remains, all attest to a once uniform climate worldwide. Tropical mammoths preserved in Siberian "frozen muck" with undigested food snap-frozen in their stomachs testify to an instantaneous climatic change.
2. DeliaGoetz and Sylvanus G. Morley, *Popul Vuh*.
3. Andrew Tomas, *We Are Not the First*, p. 13.
4. Jonathan Gray, private files.
5. Gray, private files.
6. Frederick Soddy, *Interpretation of Radium*, p. 3.
7. I accepted as approximate the year suggested by Rene Noorbergen in his *Secrets of th e Lost Races*.

   More recent evidence suggests a later date (2345 B.C.) for the Deluge and for the subsequent emergence of Egypt and its sister civilizations.

   The date November 17 is ascertained with certainty, having become enshrined in the memories of several ancient races, the Egyptian and Hindu included.

   It should be noted that the precise time is less important than the well established fact of the Deluge.

8. It is not within the scope of this work to detail evidence for the Deluge, the pursuit of which is reserved for a subsequent book.
9. Sir John William Dawson, *The Historical Deluge in Relation to Scientific Discovery*, p. 4 ff.
10. See Gen. 7:23; 9:19; 10:32.
11. W. F. Albright, *Recent Discoveries in Bible Lands*, p. 70.

Chapter 2: Search

12. Cited in Zecharia Sitchin, *The Twelfth Planet*, p. 49.
13. Francis Hitching, *The World Atlas of Mysteries*, p. 69.
14. Erich von Danicken, *Signs of the Gods*, p. 169.
15. Anthony Roberts, *Sowers of Thunder*, p. 182.
16. Cited in Louis Pauwels, *The Eternal Man*, p. 11.
17. Sitchin, p. 6.
18. Gen. 8:4.
19. William Howells, *Mankind So Far*, p. 295.
20. Sir Leonard Woolley, *The Sumerians*, p. 27.

Chapter 3: Mysterious Messages in the Canyon

1. Examples of inaccuracies in sixteenth century maps include Jean Sevei's map (1514) which renders North and Central America as one uniform land mass; Lopa Hame's map (1519) in which America's dimensions are out of scale in relation to Africa, and the outlines of the New World are scarcely recognizable; and a Portuguese map of 1520 in which South America comes to a stop in Southern Brazil.
2. The Russians say that Patagonia and Tierra del Fuego, not Antarctica, are shown (but even these were not known before 1520).
3. Interesting land changes have take place since the maps were drawn:
    (a) The Guadalquivir Delta practically did not exist, whereas now it is several hundred square miles.
    (b) Islands in the Mediterranean are shown much larger than now; they have since been eroded by the sea.
4. Rene Noorbergen, *Secrets of the Lost Races*, p. 91.

5 According to English archaeologist S. F. Hood, Irish etymologist John Philip Cohane and a number of other researchers. Noorbergen, pp. 93-95; Cohane, *The Key*, 1970.
6. Noorbergen, p. 93.
7. Gen. 11:1
8. aron Friedrich Alexander Humboldt, *Views of Nature*. Bd. I.
9. A tradition in the *Chaldean Paraphrase of Jonathan*. Cited by Noorbergen. p. 99.

Chapter 4: Operation Spider Web

1. John Michell, *The View Over Atlantis*, p. 69.
2 Stecchini, Livio Catullo, "Notes on the Relation of Ancient Measures to the Great Pyramids," an appendix in *Secrets of the Great Pyramid*, by Peter Tompkins.
3. According to the Druids, whenever an invisible magnetic current meets a water current, there is a menhir (upright stone). Whenever a magnetic current splits into two or three branches, there is a dolmen (a slab above two or three upright supports). The roofing stones of dolmens were not, as has been generally believed, in order to mark sepulchers. Human remains have been found in only 2 percent of such sites. It is very likely that they functioned as rocking stones to operate the power system.
4. Michell, p. 69.
5. Gen. 11:4

Chapter 5: Sudden Fury

1. Immanuel Velikovsky, *Earth in Upheaval*. p. 206.
2. Sir Henry Howarth, *The Mammoth and the Flood*, p. 351.
3. The *Sun*, Melbourne, Australia, October 20, 1984.
4. Gray, private files.
5. *Time*, July 3, 1944.
6. Gen. 6:1-4.
7. Peter Kolosimo, *Timeless Earth*, p. 32.

8. John C. Whitcomb, Jr. and Henry M. Morris, *The Genesis Flood*, p. 25; Rene Noorbergen, *Secrets of the Lost Races*, pp. 22, 25; Alan and Sally Landsburg, *The Outer Space Connection*, pp. 121, 148.
9. P. W. Bridgman, *Reflections on Thermodynamics*, p. 549.
10. Isaac Asimov,*Can Decreasing Entropy Exist in the Universe?*, p. 76.
11. Gen. 2:1-3.
12. Rom. 8:20-22.
13. Alan Hayward, *God Is*, p. 56.

Chapter 6: Lost Survivors

1   Charles Berlitz, *Mysteries from Forgotten Worlds*, p. 160.
2. Robert Charroux, *Lost Worlds*.
3. Most are now in the prehistory library of Lussac-les-Chateaux; some are in the Musde de l'Homme in Paris. The most revealing of the collection (which clash strongly with orthodox theories) are stored away, unable to be viewed, except by special permission, which is granted only to those individuals with "proper credentials." They are considered too "disturbing" for public display.
4   Robert Charroux, *Legacy of the Gods*, p. 6.
5. *Ibid.*, p. 59.
6. Ibid., p. 63.

Chapter 7: Somebody's Misreading The Time

1. A. J. White, *Radio Carbon Dating*, pp. 156-158.
2. In the film, *The Case of the Ancient Astronauts*, cited by Clifford Wilson in *The War of the Chariots*, pp. 148-149.
3. The *Advertiser*, Adelaide, Australia, Sept. 17, 1951.
4. Cited by Noorbergen, p. 153.
5. In an article, "Pathology and the Posture of the Neanderthal Man," cited by Noorbergen, p. 153.
6. Cited in F. C. Payne, *The Seal of God*, p. 20.
7. Henry M. Morris, *The Scientfic Case for Creation*, pp. 52-59.
8. William R. Fix, *Star Maps*.

Chapter 9: Vanishing Evidence

1   Tomas, *We Are Not the First*, p. 21.
2.   Linda St. Thomas, Smithsonian News Service, states: "What's surprising is that even if you went to every single exhibit in the 12 museums and the National Zoo...you would have seen less than 3 percent of the Smithsonian's national collections. The rest...are not on public display...some artifacts, for example, are so rare that they are neither placed on exhibit in the institution nor loaned to another museums and the National Zoo...you would have less than 3 percent of the Simsonian's national collections.   The rest...are not on public display...some artifacts, for example, are so rare that they are neither placed on exhibit in the institution nor loaned to another museum...many of our specimens are just irreplaceable...other Smithsonian treasures are kept beyond view...because they're needed for important research.   That research can later bring an artifact into public view...these artifacts [referring to a picture of mounted specimens] along with some 60 million others, are behind the scenes in the National Museum of Natural History in Washington, D.C." *Farmington Daily Times* (N.M.), May 11, 1980, p. 15.
3   Bruce Cathie, *Harmonic 288*, pp. 182-188.
4   Karl Brugger, *The Chronicle of Akakor*, p. 215.

Chapter 10: The Disappearance of Admiral Ot

1.   In *America B.C.* (p. 110), Barry Fell makes this interesting comment: "As to the relative sizes and strengths of ancient ships in comparison with those used by Columbus, medieval Europe of 1492 was in a state of nautical skill that the ancients would have regarded as benighted. Columbus' whole expedition could mount only 88 men, carried on three vessels of which two were only 50 feet in length, about the size of a small Boston fishing boat.   Contrast that with the Pharaohs of the Ramesside dynasty, 1200 B.C., who could mount expeditions of 10,000 miners across the Indian Ocean to the gold-bearing lands of South Africa and Sumatra.   Julius Caesar's triremes carried 200 men, yet he

found his ships outmatched in size, height, and seaworthiness by those of the maritime Celts."

2. Brad Steiger, *Worlds Before Our Own,* p. 81.
3. Now in the National Archaeological Museum of Greece.
4. From a statement by Dr. Price at a meeting in Washington in 1959.
5. According to Dr. Cyrus Gordon of Brandeis University, who is an authority on ancient civilizations and languages.
6. Fell, p. 263.
7. Berlitz, *Mysteries From Forgotten Worlds*, p. 145.
8. Ibid. The discoveries made by Mrs. Hearn (in La Grange), Ms. Metcalf (on the Ft. Benning Military Reservation in Columbus, Ga.), as well as those by other people in the area, were first authenticated and publicized by Dr. Joseph Mahan of the Columbus, Ga., Museum of Arts and Sciences, and later substantiated by Dr. Cyrus H. Gordon, who at the time chaired Mediterranean Studies at Brandeis University.
9. Evidence of Japanese visits has been presented by Drs. Betty Meggers and C. Evans of the Smithsonian Institution.
10. Now stored in a dusty, cramped shed on the side porch of the church of Maria Auxiliadora in Cuenca, Ecuador: probably the most valuable archaeological treasure on earth. containing 70.000 artifacts of gold and silver, perfect in workmanship and beauty, and identified as Assyrian, Chinese, Egyptian and African. The workmanship is too sophisticated for primitive craftsmen, and the materials are too precious to be fakes. This strange collection poses so many questions, it is deliberately neglected in the journals of orthodox archaeology and is unknown to historians. Called the Crespi Collection, it is now enshrined as a national treasure by the Ecuadorian government. (An assessment of the authenticity of the Crespi Collection is given in the Appendix.)

Chapter 11: Secret Planet - Are We in for More Surprises?

1. Isa. 40:22.
2. Job 26:7.
3. Job 38:14.
4. Aristarchus. Cited by Steiger, p. 129.
5. Astronomical table of *Sudya Siddhanta* (a textbook on the astronomy of ancient India). The date of its last compilation is c. A.D. 1000, but some Hindus believe that earlier editions were in use c. 3000 B.C.

6. The Mayan and Babylonian knowledge is specific; the Egyptian understanding of the same knowledge is cryptically embodied within their architectural planning. The siderial year (i.e., the precession of the equinoxes) takes 25,827 of our years. The extent of the siderial year can be recognized in the sum of the crossed diagonals of the Great Pyramid at Giza which give a total of 25,826.6 pyramid-inches. The Egyptians were adept at cryptically preserving their science.
7. *Sudya Siddhanta.*
8. Permenides. Cited by Steiger, p. 128.
9. Empedocles. Ibid.
10. Anaxagoras. Ibid.
11. Anaxagoras. Ibid.
12. Cf. "Instruments" section of this chapter, item 73, "Astronomical clocks."
13. The name of the god Sin (in Sumerian), later associated with the moon, is derived from Su'en, "lord of wasteland."
14. Published in *Ancient Astronauts*, April 1980.
15. Saturn's planetary moon Titan has a physical condition among the planets most comparable to that of Earth. "When our space probe passed over Titan its radio communication was interrupted and its photographic equipment stopped functioning almost as if it were passing through a security zone-but one not imposed by commands emanating from Earth." See Charles Berlitz, *Doomsday: 1999*, pp. 207-208.
16. Sitchin, p. 206.
17. The outer planets Uranus and Neptune have been seen to wriggle slightly in their orbits around the sun. Pluto has been eliminated as an influence. Scientists now speculate the culprit may be an undiscovered planet's gravitational pull.
18. Diogenes. Cited by Tomas, p. 27.
19. Jer. 33:22; Gen. 15:5; 22:17.
20. Biblical passages speak of beings who dwell in "the heavens," i.e., the regions of outer space (Isa. 40:22; Rev. 12:12), compared with whom the nations of earth are as a "drop of a bucket" (Isa. 40:15). Celestial beings are spoken of as participating from time to time in intergalactic conferences (Job 1:6,7; 2:1,2).
21. See details in Chapter 10, item 10.
22. According to Plutarch. Cited by Berlitz, p. 58.
23. Democritus.

24. The Pharos lighthouse at Alexandria had optical equipment to spot ships more than twenty miles out to sea.
25. The sacred book of the Maya.

Chapter 12: Travel Fast and Live Longer

1. von Danicken, *According to the Evidence*, pp. 125-126.
2. Jacques Bergier, *Mysteries of the Earth*, pp. 84-85.
3. Tomas, *We Are Not the First*, pp. 167-168.
4. The Jyotish (3000 B.C.). Described by Berlitz in *Doomsday: 1999*, p. 125.
5. Ibid.
6. Ibid. The theory of atomic rays is dealt with in specialized but unmistakable vocabulary.
7. Ibid.
8. In the ancient Hindu book, the *Bihath Sathaka*. Cited in Noorbergen, pp. 139-140.
9. B. L. Cathie and P. N. Temm, *Harmonic 695*, p. 97.

Chapter 13: Who Beat Our Computers?

1. Ken Johnson, *The Ancient Magic of the Pyramids*, p. 89. The author amplifies this point (p. 89): "Expressed another way, it allowed them to translate the four curved quadrants of 90 degrees that form a hemisphere onto the flat surfaces of four triangles.

   "The result is that the pyramid's height represents half the earth's polar diameter, and its perimeter represents the equatorial circumference. In the same proportion, the pyramid's total surface area represents that of the northern hemisphere. For all intents and purposes, the Egyptians 'squared the circle' and 'cubed the sphere'.

   "It is now clear, for example, that the Great Pyramid was built with a base length representing the distance that the earth rotates in half-a-second."

   Herodotus wrote that the exact slant height of the pyramid is one stadium long, that is, one six-hundredth of a degree of latitude.

Agatharchides (second century B C.) reported that the length of a side was one-eighth of a minute of a degree of latitude.

Chapter 14: The Sad Fate of the Gold Gardens

1. By distinction, brass is an alloy of copper and zinc.
2. Recovered from the tomb of Chou Chu, noted general of the Tsin era (AD. 265-316).
3. In the Crespi Collection. Interestingly, none of this jungle cache of artifacts bears any influence of Inca or Mayan culture.
4. Also in the Crespi Collection.
5. In the tomb of Emperor Ch' in Shih Huang, presently under excavation in Sian province, China.
6. The evidence subsists in surviving drill holes.
7. Blasted out of rock fifteen feet below ground, in Dorchester, New England, U.S.A. Reported in *Scientific American*, June 1851.

Chapter 15: Microscope on a Sexy Spider

1. These can be inspected in the Crespi Collection.

Chapter 16: Strange Ruins on the Seabed

1. This and subsequent expeditions have failed to reach the pyramids, located in eastern Peru, c. 13 degrees south latitude and 71 degrees 30 minutes west longitude. Attempts to penetrate the region have been foiled by insects, snakes and hostile natives, with the resultant death and disappearance of some of the explorers.
2. Thor Heyerdahl, the Norwegian explorer of "Kon-Tiki" fame, attempted to duplicate the accomplishment of the builders by brute power, using the "heave-ho" method. With a dozen natives laboring (with increasing frustration) for eighteen days, he succeeded in setting up one stone head, and then, satisfied, abandoned the job.
   There are several inescapable problems concerning this experiment:

(a) The stone head chosen for removal was not a typical-sized stone. (At ten to fifteen tons, as against the others weighing thirty-five to fifty tons, it certainly was a great achievement, but not typical.)

(b) His team shifted it a few hundred feet, across smooth sandy ground (which exists only in that location), whereas the other stone heads had to be moved five miles across volcanic rock, hard and uneven. Heyerdahl's "heave-ho" method, if utilized across such a surface, would have grooved the stones with long scars. None of the original statues show such markings.

(c) Heyerdahl's team utilized ropes and wooden poles. However, originally there was no wood on Easter Island. The nearest forest was 2,500 miles away. And ropes made from the local reeds were neither durable nor strong-quite inadequate for such a method. (Fortunately for Heyerdahl's experiment, he used strong, manufactured ropes from Europe.

(d) Although Thor Heyerdahl succeeded in moving one small head a short distance over a relatively flat surface, this does not explain how other large heads were moved 300 feet up and down cliff walls.

(e) The statues once wore ten-ton hats, put on after the statues were erected. How was this done? If earthenware ramps had been used to erect the hats, they would have had to be several hundred feet long and traces of them would have been found on the island, but no such traces have been found.

3. So observed Howard-Vyse, who uncovered part of the original limestone casings near the base of the pyramid. Johnson, p. 112.

4. Jeffrey Goodman, *Psychic Archaeology*, p. 97. See also n. 1, Chap. 13.

5. Details of corroboration are too complex to enter into here, but they may be studied in Ken Johnson's *The Ancient Magic of the Pyramids*, pp. 60, 104-105, 146. Additionally, Richard Wingate ventures the opinion that where tombs have been found in some pyramids, "the situation may be similar to that of Westminster Abbey, where many historical figures were buried, but whose main function is not that of a burial vault." (*Lost Outpost of Atlantis*, p. 116).

6. An inscription in the Pyramid of Snofru (Sneferu), which is two-thirds the volume of the Great Pyramid, shows it took only two years to construct. By similar methods, the Great Pyramid would have been completed in as little as four years. Furthermore, excavations at the

Great Pyramid have uncovered only 4,000 laborers' huts, which in no way could have housed 100,000 workmen. The problem that emerges for conventional historians is how only 4,000 men could build the Great Pyramid with 2,300,000 blocks in just four years, during just three months each year, if wooden sledges and barges were used.

7. If we are to believe in the use of wooden sledges and barges, mathematicians tell us that 26 million trees would be required just to fashion the necessary number of sledges and rafts - more than Lebanon or the ancient world could have supplied in the twenty years we are told the job took. Two tomb paintings of the Twelfth Dynasty which show sledges and barges being employed to transport a few statues were concerned with methods used, not in the Fourth Dynasty (when the Great Pyramid was built), but a thousand years later in the Twelfth Dynasty. Hieroglyphics from the different dynasties indicate a decided decline in the technology and life-style of Egypt after the time of the Great Pyramid. This is supported also by the funerary texts in the Book of the Dead. The Egypt of the history books, with which we are familiar, was but a vague shadow of the supergreat early Egypt.

8. Gray, private files.

Chapter 17: Journey into the Unexpected

1. Aiphius Hyatt Verrill, *America's Ancient Civilizations*, pp. 243-245. Cited in Berlitz, *Mysteries from Forgotten Worlds*, p. 79.

2. *Ibid.*

3. The Spaniards in Peru discovered whole walls adorned with gold and silver animals, birds, plants and climbing vines which seemed to have grown on the spot, imitated from life and fitted into the wall, as a tapestry.

Chapter 18: Perfume Please, the Game Stinks!

1   An unconfirmed though persistent legend, this one item should be regarded with caution.

Chapter 19: Forbidden Tunnels

1. Alec Maclellan, *The Lost World of Agharti*, pp. 24, 193.
2. *Ibid.*, p. 193.
3. *Ibid.*, p. 206.
4. *Ibid.*, p. 207.
5. Accounts of these tunnels come initially from the Spanish invasion of 1531.

    Searching for the entrances was recommenced by the Peruvian authorities in 1844, after a dying Quiche Indian (a direct descendant of the Incas) confessed their secret to a priest.

    One tunnel apparently runs from Cuzco via Catamarca into what is now the interior yard of Lima cathedral. Access from the outside world is disguised through a stone slab cleverly sunk into the foundation among the other slabs. Only those who know the secret can open it.
6. According to the London journal *Economist*, May 15, 1968, the Brazilian government reporter Jader Figueira related that, of all people, employees of the Indian Protection Service were very active in these crimes.
7. Brugger, *The Chronicle of Akakor*, p. 105.
8   "A war...over the whole earth": compare Rev. 16:14; "The mountains...will tremble": compare Jer. 4:24. "Blood...from the sky": compare Joel 2:30. "Man's flesh...will disintegrate": compare Zech. 14:12.
9. Brugger, pp. 191-192.
10. Kolosimo, *Timeless Earth*, p. 66. Some Soviet archaeologists believe that the tunnels are part of a huge network stretching out toward Iran and perhaps linked with those discovered near the Amu Darya in Turkmenistan and on the Russo-Afghan border.
11. Alec Maclellan, *The Lost World of Agharti*, p. 196.
12. Nicolas Roerich, cited by Tomas, *Atlantis: From Legend to Discovery*, p. 45. Specifically, there are entrances to caves in the cliffs towering over Kurlyk. Secret passages go "from Tibet, through Kuen lun, through Altyntag, through Tourfan."
13. Kolosimo, *Not of This World*, p. 161.
14. Maclellan, p. 75.

15. According to tradition, this includes many of the majestic ruins of India, Ellora, Elephanta, and the caverns of Ajunta (Chandor Range).
16. From a statement made in London in 1945 by Harold Wilkins, explorer and historian. Professor Friedrich Max Muller (1823-1900), in *Sacred Books of the East*, states that this inland sea occupied what are now the salt lakes and deserts of Middle Asia north of the Himalayan Mountain Range.
17. Maclellan, p. 185.
18. An article, "About Caves and Other Secret Hiding Places in the World," by George Wagner, Jr., published in the January 1967 issue of *Search*, discusses this metropolis. It is referred to by Maclellan, pp. 162-163.
19. Maclellan, p. 187.
20. John Lloyd Stephens, *Incidents of Travel in Central* America, Chiapas and Yucatan, cited in Warren Smith, *This Hollow Earth*, pp. 80-81.
21. Extending from the pueblo of Puchuta, to Tecpan.
22. The account was written down 700 years ago by Ralph of Coggeshall and later by the chronicler, William of Newbridge.

Chapter 20: Mystery of the Screaming Robot

1. In the Crespi Collection.
2. Crespi Collection.
3. Crespi Collection.
4. Discovered in pre-Columbian graves in the 1920's and now on view in the University of Pennsylvania in Philadelphia. Constructed in the form of a modified jaguar, it has been examined in detail by Dr. Ivan Sanderson, who has noted that "the joints of the legs are hinged the wrong way for an animal but the right way for heavy-duty shock absorbers."
5. In the Crespi Collection.
6. Found in the Chicama Valley, on the northern coast of Peru, it is now in the private collection of Senor Gerardo Niemann (Hacienda Casa Grande, Trujillo, Peru).
7. See details in Chapter 10, item 10.
8. See Chapter 25, item 2.
9. The Chinese chronicler Suma Chien, 100 B.C. Cited by Noorbergen in *Treasures of the Lost Races*, p. 113.
10. Ibid.

Chapter 21: The Photo Spies

1. Cited in *Ancient Astronauts*, July 1976, p. 45.
2. Tomas, *Atlantis: From Legend to Discovery*. pp. 112-113.

Chapter 22: Bikini Girls of the Mediterranean

1. The shoe print in Fisher Canyon, Nevada, was embedded in a coal seam "15 million years old," according to the evolutionary time scale (thus posing an insoluble enigma for the conventional view). The Gobi Desert discovery was in sandstone rock, likewise "millions" of years old.

   However, these relics can be interpreted more logically as belonging to pre-Flood civilized man (and therefore slightly over 5,000 years old).
2. The clothing was reconstructed from remnants found on Paleolithic man uncovered near Vladimir by Professor Otto Bades of the Ethnographical Institute of the Academy of Soviet Sciences.
3. On frozen bodies of humans found in ancient burial places 120 miles northeast of Moscow.
4. Pictured on flat engraved stones discovered in 1937 in a cave near Lussac-les-Chateaux by Leon Pencard and Stephane Lwoff.

Chapter 23: The Crystal Skull

1. Kolosimo, *Not of This World*, p. 204.
2. "Laser" means "Light Amplification by Stimulated Emission of Radiation," i.e., a reinforcement of light. In laser guns a light ray is intensified through forced emissions of "stimulated" atoms and molecules, and a light is created ten million times "cleaner" and much brighter than sunlight. Ray guns can cut holes in walls, or vaporize objects. Was this the method by which the vast tunnel network under the earth's surface was cut?
3. One is in the Museum of Mankind (part of the British Museum, London). Another is privately owned.

Chapter 24: What Happened After the Car Crash

1. Ps. 139:16.
2. Gen. 1:29; Lev., Ch. 11; Deut. 14:21; Lev. 7:4,19, 26-27; 19:5-8. Scholars believe that these laws were for religious reasons: those who were unclean were not fit to approach God. I will give them no argument. This is exactly what they were intended to be on a superficial level. But their real purpose was to improve the health of the people. The health benefits that accrue to people living under the mandate of these laws have been demonstrated time and again.
3. Lev., Chs. 13 and 14.
4. Lev., Ch. 15; Num. 19:11-16; Deut. 23:12-14.Ibid.
5. Lev., Chs. 13 and 14; Num. 31:21-23.
6. In the *Sactaya Grantham*, which belongs to the *Vedas*.
7. Ps. 51:7 (an active ingredient in hyssop is penicillin).
8. 2 Kings 4:34.
9. An Egyptian formula derived from honey and acacia gum was an effective spermicide.
10. Gen. 17:12; Lev. 12:3.
11. *Scientific American*, October 20, 1900. Cited by Steiger in *Mysteries of Time and Space*, pp. 63-64.
12. In the British and Cairo Museums.
13. In October 1975, Don Crabtree of Kimberly, Idaho, one of the world's top authorities on lithic technology, allowed a local surgeon to remove a tumor from his lung-entailing the cutting of an incision three-fourths of the way around his trunk.
14. X-rays (cathode rays that pass through opaque bodies) were rediscovered by Konrad Roentgen in 1895.
15. This account of an operation by two Arab surgeons is recorded in the *Enciclopedia Christiana*, the official Roman Catholic reference work. It is also depicted on an ancient wood carving at the Cathedral of Palencia, Spain. The cathedral's records back up the fact that the leg transplants took place.
16. Found among hundreds of pre-Inca stone carvings collected by Dr. Javier Cabrera, of Ica, Peru.
   Dr. E. Stanton Moxey, fellow of the American College of Surgeons, says,..."in the photographs of stone carvings depicting heart surgery, the

detail is clear-the seven blood vessels coming from the heart are faithfully copied. The whole thing looks like a cardiac operation, and the surgeons seem to be using techniques that fit with our modern knowledge." Quoted by Noorbergen, p. 156.

Natural surface oxidation covering the engravings, as well as microorganisms in the grooves under a fine glaze, as seen through a microscope, confirm these stones as genuine, rather than modern forgeries. Many are still being uncovered in undisturbed strata near where Cabrera found his. In fact, they were first observed by Europeans in 1555, and thousands are in other collections.

17. The examinations have been performed by Professor Andronik Jagharian, anthropologist, and director of operative surgery at the Erivan Medical Institute in Soviet Armenia. The discovery site was at Ishtikunny, near Lake Sevan. (Reported by William Dick and Henry Gris, "Delicate Head Surgery Was Performed 3500 Years Ago," *National Enquirer*, September 10, 1972, p. 30.)
18. *Ibid.*

Chapter 25: Ruins That Glow in the Night

1. Noorbergen, *Secrets of the Lost Races*. pp. 45-46.
2. A fragment of a Sumerian text cited by the noted archaeologist S. N. Kramer in *History Begins at Sumer*, p. 200.
3. Discovered in sedimentary rock in the Coso Mountains six miles northeast of Olancha, California, on February 13, 1961. It was offered for sale at $25,000.
4. The ancient Jewish manuscript, *The Queen of Sheba and Her Only Son Menyelek*, tr. by Sir E. A. Wallis Budge. London: Philip Lee Warner, 1932.
5. Eliphas Levi, *Histoire de la Magie*, cited by Noorbergen, p. 51.
6. In Room 17 of the Temple of Dendera.
7. Identified among relics in the basement of the State Museum in Baghdad, Iraq, in 1938, by Dr. Wilhelm Konig, a German archaeologist.
   Those at Ctesiphon were uncovered by Professor E. Kuhnel of the Staatliches Museum in Berlin.
8. Richard Mooney, *Gods of Air and Darkness*, pp. 151-152. This ancient manuscript, the *Agastya Samhita*, is preserved in the Princes' Library in Ujjain, India.

9. Discovered in caves in the Bayan-Kara-Ula Mountains, they were sent to Moscow for scientific study. Reported by Viacheslav Zaitsev, in the Soviet magazine *Nemon*, November 12, 1966.
10. Johnson, *The Ancient Magic of the Pyramids*, pp. 15-19.
11. A theory of the old alchemists held that lamps could be created by reducing gold to an oily fluid; in a lamp correctly made, the gold reabsorbed its oily fluid and gave it out again.
12. Colonel P. H. Fawcett, *Exploration Fawcett*, pp. 269, 285-286.
13. Tomas, *Atlantis: From Legend to Discovery*, p. 87.
14. C. S. Downey, at a conference on street lighting and traffic in Pretoria, South Africa, in 1963, described it as "a system of artificial illumination equal, if not superior to, the twentieth century."
15. An article in *United Press*, by Harold Guard, London, 1963.
16. Ibid.
17. Lucian, Vera Historia.
18. Brugger, *The Chronicle of Akakor*, p. 31.
19. Tomas, *We Are Not the First*, pp. 166-167.
20. Job 38:35.

Chapter 26: The Mercury Secret

1. Kolosimo, *Spaceships in Prehistory*, p. 298
2. Noorbergen, *Secrets of the Lost Races*. p. 121.
3. A Chaldean text, the *Sifr'ala*, deciphered by the archaeologist and ethnologist. Y. N. Iban A'haraon.
4. *China Pictorial*, Peking, Nov. 8. 1958.
5. von Danicken, *Chariots of the Gods*, p. 79
6. Cited by Soviet scholar, Gorbovsky, in *Vie Nueve*, June 29, 1962.
7. An oral tradition recorded in the twelfth century *Budhasvamin Brihat Katha Shlokasamgraha* of Nepal, reported and commented upon in Noorbergen's *Secrets of the Lost Races*, p. 123.
8. Noorbergen, p. 124.
9. von Danicken, Signs of the Gods, pp. 36-5 2.
10. A description in the ancient Indian *Samarangana Sutradhara*. Referred to in Berlitz, *Mysteries from Forgotten Worlds*, pp. 126-127.
11. From a speech delivered at Cambridge in July 1946 by the British nuclear physicist Edward Neville da Costa Andrade (citing Newton).

12. A description and illustrations of the pots appeared in the Soviet periodical, *The Modern Technologist*. Cited in Noorbergen, p. 131.
13. In the *Mahavira of Bhavabhuri* (eighth century).
14. Kolosimo, Not of This World, p. 44.
15. Translation, *Aeronautics, a Manuscript from the Prehistoric Past*, was published in book form by Coronation Press, Mysore, 1973.
16. Originally, it was thought to be a model of a bird. However, the tail of the plane is vertical-a feature never seen in birds. The glider's design is ample proof that it is not a model of a bird. Birds, with moveable feathered wings and tails, are built differently from planes. The glider's design (demonstrating camber, the angle of the wing back-sweep, the dihedral angle, the angle of lift or depression in regard to the fuselage, and the wings formed to create a vacuum for lift) is ample proof that it is not a model of a bird. Additionally, it flies some considerable distance when hand thrown. A legend related to ethnologist R. Baker, by a wise man of a dying totemic cult of northern Canada.
17. A legend related to ethnologist R. Baker, by a wise man of a dying totemic cult of northern Canada.
18. Frank Waters, *Book of the Hopi*, cited by Noorbergen, pp. 145-146.
19. Robin Collyns, *Laser Beams from Star Cities*. p. 134.
20. Their features are more mechanical than biological (wing positioning, fuselage shape, front delta-shape wings tilting downward, as in high-powered jet aircraft). From the wing edges there is something which clearly resembles mechanical elevators. The tail is right-triangular in shape, flat-surfaced and rigidly perpendicular to the body and delta wings. No bird, insect or winged fish has a tail like this-but it is the standard pattern on modern aircraft. These artifacts also carry an insignia on the tail.

   On the tail of the Colombian model, the early form of the Hebrew *beth* (B) appears as an insignia, in exactly the place where identification marks appear on many modern planes. This puts the original aircraft before the second millennium B.C.

   There seems also to be an indented seat at a point where a cockpit would normally be.

   The objects are displayed in the Field Museum of Natural History (Chicago), the Museum of Primitive Art (New York), the Smithsonian Museum of Natural History (Washington, D.C.) and in Bogota, Colombia.

1. D. W. Hauck, "Israeli Commandoes…A Crack, Well-Planned Attack," p. 8, *Ancient Astronauts*, May 1979.
2. Smith, *This Hollow Earth*, p. 70.
3. Brugger, *The Chronicle of Akakor*, pp. 58-59; also reported in von Danicken, *According to the Evidence*, p. 136.
4. 2 Sam. 21:20.

Chapter 27: Were We on the Moon in 2309 B.C.?

1. Anthony Roberts, *Sowers of Thunder*, p. vii.
2. Another passage in the *Mahabharata*. Quoted by James Churchward in *The Children of Mu*, pp. 188-189.
3. The *Surya Siddhanta*. See Tomas, *We Are Not the First*, p. 149.
4. See no. 7, Chap. 29.
5. Maya folklore.
6. The ancient *Samsaptakabadha*.
7. The *Puranas*.
8. A seal cylinder depicting Etana flying on an eagle's back between the sun and the moon is in the Berlin Museum.
9. Tomas, *We Are Not the First*, p. 146.
10. *Ibid.*, p. 47.
11. *The Collection of Old Tales*, a Chinese work compiled in the fourth century, from ancient sources.
12. Tomas, *We Are Not the First*, pp. 148-149.

Chapter 28: Could Science Make You Invisible?

1. First related to O'Connell, who lived there 1826-1837, and again to the German scientist, Dr. Paul Hambruch, who led an expedition in 1910. Reported by Bill Ballinger in *Lost City of Stone*, p. 45.
2. English historian Geoffrey of Monmouth (twelfth century), *Historia de Gestis Re gum Brittanniae*.
3. Francois Lenormant, *Chaldean Magic*. Cited by Tomas, *We Are Not the First*, p. 128.
4. The *Mahabharata* and Ramayana.
5. Kolosimo, *Timeless Earth*, p. 193.

6. Clement Durell, *Readable Relativity.*

Chapter 29: Too Late for Escape

1. Democritus. Cited in Tomas, *Atlantis: From Legend to Discovery*, p.80.
2. Lucretius. Cited in Tomas, *We Are Not the First*, p. 72.
3. The *Yoga Vasishta.* "Readers of the Buddhist Pali sutras and commentaries, who studied them before modern times, were frequently mystified by reference to the 'tying together' of minute component parts of matter; although nowadays it is easy for a modern reader to recognize an understandable description of molecular composition" (Berlitz, *Doomsday: 1999*, p. 125).
4. Mooney, *Gods of Air and Darkness*, p. 83.
5. Noorbergen, *Secrets of the Lost Races*, p. 139.
6. Berlitz, *Doomsday: 1999* (p. 120) relates that "seven years after the first successful atom bomb blast in New Mexico, Dr. Oppenheimer, who was familiar with ancient Sanskrit literature, was giving a lecture at Rochester University. During the question and answer period a student asked a question to which Oppenheimer gave a strongly qualified answer.
   "Student: Was the bomb exploded at Alamogordo during the Manhattan Project the first one to be detonated?
   "Dr. Oppenheimer: Well-yes. In modern times, of course."
7. Quoted from the *Mahabharata*, a compilation of 200 verses translated completely by 1884. Although the document dates back in its present form to 500 B.C., textual evidence indicates that it refers to events that occurred 1500 to 2500 B.C. The chief translator (decades before the appearance of aircraft, war gases, rockets and nuclear bombs), commented that much in the book would to the purely English reader seem "ridiculous."
8. Von Danicken, *According to the Evidence*, p. 164.
9. The *Stanzas of Dzyan*, translated during the past century, date back several thousand years.
10. The *Popul Vuh*, the sacred book of the Mayas, which, according to ethnologists, is the oldest surviving document of human history.
11. Baker. See no. 17, Chap. 26.
12. "Kuskurza," the "Third World Epoch," in Frank Waters' *Book of the Hopi*. Cited by Noorbergen, pp. 145-146.

13. Noorbergen, p. 140.
14. Berlitz, *Doomsday: 1999*, pp. 123-124.
15. Erich von Fange, "Strange Fire on the Earth," *Creation Research Society Quarterly*, December 1975, p. 132.
16. *Ibid.*
17. Visitors are told that the rock was ground by glaciers. On the contrary, a glacier would flow down to one side-not in six different directions over an area of 18,000 square yards!
18. In 1850, explorer Captain Walker discovered the Death Valley ruins. An associate gave this description of the area. Quoted in Noorbergen' s *Secrets of the Lost Races*, p. 128.

Epilogue

1. 2 Pet. 3:12.
2. Isa. 46:9-10; 41:21-23; 42:8-9. Jer. 28:9.
3. Amos 3:7.
4. Luke 21:24.
5. Luke 21:25-26.
6. Rev. 13:16.
7. Rev. 18:11-19.
8. Rev. 17.
9. Dan. 12:1; Matt. 24:21.
10. Matt. 24:22.
11. Matt. 24:37-39.

Printed in the United States
21704LVS00002B/124